Room
to
breathe

Room to breathe

by Jenny James
with letters and poems
by David Boadella

CALIBAN BOOKS

Contents

To Becky and Pepe

To Volkhard, who set me on the right road

To my Mother and Father, both dead now, who gave me enough life and laughter despite all the pain, to carry me through this journey.

Your children are not your children.
They are the sons and daughters of Life's longing for itself.
They come through you but not from you,
And though they are with you yet they belong not to you.

You may give them your love but not your thoughts,
For they have their own thoughts.
You may house their bodies but not their souls,
For their souls dwell in the house of tomorrow, which you
        cannot visit, not even in your dreams.
You may strive to be like them, but seek not to make them
        like you.
For life goes not backward, nor tarries with yesterday.

Kahlil Gibran (The Prophet)

Preface

to the new edition of 'Room to Breathe'

Jenny has asked me to write this preface to the new edition of
'Room to Breathe', which is a bit of a cheek really considering all
the horrible things she has said about me in the book. However,
since I am a very nice forgiving sort of person and bearing in mind
that she recently called me her 'favourite human being' I'll
overlook these little comments and ask you dear reader, to do the
same.

After all, rather a lot of water has gone under the bridge in the
nine years since this book was first written. Jenny's Lake District
retreat swiftly turned into a busy therapy centre, which in 1974
Jenny transported to Donegal, Eire, naming it Atlantis, and
although this was even more remote it became even more busy
and famous and infamous. I have lived in Atlantis with Jenny for
over four years now (I came for a week's holiday) growing and
developing, assisting and watching changes take place until today
it is barely recognisable as the primal therapy centre I joined,
where people would often spend all day in a sound-proofed room
screaming out their pain. Today Atlantis is a very successful
organic farm where untangling emotional knots is entirely
integrated into the work of the garden and peat bog, and where
the adventure of self-exploration has extended into a plan to
sail across the Atlantic ocean and explore the South
American continent with a view to settling the whole commune in
a wild and unspoilt piece of land there. To this end we have bought
a beautiful old wooden sailing ship, which I am living aboard with

other commune members, preparing the boat for our adventure. As I write in the main cabin there are sounds of sawing and planing as Fergus replaces some rotten wood and the rhythmic tap, tap of Alex's caulking iron. Alex has been with the commune, on and off, from the outset with Jenny in PNP house in London and the change from banging cushions to banging caulking irons is something he has adjusted to with surprise.

So, as I varnish spars or tar the deck, back home on the farm Jenny lives on Innishfree Island, a youthful 40 year old grandmother, with her man and their year old daughter; with her now grown-up daughter Becky and her boy friend and their new born son – born by the cottage fireside this spring with the whole commune present.

Jenny is the founder of this famous therapy commune, but if you went there now (and you are welcome) you might be surprised to find her planting out cabbages, weeding onions, washing nappies and organising building work on the new greenhouse. For Jenny has certainly found a lot of room to breathe – to breathe the fresh clean air of Innishfree Island where you will find no roads, no cars, no electricity, no running water – except that which runs from the sky. Her journey of self-exploration, which led her headfirst into an often chaotic jungle of overpowering emotions is now taking her more and more into the clearings and wide open spaces, where there is room not only for breathing but also for singing; not just for crying, but for laughing too; for self sufficiency as well as self-expression; room not only for regressing into childhood traumas, but also for having babies in a natural and healthy environment; space not only for psychological exploration, but also for psychic delving; room for attention to the philosophical and political as well as to the personal; room not just for a therapy commune, but also for a home and a family.

'Room to Breathe' is a close look at the tangle and knots and chaos that anyone seriously considering 'growth' work has to be prepared to go through. Jenny was not particularly neurotic or unhappy. She's a fairly averagely messed about human being with a large desire to tidy up that mess, and this book shows one way of doing just that. I have followed a very similar path myself and maybe therapy will be the way you choose. But whichever journey you take, one thing is for sure – there is absolutely no guarantee where it will take you. Jenny and I certainly had no idea that self-exploration, therapy and growth would lead to organic vegetable gardening, goat rearing and cheese making, let alone boat repairing and sailing to South America and beyond. . . . And when we began our gutsy journey we never expected to enter the psychic realm. . . .

So, dear reader, while reading this book (apart from ignoring anything disparaging said about me) be sure to expect some surprises and if you decide to find your own room to breathe, you should expect to have to crawl through some suffocating corners before you reach the fresh air.

Snowy James
'Atlantis Adventure'
Dartmouth,
Devon.

Preface

This is the story of one person's struggle to breathe: to find space inside my own body to take air in and let myself out, and room around me to work out the aches and pains of a cramped childhood. The pathway I took hasn't really got a name, though the therapist I went to called himself Reichian and it was through reading Reich that I found even the hope of a way out of my suffocation. Today it is Janov who is in vogue; but in the end, it's not the names that matter, but whether, when they'd finished with you, they left enough life in you for you to want to carry on. I hope the account of my journey helps you a little with yours.

Jenny James
Atlantis
Burtonport
Co Donegal
Eire

Introduction

Jenny wrote to me from Germany in September 1968 to ask could she have therapy. Sent me the story of her life and said her main problem was nymphomania. I said I would see her when she got back to England, but several letters passed between us before we even met. The next I heard, she was back in England, having been deported from Frankfurt the day before for taking part in a political demonstration. But not to stay. Before there was time for a session, she was off again, to visit a friend imprisoned in a Swedish jail. She sounded rather desperate with all this rushing around. I kept replying to letters, but the answers always came from somewhere else. Next she was back in England, writing from Kent, saying that she was homeless, jobless and aimless, and that if she were not to undergo therapy, she would probably wander around abroad, earning now and again, with no specific destination. She was also dragging herself out of a terrible depression and bewilderment brought on by breaking up with her boyfriend. A girlfriend had just at that time been committed to a mental institution where she was under forcible sedation.

The next time she wrote, it was from Wales. "The address is that of my caravan, which I had to move here in August. I got so depressed with not being able to find even a perch to jump off from into more permanent accommodation in the London area, and with discovering how few friends one has when really in need, that my pride got the better of me and I came 'home'."

We were still trying to arrange, in this shifting situation, where and when to have the first session. "I hitch-hike everywhere I go and the distance presents no problem to me; I will just have to find somewhere to stay the night. You tell me the address and time and I'll be there."

Finally she came for the first session. Her breathing was very shallow, she lay wrapped in a kind of numbness. I forget exactly what she talked about, but the most conspicuous thing about her was her averted face, her eyes that never looked directly at me, but turned away as though already resigned to expecting a blow. Even lying down, she was running away.

It was nearly six weeks before she came again. The next letter I had was from Newcastle, to tell me that she had had a telegram sent to her in Malaga to let her know her father was dying, quickly, of cancer. "It's all over him. He doesn't know. Please write to me."

Her father declined horribly fast. She travelled to and from Newcastle on hopeless visits. "I think it's sadistic to just let him suffer all this, to no end whatsoever. I can't understand the nurses and doctors. He hates himself and the world and he just can't bear it any more and nor can I. All this has happened in just a few weeks, he can hardly talk or eat now so I pray he may go very quickly."

So she had to miss another session, so as to sit there each evening trying to say something ordinary and seeing her stiff-upper-lip father writhe in pain. It was a terrible end, and a terrible beginning, but he died, and her therapy with me began. And something else started too:

"As I have been so bad lately, I thought that it would provide relief to keep a sort of 'psychiatric' diary, that is, containing dreams and feelings rather than events. But does it make you worse to get introspective? "

She had remembered every incident from her childhood since before the age of two, yet she could not remember what had taken place in the previous session. Her tendency not to look, to run away, not to join up or relate to what had gone before was one of the biggest obstacles I had to face in trying to help her. Her problem was a desperate extroversion, running half way round the world looking for solutions. The solutions lay inside her if she could only start to hear them, if only she could get in touch with her body, with her feelings, and what went on at the back of her head she felt was falling off.

David Boadella

David Boadella is the author of Wilhelm Reich 'The Evolution of his Work' and is also the editor of Energy and Character, the Journal of Bioenergetic Research.

Ice

I suppose the most remarkable thing about my childhood is its ordinariness. Now that I have seen so many people through the horrors of their pasts, I realize I am perhaps one of the luckier escapees, which doesn't say much for what is being done to the young of our species in this hemisphere.

My mother was a nervous energy-bomb who spent all her time controlling other people and throwing fits when thwarted. She was a dreadful snob and had such a high opinion of herself that no-one could share it with her, except perhaps her devoted second husband. She was extremely clever with words, which she used to cut me and other people to pieces. Her best characteristic from my point of view was her inconsistency: being highly emotional, she would often forget her own rules.

She managed to make absolutely everything in the world seem a source of potential danger: fire and water and roads and heights and other people. I came to care obsessively about pain and death, becoming vegetarian at the age of twelve and plaguing myself daily and deliberately with the thought of the millions of animals being vivisected or killed for food.

My body she stole from me almost completely: I was not allowed to wash my own hair or choose my own clothes. I was not allowed to play with the 'scruffy' children in the street. I must not pick up their accent, nor shout or rush about. I was destined for university from the age of five, and it was there that I would meet a nice young man of my own class and marry him. My mother, a member of the British Communist Party, delighted in retelling me stories of her French aristocrat forbears.

Thirty-two when she had me, my mother had been raised in true Victorian fashion. For her day, she was a rebel, leaving home at the audacious age of twenty-two, before getting married, and going to live with a girl-cousin. My mother showed a nosey interest in sex, but only on the level of my body and its development. Men didn't exist, and nor did women's feelings towards them, except ones of disgust. Sex was evidently something engaged in twice in a life-time to collect the two dear little children that every natural woman must long for. Out bursts of violence speckled my teenage whenever my mother felt the threat of lively energetic sexuality entering the house. She once stormed through the house like a hurricane because a friend of mine had come in 'with her eyes sparkling and her cheeks flushed'. 'How dare she come in here *like that*.' I never knew exactly what my mother meant and never felt the inclination to probe further. I just knew I hated her and I knew I wanted boys, and that was enough for me. What I didn't know was the damage that such clouded explosions were wreaking in my body. I came to associate 'excitement' with the most disgusting state imaginable, and I was many years into my therapy before my eyes cleared sufficiently for me to see that my face when red could also be quite beautiful.

My father, the defeated one, a Gemini with two tragically conflicting sides, was cold and unapproachable in his pale misery when I was little. Once I became a grown and flirtatious woman, his face flushed in my company and he behaved more like a visiting lover than a father, though he would have been shocked and furious had anyone pointed it out. Raised in a totally materialistic tradition, anything that smacked of emotion was to be ridiculed. My Dad was a sneerer, his contempt could kill. But what keeps me in love with him, though he is many years dead now, is his boyishness. Spurts of good humour would bubble up through the heavy layers of depression, he would come swinging down the path whistling to visit me and was shy when I kissed him. The love he never dared show was deep and real. He was your average stiff Englishman, crotchety and retiring, yet with passions seething just below the surface. He was an impatient bastard and there was only ever one point of view on any subject, namely, his. He could get into arrogant anger over issues such as Vietnam (I was trying to put the pacifist line, which I now heartily disagree with myself). My father was a puritan, yet he loved sex, 'nature's finest invention' as he called it. He did not try to twist or change me, but then, he wasn't around much to try. The worst favour he ever did me was in marrying his second wife, a cold, uptight woman. He spoke disparagingly of her himself, but there he was, and he had a son by her when I was thirteen, and when it was time for my father to die, she successfully came right between us.

I had practically no contact at all with the man my mother married, because I would not accept him or speak to him. He was not my father and that was that. Worst of all, he had no identity of his own but seemed just a shadow to execute my mother's commands. It is only since my mother's recent death that I have come to know and like him as an individual in his own right.

I was born in 1942, during the war, my parents' eldest living child. We lived in digs in the war, and I remember playing with the landlord, but not with my father. When I was two, my sister was born; I punched her in the stomach as soon as I was left alone with her and hated her all my childhood. I sensed very clearly that there was not enough love in our family to share with yet another baby; I was already hungry myself.

My parents were always quarrelling and fighting and finally split up when I was about five. My mother married one of our lodgers a year later. My dad went off and lived alone for a while and then got married. Throughout my father's life, I saw him once a fortnight or once a month, but in my head I lived with him always.

I clung closely to my mother in my early years, refusing to speak to strangers, even if they were children. I wouldn't go to the toilet unless she was standing there. I would wet myself rather than go to the lavatory in anyone else's house. I was eneuretic until I was fifteen. Yet when I started school, I enjoyed my new-found separateness. I remember even now the exact lay-out of each classroom, who sat where, the children's and teachers' names, even my first reading books.

At eight, I consciously withdrew from my mother into a secret little world of my own. I fell in love with a boy in my class and loved him silently and secretly for four years. He was pale and shy and had grey-blue eyes like my father. He never spoke to me, but I spoke to him all the time in my head. Whatever I did at home, I phantasized him standing by me approving or disapproving of how I was being, of how I looked, of what I did. Only when I went to the toilet did I leave him outside the door. I put an enormous tension on myself to be perfect so that he would always love me.

At the ages of ten and eleven, I was happy for perhaps the first time in my life. I had become much more extrovert; I was popular with the boys at school; my form-master obviously liked me. He was tall and had white hair. At ten, I started a childhood romance with a lodger's son. We used to creep into bed with each other every night, until somehow my mother managed to turn me against him, and I never spoke to him again. I didn't know myself why I was being so cold, yet somehow I enjoyed the power such cruelty gave me.

At eleven, the energetic little world I had carved for myself was stolen away. I had the misfortune of passing the 'eleven plus' and ending up in a cold, hating, strict, uniformed, one-sex grammar school, ruled over by a smiling tyrant whose life was devoted to killing little girls. I fell very ill after only a week at the school, and spent the next five years growing in hatred and rebellion, learning to despise sterile dehydrated 'knowledge', acquiescent, spineless 'friends' and everything that was anti-sexual.

Between the ages of eleven and fourteen, I thought of nothing else but finding a boyfriend. I lived for Fridays, when I went to a youth orchestra, dressed-up and made-up, and fell in love with the boy who played the double-bass. He had blonde curly hair and blue eyes. Just like my father. I cried nearly every day of my life during these years, and fought more and more with my mother, who was quite determined that my sexuality should be turned nowhere but to her.

At fourteen, I at last managed to find a man willing to take from me my hated virginity. I didn't even have periods yet, and I still wet the bed. I didn't even know how intercourse happened, I just knew that something did, and that it must have more meaning than mothers and school and nice clean socks every day. My lover was twenty-three and we stayed together for a year and a half, until, in fact, I found him as oppressive as my mother. They had both decided I was to marry him, and that I shouldn't wear make-up or sexy clothes. Some of the time he lived with us, and most of the time he slept with me. My mother twisted herself and me in knots playing the double game of 'I know he will take care of you', meaning he wouldn't dream of having sex with me, whilst at the same time making such remarks as 'Don't make the bed squeak too much.' I pretended never to know what she meant.

Apart from my need simply to be held, sex for me meant the passion of secret rebellion: my black-ringed eyes and aching genitals carried me through morning after morning of exultation, standing in my hideous uniform, freezing, in military lines, waiting to file in and pray to a god I knew didn't exist, watched over by rows and rows of bitter old maids and frustrated young ones. Making love in itself was a terrible tension for me: a constant terror of my mother bursting in. I would lie holding my breath, hating my lover for every sound he made, hating him for his quick breathing and his ability to let passion take him over without a care for the danger I was in.

By fifteen, I was weary of his jealousies and controls. I wanted teenagerhood, boys who were young and fresh and didn't know how to kiss. So I broke away from him (years and years later he was still visiting my mother), and started hunting again, a sophisticated little fifteen-year-old newly menstruating, finally having stopped wetting the bed, and armed with the sexual experience of a twenty-year-old.

At sixteen, I met Graham. He was blond and blue-eyed and

shy and scruffy and withdrawn, and looked like my father. He was only one year older than me, a local English working-class boy, and a virgin. We spent a beautiful year together before we had sex, a year during which I guided him through and sometimes out of several outstanding neuroses of his such as not daring to eat in my house in case his table-manners weren't right. We were happy and close. I'd walked out of the ridiculous grammar school and my world opened up briefly as I sailed happily through a year at a co-ed., no-uniform, happy-go-lucky technical college where I did 'A' levels and shorthand and typing.

At seventeen, I made a bad move. I went abroad, alone, to work and to live with a German man penfriend I hardly knew. I left Graham and my childhood and discovered the cold and killing world of unskilled labour, first in a Coca-Cola factory, and then in a hospital. My teenage dream romance with my German local newspaper reporter ended up in getting hit and being told that 'women like it'. After four months, I returned home, broken, but angry. Six months later, at eighteen, I was married to a soft-spoken Spaniard I'd met at a dance two years before. We hardly knew each other, and our marriage was empty. All I wanted from marriage was the security of guaranteed sex. That's how I thought of it anyway; I didn't yet know that what I really needed was to be held and cherished; I also didn't know that my constant frustration was due to the fact I'd never heard of orgasm, let alone had one.

Meanwhile, at eighteen, I got into politics. My parents were in the Communist Party, so I joined the YCL (Young Communist League). It didn't take me many months to realize I was with a load of well-meaning dummies. I branched off into the CND — the anti-bomb movement — and this at least was meaningful. I became super-active, organizing first the local group, then the Kent region, and finally working at head-quarters in London. I went on every Aldermaston march, I marched from Edinburgh to London, but when I wanted to join the San Francisco to Moscow march, my husband put his foot down, picked me up bodily and put me on a coach for home, locked me in our room for several days and alternated between tears and threats until I agreed to abandon the project and come with him to Spain.

Four months we spent in his country, me miserable as hell. There was nothing in our marriage for me; I was desperately hungry for physical contact and he, nine years older than me and brought up a Catholic by a cold father and withheld slave-mother, seemed to find sex abhorrent.

In the autumn of 1961, it seemed there was going to be a nuclear war over Berlin. We set off for home on our scooter, but four hours later watched helplessly as a huge tree-trunk bounced off an oncoming lorry in front of us. We hit it and flew through the air. My husband, ignoring his skinless, bleeding legs and my hysterical sobbing, inspected his ruined scooter. I stayed in deep shock for days on end, tossing and turning, my face a swollen mess. Pepe, my husband, got the scooter mended and we drove home on it, both in pain. At night, he agonized, not being able to bear even a sheet on his wounds. I lay beside him in the other agony of needing to be held and loved and having a fierce, unapproachable husband. I developed a neck tic which jerked my head to the side every time a lorry passed, and when we got home and my face healed, I noticed one side of my neck was starting to grow. It grew and grew during the following weeks till a fist-sized tumour formed. Secretly suspecting cancer, the surgeons had me in hospital — for the first time in my life — and cut open my neck, discovering TB, though I knew for myself that the horror and shock and loneliness of my accident had more to do with it than any unpasteurized cow-milk. A week after my operation, I was better. It was a sunny October and I was nineteen and wanted to jump up and run about. The grass outside my isolation ward was green and called me. I wanted to go home. I was laughed at. 'You'll be in here to make decorations for Christmas' the nurses said. The grammar school, working in the hospital in Germany, and now this. Shocked, furious and impotent, I was having another taste of that other world, the one where life is stopped and individuality scoffed at. For five weeks I spat fire, I argued and I cried; I was told to mind my own business when I asked what was in the pills I was expected to take into my body. I got a bad name, finally sunk into depression and got really ill. Then they sent me home.

I soon went to work again, fell in love again, went back to politics, and got more and more distant from my husband. He got a girlfriend, but got me pregnant first. I decided to throw in everything and try to make things work between us. He decided to leave me. I couldn't believe it. Twenty years old, pregnant with twins, crying every day, locking myself in the bathroom with razor-blades, wanting only to have back this husband I hardly knew, I finally fell really ill and had no will to recover. My mother, alarmed, fetched Pepe home. I asked no questions, took what warmth I could, and held in my revenge for later.

With such a nightmare pregnancy, only my ignorance made me hope for a natural birth, at home. After three days and nights of labour, I was finally whisked into hospital and operated on. A deformed baby, who died after three weeks, and my daughter Rebecca, perfect, nearly twelve years old as I write today.

My father collected me from hospital; another autumn, and another near nuclear war, over Cuba this time, just when my babies were being born. Milk poured from me and wetted my nightgown and fed the incubator babies in the hospital, but no love flowed from me as I breastfed my one baby; I was too cold and unloved myself for that. My father was vacant and silent as he took me home to Mum's big, cold house. He didn't know of anything to say to me, and he soon left. I spent a few night-marish days there, in the house of my mother who knew every-thing about bringing up babies; she bossed and she freaked and what life was left in me took me away from her and into the caravan Pepe and I were buying. I was scared to go there, but I went and it was better. I wanted Pepe to take from my breasts, to see me feeding our baby and to join in. But he was on hospital shift-work, bad-tempered if woken, busy and cold.

After three months, I deliberately dried up my milk supply so that I would be free to run away from home if I needed to. The fight was still very much in me, though my baby got bruised in the battle. My only passion was for my freedom, I was too unnourished to be a mother. With Becky nine months old, I escaped for two weeks on a political campaign to Greece. I met Volkhard, a nineteen-year-old German boy, and my life began again.

Volkhard introduced me to rationality; to the idea that women are people and have a right to stand up in the world; to the concept that I could be in charge of my own destiny; to the existence of the unconscious and its geographer, Freud; and to the world-shattering fact that females have orgasm. I was twenty-one. I began the relationship in a light-hearted, arrogant fashion; yet after a year, he had become a loving and supportive daddy for my bright-eyed baby, and a patient, interested therapist to his neurotic but passionate girlfriend. When I first experienced orgasm, at the age of twenty-two, my troubles — and his — really began. I expected him to know my feelings as if he were me. I was dashed to despair when I found his responses lacking. A pattern so familiar to me now that I give therapy, but at that time neither of us knew what was going on: Volkhard had opened me up to my feelings, given me back my self, taught me to love and trust again, and to take a pride in my sexuality. Given so much, I wanted so much more. For three years he patiently rode my storms with me, until I finally left him. We both gained a lot and hurt a lot. Plunging into Freud, I discovered the wonders of dream interpretation and started writing down my dreams. The German fetish for rational thinking, until I outgrew it and learned to hate it for the killer it can be, was a very opportune tool for me in the chaos I was in. I treated Volkhard rough, demanding he exist for me and look after me and my problems; and I gave a lot, fun and love and life force.

It was the death of my girlfriend that became the final death of our relationship. I had known Vicky only a few months. She was an Aries like me, tall and dark and fierce. I fell in love with her passion, her hatred of coolness and rationality. Her boy-friend was like mine, conventional and cool. We fumed one evening together, gaining new strength to fight the climate we lived in and the men we lived with. But we lost, she forever, I temporarily. I grew a tumour in my womb and sent myself home to England. She wrote me this letter the day before she killed herself:

Dear Jenny,

Your letter arrived today and I was very pleased. But I cannot comfort you because I am myself in need of comfort. My boyfriend wants to move out, to live alone.

We have been living together for six months and have often quarrelled, sometimes quite fiercely. He said I ought to change my ways, the trouble with me was my hyper-sensitivity, and I couldn't expect him to make allowances for it. I was desperately miserable and suffered greatly but he never did anything to comfort me. When I met him, I was completely resigned to expecting nothing from men but frustration. He gave me hope and sometimes I was even happy with him, which I had never been before. When we quarrelled, I was always horrified by his brutality. During the past few weeks I began to suspect that he doesn't love me at all, he is just using me. I asked him: 'What am I to you? Am I just a machine that supplies you on call with sex or discussions on how to change society?' He said: 'Yes, anything else was just metaphysics, ideology.' Ideology to want to be loved, to want to be understood and cared for?! So, it now turns out that for him the fault in the machine 'Vicky' is irreparable, she is neurotic and has to be sent to the doctor, like a washing-machine to be mended when it breaks down.

When I first got to know him, I told him I was neurotic, that a psychotherapist had told me so; I told him I had already been in a hospital for psycho-somatic disorders, and that I had discharged myself after four days because it seemed to me I was relatively quite healthy. I told him I needed to see a psychiatrist. He reckoned he could help me and said things weren't really so bad with me. And he was right; I felt better than ever before; suicide thoughts which I used to carry around with me all the time only came back when he was cruel to me. But now he has come to the conclusion that I am not curable, not by him at any rate.

I promised him I would be less sensitive, that I would stop

making demands that had always caused trouble, I begged and implored him to spare me this pain, but he remained unmoved, stony. If I am to be logical, I must end it, but it is so difficult for me and I will suffer so much.

So that's how things are with me, Jenny.

I had wanted to ask you to write to me, but I didn't dare to. I am so pleased that you have written to me anyway, especially now when I am feeling so bad; it makes me feel less alone.

Is your father good to you?

How is Becky?

Vicky

When I received this letter, I was scared for Vicky's life and wrote back immediately, a 20-page letter, outlining in detail how we could live together in England, give up our boyfriends, and find contacts that were right for us. I was ill myself when I wrote, homeless and rootless. My phantom tumour, which had got me out of Germany, had dissolved in a flood of grey water which ran from me for one whole day. I had left the intolerable atmosphere of my sister's house and had travelled far north to Newcastle and the coldness of my father's house. My Becky was ill with a high temperature, but my stepmother said it wouldn't be right to fetch a doctor out in the night. By morning when he arrived, my baby was better, but I was laid out in the terrible pain of migraine. Vicky was already dead by then, but I wasn't to know that for several weeks.

I was in London when I heard the news in a letter from Volkhard. He didn't know how she died but suspected suicide. Finally the official version came through, from Vicky's mother, and via Vicky's fiancé: the story was that she had got killed crossing a road. I knew for sure this was a lie as she was as 'neurotically' careful about crossing the crazy roads of Frankfurt as I was. I thought maybe she'd thrown herself under a car. I wrote screaming letters back to Germany telling them they were all liars. Her mother pleaded Vicky's shortsightedness and the fact she had a period at the time! So then I knew there was a plot afoot. Volkhard wrote me a groovy letter about Vicky's funeral, how they held discussions with the priest, and how they should have played Beatle music, and how he couldn't pretend he cared because Vicky never did like him anyway. I wrote back to him in a white fury, sick with grief and impotence:

After a week maybe, when the pain isn't so strong, the pain of knowing that my Vicky can't love any more, can't laugh any more, can't scream when she hears pigs like you talking; perhaps after a week I will read your letter again and answer you 'sensibly'. But rationality and cool thinking are completely out of place at this moment. Your letter is out of place too. Vicky killed herself twice in vain if her boyfriend is anything like you. Thank god, that's all I can say, thank god that I didn't do it.

I will surely come back to Frankfurt one day. I would have come back for Vicky's sake anyway, and now I will still come back for her sake, to make sure her murderers don't kill anyone else. Even if a girl throws herself under the wheels of a car, she doesn't have to be killed; to be injured perhaps, maybe she wanted it that way, just to be badly injured so that the world would open its eyes. But then she wanted to live on, she wanted to live and be loved, properly. She was so good, so stupidly good, still so young and still so soft and not bitter yet, and yet so shortsighted that she couldn't see that all the unfeeling people would carry on just as before. Thank god she was spared the pain of reading your letter, of knowing that you dared to make a rational assessment of her character a few hours after her burial, and that you are not ashamed to express sympathy for her boy 'friend'. Dead already, and you want to kill her again. Not satisfied with already having killed her, you want to make sure that she didn't deserve to live anyway, that she was wrong in her life.

So she treated her boyfriend in public like shit? Oh Vicky, such a sin: you must die for that! Go on, kill yourself quickly, or else we will kill you. Making a man look ridiculous? Have you no shame? He makes you unhappy at home, in private? You cry and he doesn't comfort you and you have become bitter and you seek revenge? But that just won't do, you are a woman, you must hide your pain and your unhappiness, you must pretend that your man knows how to make you happy.

You must lie, or die. And after your death, you will, of course, not be missed. You were a burden, you and your damnable everlasting demands for happiness. At last we've got rid of you. Now we can get on with our studies, now we can spend our strength on really important things like changing society and making the world happier. When we had to fuss over you all the time, we had no time to help the working classes. You wanted your happiness immediately. Why weren't you patient, like the working class, why couldn't you learn to suffer quietly, why did you play your woman's role so badly?

Well, I am even more shameless than Vicky. Not only do I refuse to accept these norms, I also refuse to die.

I came too late to help Vicky, but I can be her revenge. I will not fight just against capitalism, but against all the cold people who kill those who are warm and alive. At least Vicky has done her dying; I still have that to go through and I am very frightened of it.

So you went to her funeral, Volkhard? Why? To hold discussions with the priest? And Dieter went too! And didn't you both once scream out SUICIDE! Vicky didn't die, she was killed! You'd have done better to stay at home and cry and promise yourself that such a thing would never happen again, that you would never again lead 'private lives', that you would concern yourselves with the problems of this world today now in Frankfurt, that you would never again stay at home studying books on how to change the world, but would go out and talk to people, talk to them about their problems — not with priests, who in any case think they've got a second life. You sneer at Carsten's mother because she cried for Vicky, yet she was ten times better than you: at least she was ashamed, at least she felt uneasy; maybe she didn't know why she was crying, but she did know there was something to cry about. Beatle music? Very clever. Only trouble is, Vicky wouldn't be able to hear it, her ears are full of earth.

You won't see me for a long time. But not a very long time. I will come and live in Frankfurt with Werner, and we will collect all the Vickys around us so that they will never feel alone. And we'll smash up all the cars of all the fast drivers so that they can never again help lonely girls to their death. And we'll wear scruffy, dirty clothes and parade around, to disturb people because they know that sex is messy and dirty; and we'll make noise and loud music, because people can't bear that, for they know that sex is noisy and like loud music; and we'll have really long hair, lots of it, and the men will have beards, and we'll laugh when we see how uneasy it makes people feel, because they sense what Hair means. And we will Do Nothing, Do Nothing in public, because that's not allowed: you can only Do Nothing at home secretly, behind closed doors, and then only when you're pretending to be Doing Something. And we'll knock on all the doors, and when we hear a girl crying, and the screaming silence of a man, we'll drag her out of there quickly, so that there won't be any more suicides in Frankfurt-am-Main.

Well, Volkhard, if you are reading this today, I can't take back one drop of the passion of my hatred and hurt, but I will tell you, now that I know my life better, that you helped me more than any other boyfriend before therapy, and that it was through you that I began to find myself.

For a few months after splitting up with Volkhard, I lived alone, working in dingy local offices. I felt cold and stunned. I sought out my former acquaintances in politics and found they had moved from theory to direct action, which suited me fine: they were engaged in a campaign to improve conditions in hostels for the homeless, which meant amongst other things allowing the husbands to sleep with their wives. I met Derek, and threw myself into a total relationship almost diametrically opposed to the one I had had with Volkhard. I did not develop in myself at all, but had the emotional, irrational, mystic side of myself confirmed, which in the early months felt like floating on a warm cloud. Derek was a Pisces (Volkhard a Virgo) and with him I crept back into the intuitive side of myself which had been so sorely abused and trodden on during my trip into German materialism. Sex was always bad and started corroding our relationship right from the beginning. Still at least Derek was into reading Reich and didn't call him 'the one who went mad' as Volkhard had. Both Derek and I had the devil of a time coping with our aggression, though we didn't realize this then, and our relationship ended some eighteen months later with me with a bloodied head standing in cold defiant fury, but never fighting back, something in those days which I felt to be 'beneath me'.

It was through politics again that I met my final boyfriend before therapy. I met Nigel in Cambodia on a 'peace mission'. The trip didn't bring me much peace: for confusion and misery, this relationship beat all previous ones. I had finally found a man I thought would solve all my problems: one who wanted sex more often than I did. The result was I went completely cold and found myself praying that he would fall asleep at night and not want sex. But at least this gave me my first inkling that there was something very much the matter with me, and not just with my boyfriends, which is what I had previously imagined.

It was in the summer of 1968, in Frankfurt once more, this time with Nigel, that circumstances combined to cause me to write off to get therapeutic help. It was now two years since Vicky had died. I went to visit an aunt of hers and finally heard the truth: Vicky had hung herself. Her mother and fiancé had indeed concocted the story of her death on the road, the very same day that she was found hanging there, made-up and dressed-up, in her bedroom. I thought my body and mind would crack wide open with sobbing. I cried for days and nights on end. And then I knew there was some frightening uncontrollable force inside me that could lead me to disaster, for my despair was followed by a passion to get Vicky's fiancé, sleep with him, have him love me, succeed with him where she had failed. Carsten had blond hair and blue eyes and, of course, looked a little like my father. I got as far as sleeping with him before I realized I was going crazy. It was Nigel's patience and hurt which brought me to my senses enough to avoid any macabre theatrical ending to the story. I wrote to a Reichian therapist I had heard of and David Boadella answered me, and that's really where my life begins.

Undercurrents

Beneath the bravado, the bloody endings and the fresh beginnings of my swirling emotional life before therapy, one thing remains constant: terror.

Ever since Volkhard introduced me to Freud and his dream interpretation method, I got into the exciting and rewarding habit of writing down my dreams. Until the start of my epic correspondence with David, dreams are all that remain to chart the storms and whirlpools of those floundering years. I reprint some of these nightmares here, without comment; I believe they say much for themselves.

Wind Dream, 7th May, 1965
Suddenly horror. The door is flung violently open and a strong blast of wind and darkness comes in. The horror is the fact that no-one comes in, it is simply The Wind. The Wind wishes me evil, it is punishing me, watching and controlling my actions by spying.

I become suspicious of everybody, frightened to let anybody in, scared of opening doors and windows in case The Wind gets in. It seems to be laughing in the background all the time, it knows it will win in the end, because it is stronger and has more weapons and is cleverer.

Gas Dream, 27th March, 1966 (A month after Vicky's death)
It is wet, dark and cold. I am with about four people, including
Volkhard, by a river or canal. We enter some sort of concrete
building. I go in last.

As soon as we are inside, I realize something very strange is
happening to the people I am with. They are changing from
quite ordinary, generous human beings into savages, like the
Nazis in Germany: they are tormenting people and are
preparing to cut the throat of one boy or man. This is accom-
panied by general laughter and merriment. I am absolutely
horrified, filled with anger, yet almost powerless to do anything
about what's going on. I turn to Volkhard thinking, 'He's not
like them, he'll help me do something about it.' To my utter
horror, I realize that he is 'turning' too, he is starting to giggle
and get silly and yet monstrous like the rest. I am nothing to
him and I know that any minute he'll join in. I think everyone
is going mad, when suddenly it occurs to me that there must be
something strange about the place we're in, something funny
about the air, something which is overcoming all these people
who were previously so nice and kind. As I'm thinking this, I
feel suddenly that it is affecting me too, this gas, or bad air, or
lack of oxygen or poison or whatever it is. With a tremendous
effort, I decide frantically that I must get these people out
before we all go mad and kill each other.

Even as I decide this, I feel a light-headed sensation come
over me, like the first effects of a gas anaesthetic. My knees
start to give and I feel like giggling too. I have a strong
inclination not to care, not to give a damn about anything, to
laugh and be silly with the rest. But with a tremendous effort, I
get hold of Volkhard and start to pull him out of the shelter.
This is terribly difficult and I keep thinking I'll have to give up,
he is so strong and heavy and resistant, and also because the
effects of the gas on me are more and more difficult to overcome.

Finally, when I think we are both dead, I find that with my
last drop of strength I have managed to drag Volkhard out of
the building. We both collapse in the fresh air outside by the
canal and slowly revive. I experience tremendous exhaustion.

Double Nightmare, 4th May, 1966
I dream that I have just woken up from a dream. It is the
middle of the night and pitch dark. I don't like being alone.

Suddenly, I have a strong sensation of the door opposite my
bed being opened and of someone making their way up to me.
I can feel the horror and stinging in my eyes and nose as I write.
I force myself to say 'Who is it? What do you want? Who are
you?' There is no answer, yet I still feel this Someone coming.
Feeling dreadfully alone, I force myself to get out of bed and
put the lights on. The light doesn't work. In terror I move along
the wall to the table lamp. I press the switch. It doesn't work
either.

In panic, I awake, amazed to find that it was a dream, I was
so sure I was awake already. I lie absolutely electrified, petrified,
in the pitch dark. I can't move because of the electric shock in
my limbs. Somehow I dare to open my eyes. Forcing myself to
move, I get out of bed and switch on the table lamp. This time
it works, and I leave it on all night.

Pig Dream, 3rd January, 1967
A pig, large and ugly, appears. It comes straight for me. It is
grinning, but I know it wants to get me. I am in great danger
and turn and run as fast as I can. I dash through door after
door, slamming them behind me. I rush up stairways and round
corners, each time only just making it, the pig hot on my heels.
I run on and on and finally get to the top of the house where
my father is asleep in bed. The pig is close behind me. I scream
aloud, hysterically, for my father.

Jinx Dream, 4th January, 1967
A curse is set upon someone I know: the effect of the curse is
that he has to dog me wherever I go, whatever I am doing, who-
ever I'm with, by unexpectedly, erratically, appearing before
me in different guises, quite unrecognizable to me at first sight.
The imposition of the curse is sudden and shattering; we both
suddenly know we are in it, inextricably, for ever.

What happens is I may go up to someone and start talking,
treating him politely. Suddenly he will grin maliciously, say,

'Hullo, it's me' and then disappear. The curse makes living itself unreal and impossible, as I never know who is a real person and who is my jinx. I realize I cannot live on like this, cut off from the ordinary world, so I try to escape each time I sense him coming. I rush at great speed along corridors, in and out of rooms, down fire-escapes, down and up lifts, through underground air-raid-shelter-like places. Many people see me running, but no-one can help me. I daren't stop anyway, because they might turn into the jinx; I can turn to no-one. My flight is full of fear and horror, yet it is somehow satisfying to feel I am at least doing something positive and daring to change my destiny, even if I have little hope of winning out against such a terrible power, and even though I may face horrible punishment when I fail.

Spaceship Dream, 17th February, 1968 (Sleeping out on a beach in Thailand)
I dream I am in bed. There is a loud alarming noise of jet aeroplanes, war planes. I look at the sky and see a strange contraption, enormous, a great machine with flashing lights. It is making a hell of a noise and is coming nearer. It is coming directly for the house from outer space. It lets down a small capsule, box-shaped, which falls down, unreally, clumsily and heavily on to our bed. It just misses me and falls on to my sister's stomach. I shift it over, wake her up and she frees herself. I have a sense of urgency and great evil. I rush into the next bedroom where my mother is sleeping to ask her what to do. I am very scared and have changed into a child. I rush back to my dreaded bedroom and see that the satellite is very conspicuously absent. There is a sense that it has escaped or been reclaimed. The feeling of the presence of superior powers that can work this kind of trick is strong and frightening and makes me feel alienated from the natural world.

Bomb Dream, 28th February, 1968 (First night in Bangkok prison)
I am in my garden with someone I know. The sky is gloomy and dark and there is a feeling of mustiness and sterility about the

scenery. Suddenly, a cylindrical bomb or rocket or space-ship is taking off from a stony spot further down the garden. Fire appears all around its base and the top separates and takes off. I imagine a mushroom cloud in the sky. I rush behind a wall with my companion and we throw ourselves flat on the ground and cover our eyes. I wait for the flash, the boom, and the wind, and have no hope.

Execution Dream, 3rd April, 1968
I am with a large group of people, all involved with me politic-ally. We are moving forward along the side of a house, which is my grandmother's house. Suddenly a message is called through the air: Everyone who belongs to the Communist Party, STOP! Some of us stop dead in our tracks, including my father and other old commies. Immediately upon hearing the message, my legs go weak and my feet drag and I have a terrible compulsion to stop. I don't belong to the party, but it's as if the force of my family tradition is having an effect on me; I fight against it and move on, very slowly and painfully. Others are passing me by.

As we near the end of the building, there is a large stage from which a light is shining. Most of my people have moved on and are standing in front of it. I hear another announcement and see some sort of leader organizing things. The announcement is that all those who are not communists are to be gassed. The news is taken stoically, tragically. Some are terribly affected, but quiet and accepting. I see Derek in the back row and feel with him despair and anguish at the point of death. He turns his head to one side and puts his hands over his face. I am the last to round the corner, and as soon as our fate is announced, I slide back-wards, mechanically, without any conscious decision. I pretend out of my fear that I too am a communist. I am scared, feeling guilty like a child. I am scared that the leader, a woman, will call me forward to stand where I belong. But she is looking away and now I deliberately move back a good ten paces to make sure I am not with those who are going to die. All is in darkness except the light shining from the execution stage. I am heart-broken for my friends, I can feel their fear as if it is happening to me. Then the gas is turned on, and all my comrades die. I am filled with hatred for the power that is doing this thing.

Then a change comes. I feel my friends are not dead, but only deeply unconscious and there is at least the chance they can be woken up. I rush around, tending to all my people, who are slumped on chairs or on the floor. I try to rouse Derek; I feel they must not be left unconscious for long or they will never come to. Derek's head keeps lolling about. I feel very gentle towards him, terribly responsible and concerned. Another person, my Mum's maiden sister, has shrivelled to a pancake. I think she is really a hopeless case, because being so much older, the gas will have affected her disastrously. But I battle on with my work, rushing around to each in turn trying to revive them. I have a feeling I will win in the end and save them all.

At one point after the gassing, I see news flashes, slogans which fill me with red-hot impotent fury. They are put out by the government that has done the executions. The notices are in capitals and excuse the gassing, saying how necessary it was and how the deaths don't matter, it was all for the good of the regime.

Gas Again, 16th July, 1968
I am standing on a bridge looking down at the murky water a long way below. Someone persuades me to go down into the water. It is cold and grey and dark. I go into the water and am just a few feet from the bottom, and worried I might not have enough breath to get up again. A female person comes up behind me and puts a mask before my face, which is supposed to be an oxygen mask. I would much rather rely on holding my breath than be given oxygen. My anxiety increases as the mask comes nearer to my face, and I am near panic as it closes over me. The attitude of the woman is one of silent, gentle authority, of knowing what's best and of looking after my interests. When the mask is right over my face, I still fight against breathing in. I hold my breath because I can't be sure it isn't poison gas.

Death Dream, 19th August, 1968 (With Nigel in Frankfurt)
Nigel and I are sitting in a rocket with Becky on some sort of round-the-world trip. The rocket goes straight up, and will then be intercepted by another vehicle which is to take us into orbit. Becky is on my lap and she is fed up. As the dream starts, she is saying, 'Why do we have to go up in the air, why couldn't we stay on the ground?'

I put my hands gently over her face and press her to me and say, 'You go to sleep and don't worry, it'll all be over when you wake up.' She settles, but just then Nigel and I simultaneously have a flash picture of the vehicle we're in prematurely separating from the rocket and falling. We know immediately that this is the end. We are filled with unspeakable sadness and helplessness. I hug Becky to me and put my hands round Nigel's face and kiss him. I keep repeating to him, 'I love you, oh I love you, I've loved you so much.' He says grimly, 'Another bloody tragedy, another tragedy they'll read about in the papers tomorrow.'

Then we start to sink rapidly, knowing the sea is thousands of miles beneath us.

The horror wakes me up, and I am amazed to find I have not died.

The thaw

Kindling

Lighting a fire is therapy enough: stoking
can be as grim as breaking rocks
or hewing at the face below the earth,
for when the dead coals settle in the body
of the grate, and all the fire is choking,
only a poker-fist seems fit to smash it open.
But fires are subtle as roses, need careful nursing,
so the hands that feed the flames must feel
sure as a surgeon's to where the bright heart beats.
Test your skill then on the blackened fuel,
coax in the air, and start
the red life drawing to the stove's lips.
Learn at last the delicate fire's art.

David

It didn't occur to me to write much during the first year of my
therapy. Basically, what was going on was that I would go and
see David for an hour a fortnight and my contact with him
would charge me up with the energy and confidence I needed to
carry me over till I saw him again. The essence of the healing

effect he had on me lay in his capacity for responsive, energetic listening and the magical way in which he would feed back into me the chaotic outpourings of life force I delivered him, in the form of sparkling crystals of insight. David received me with excited approbation: no criticisms, no deadly Helpful Advice; just this really straight little man looking right back at me with unguarded blue eyes and touching me now and then with electric, undemanding fingers.

My first year with David was a period of adjustment: a pause from my frantic relating to the world outside me, a tentative step towards looking at the world inside me.

My father died. I settled down in London. For the first time since I was fourteen, I was not in a single marriage-like relationship. I was beginning to stand up, open my eyes, breathe deeper. I bought clothes for myself that were not absolute necessities. I even painted the walls of the room I was squatting in. For a change, I was in the world, not simply passing through it.

Then, with an office job and a typewriter in front of me all day long, I started to open myself to David.

8th April, 1969
Dear David,

I sunk into a depression at bedtime which carried on till yesterday morning, deep, terrible, total. Normally when this happens, someone is hitting or hurting me, or not caring. This was the first time it had ever happened with someone being completely loving and sympathetic. It was worse in a way, knowing something inside me was wrong. I just sat and looked at the wall. I couldn't do anything, not clear up or work or cook. I cried, but only halfheartedly, if Steve touched me or spoke to me. I couldn't go out. I missed the sun I love, and I missed the Easter marches for the first time in nine years.

23rd April, 1969

Well, if you want a negative transference, David, and hate and bitterness, you should be here now because it would be easy. For you it's just an intellectual exercise, the sessions are great fun for both of us, and also totally irrelevant. In real life, all that counts is the crushing and the ropes tying you up and helplessness of the people around and ultimately the knife in the kitchen. So one day when you hear, 'Sorry, she can't come to sessions any more', you'll have to shrug and say, 'Oh dear, one of my failures.' All the things you suggest I do when in trouble only work in a world of dummies and not where sick humans are concerned. If I let out some of my aggression and bitterness, how can you think the other person is going to stand there and do nothing? They react, they hit out, they make it worse, then I'm back where I started, only much worse, and even more determined to keep free of contact, not to let anyone know what's inside, because they only hurt you more when they know; they're all babies too, so I don't see how it's all supposed to work, and I don't believe it ever can.

The distended bladder must burst, and as there's never anyone else there to do it for me, because they're all deflated, dead bladders, I must do it myself, and as far as I can see, a knife is the quickest way.

5th May, 1969
Dear David,

Well, the whole world is crumbling about me and I don't care and am even glad; I love chaos, it relieves my energy tension. I am still besieged by dozens of hungries each weekend and haven't reached the NO stage, though I'm angry enough now to jump that hurdle soon. Perhaps one day I'll get angry enough to chuck everyone out.

When you met me, I think I was basically a smiley person outside. Now I feel I am a scowly person. I don't like you very much either, nobody, in fact, except Becky who I think is bloody marvellous, she's started to be scruffy and messy like a good squatter's kid — I can't stand it, that's why I think she's marvellous, to have broken out of her upbringing already.

6th May, 1969

I have told Trev he can go to hell, and everyone else too. I told him quite openly; I just don't want anything to do with restrictive, non-revolutionary, vindictive, clinging men. I enjoyed telling him to sod off because I didn't feel I was doing something cruel, I just felt I was legitimately asserting myself. I feel free, and not alone, although the memory of being close and warm and sexual with someone often causes me a pang. I feel very alive today.

There hasn't been a revolution. I am not independent. It hurts me when my bloke doesn't come home till the early hours of the morning; but I don't sink into it. I'm aggressive at home, not in a petty way, but openly and laughingly. Everyone thinks I'm mad of course. I haven't any illusions, I know that I'm not strong enough for this to last, but I feel it's a marvellous breakthrough to have experienced even a taste of what it will be like to be me instead of someone else. I'm enjoying my freedom, even though it means a lot of loneliness.

13th May, 1969
Dear David,

On Sunday, I distributed a large bowl of grated cheese all over Stephen and over most of the room as well. The whole passion lasted only as long as an orgasm and I dissolved into helpless giggles afterwards which left me feeling absolutely marvellous.

I still feel wonderful, not high, just wonderful all over. I am convinced that my hair, which was dead, has come to life and I wouldn't be surprised if it started to grow (it stopped growing seven years ago when Becky was born). Also, my breasts have suddenly come back to life and I've put on a bit of weight which makes the difference between feeling empty and feeling alive.

Through the newfound aliveness and confidence which David's therapy gave me, I was able to allow myself also to start to feel the layers of deadness inside me; these show up in the following dreams which I had in Spain, summer 1969. (For those of you not familiar with feeling out the significance of dreams, the simplest and most powerful method is Fritz Perls' approach: consider every symbol in the dream to be a buried part of the dreamer.)

*I dreamt I had a beautiful penis, but that when I touched it,
I could feel nothing, it was dead.*

*I dreamt I had a baby, without fuss and without letting the
nurses know. I was proud, but anxious because I wasn't sure
whether the baby was alive or not. It didn't seem to be
breathing. I asked someone whether it was dead. They said, 'No,
that is quite normal, babies are always like that, you don't have
to hit it, it will just start to live of its own accord some time.'*

*I suddenly remembered in my dream that I hadn't been for
ages to see my rabbit at the bottom of the garden. I rushed to
it, sure of disaster. The animal was very ill, dying of neglect. It
had a sort of myxamatosis-looking disease, eyes glazed and half-
blind, a big abcess on one cheek, ears flopped, weak and
immobile. I gathered it into my arms and held it close, full of
love and misery. The animal leant close to me, enjoying my love
and warmth and saying, 'Ah, that's better, that helps.' I was
overwhelmed with love and pleasure and misery for the waste of
its life.*

Also in Spain that summer, a poem came to me, for just the
second time in my life. I had been thinking of how I'd been
with Becky when she was a baby.

surrounded
by her inner space
the unsuckled mother
flounders, unfilledfull
and spurting forth a flood of emptiness
from her weeping nipples
drowns her child.

                                        Jenny

Apart from Therapy

In the summer of 1969, two movements were born in England
that were to accelerate the changing of my life and the lives of
many others.

One evening I went to the first PNP meeting*. 'People Not Psychiatry' was an attempt by a mixed group of people, myself amongst them, to take the treatment of emotional disturbance out of the hands of 'experts' and bring it back to the community. Thrilled with my own therapy, I put my name on the 'network list' and determined to use what I had learnt about myself to help others.

That same evening, I left the meeting early in order to go to my first encounter group, one of the first ever to be held in England. It left me, like my first therapy session nine months before, walking several inches above the ground. A whole new area of experience had opened to me. The group was run without structure or leaders, though the main instigators were Layla Shamash and Till Norland. I needed the group very badly. I was living alone, having moved out of a crowded Ilford squat to a more middle-class squat in Lee Green. I was very lonely and lived from one group to the next, one session to the next.

Then one day, Pam Barnett, wife of Mike who had conceived the PNP idea, asked me to move into her Belsize Park flat with her. I was no longer in the suburbs, but right at the centre, in the first PNP house.

*See 'People Not Psychiatry' by Michael Barnett, published by George Allen and Unwin, 1973.

Learning to swim

During the autumn and winter of 1969, I was studying for an M.A., translating an article for David's new Reichian bulletin, 'Energy and Character', helping Pam cope with the influx of cries for help which followed the PNP advertisements, and still trying to deal with my own inner sadness and chaotic relationships.

At Christmas, Pam's husband moved back in with her, and I had to go. I lost my first woman friend and went to live with a man. It didn't work and I ended up in a dreadful little attic room in Notting Hill Gate, feeling abandoned and very alone. For several months, I'd been hearing tales of an American guy called Jerry who was in the same encounter group as a friend of mine. He sounded strong and non-conforming, and I wanted a fruitful relationship with someone who would help me forward instead of dragging me down. I phoned Jerry up and started my first matter-of-fact relationship (no love-at-first-sight or 'forever' promises). We saw each other for a whole year before finally moving in to live together.

In the spring of 1970, the sun shone again for me. Unbelievably, I was being handed a house to set up a PNP community.

I wrote to David in May:

I was twenty-eight in April, and for the first time I am not having fits about the passing of time and advancing years. This is not just an absence of anxiety, but a positive feeling of liking to be the age I am. I feel alive and better and in-myself more, ! enjoy being me. And as I feel fulfilled, there is no nostalgia, I'm happy to be where I am.

The therapy experience for me is like a simplification, a quietening down and a straightening-out; no accent on the mind-shattering experiences I expected, no magic changes so that people look at me and say, 'gosh, isn't she different!' I suppose I always thought that I'd change beyond recognition, yet somehow it's not like that. It's more that the hysteria is an overlay, and I'm underneath it, quite sane and calm really.

Dream about David, 4th June, 1970
I go to my mother's house. There has been a plane crash and David is dead. I feel the most heartbreaking, shattering sorrow. I feel I cannot live. His body has been brought home and he is lying under a sheet. The whole dream is drowned in my crying.

Suddenly, I see the sheet move, as if David is trying to sit up and is failing. I tell my mother. She goes to see, but says that it's only the last of the death agony and that now he really is gone. I feel something not-quite-final, which increases my aching sorrow because it allows room for hope.

Letter to David, 6th June, 1970
David, I've got to rethink the whole universe. I'm travelling so fast I can't stop. Listen to what I've seen:

If the distinction between 'material' and 'spiritual' is one we've created for our own comfort, and if, in fact, there's no gap, just a gradation, then babies come out of you only from what's there; you can't invent them from what you're not. So you make a baby, like you make a dream, no-one helps, it's all your own work.

So, look, David, I made two girls. I made one totally perfect. Becky is flawless. And then there was Nicole, with my face, born to die, with all those deformities: Look! a head so big, so full of water she couldn't hold it up; a backbone with a great big hole in it, as good as no backbone at all, so she'd never hold herself up in the world; and her legs, pathetic, paralysed, she'd never be able to stand up for herself, never be able to kick out at the world. And she wasn't allowed to cry; she was in so much pain they kept her permanently drugged up to stop her screaming the hospital down with the agony of the three endless weeks of life to which she was condemned.

So I let Becky live, and hated her rounded perfection; and I reproduced myself in Nicole, loved her pointed little face; loving her was easy, I knew she was going to die.

Letter to Jerry, July 12th, 1970

The jagged rays of energy that flash out of me tell me I want you very much. But how can I stop eating you and stop paining when I don't eat? Jerry, it's a full-time nightmare and it's not fair to you to have to solve it. It's a pain for me to go away, I'm not brave, I'm lonely and frightened, with a gay grin. But I can't stand my plague, the fury I feel when I don't get the solidarity from you that I need. Circles, circles, but at present I can only see me working it out alone, loving you from a distance, weaning myself. David says, 'get close', but closeness is death for me. I couldn't get up today. I need to lie forever in a warm bed with you, to suck you in, digest you, fuse with you, and then to lie forever as one single maggot and die warmly. That is the extent of my present horizon — be horrified and run, Jerry, run.

I can't stand separation, I can't bear the fact that our two bodies are separate. When I see you, I am not me because I am breathing through you, lost completely. It'll take a long time Jerry, I don't know if there's an end, there must be an end. I used to think that if I were satisfied sexually, the clinging squashing would stop, but that was when I believed sex was the whole world, and now I know it's just a metaphor: to be joined, to be touched, to be hot all over, to be flowing with energy, to be the sole focus of another's attention, even if just for a second. No, sorting out my ego will solve my impotence, and not the other way round. I'm really lost at the moment, I can't be anything for you, except a damned nuisance. Such fun I am at other times! all smiles and jokes and emptiness inside. The sad me, the useless, ugly, helpless me you see is far realer. I've danced and bounced and sparkled my life away for others, and leaned and drowned when in close contact. It doesn't stop, and I have no answers, only spinning circles, whirling labyrinths, endless trick mirrors reflecting a nightmare cycle. So the riddle is how to love you for you, not love you for me, how to look at the kittens and love them and let them be, not want to squeeze them to death to absorb their beauty and sensuality.

Whatever happened to me in the womb? What went wrong? Did they send a blast of cold air down there and cut the cord too soon?

I hate you for needing crutches, and because I am not the main crutch you need and that is the only thing that could keep my neurosis in order. And at present it is very disordered, getting frayed around the edges, bald on top, thin in the middle. It's breaking down and I haven't found a replacement. I'm desperate, breathless, the breakdown engulfs everything, the world around me is catastrophic, everyone is sick and I am helpless to help, so I hate them for being sick. I can't think rationally, nor feel coolly, gently. I'm swimming in a muddy pool full of grey, confused goldfish, wild with staring eyes; the universe is going mad, popping with the swelling of Bad Energy, undischarged energy that is clogging up my system.

○   ○   ○

I went to Spain to get away, and to find myself, alone without Jerry. When I was there, I took some LSD.

I want to say something about my attitude to drugs. I had been a puritan about everything except sex. I disapproved of people who indulged themselves with food, clothes, cinemas, cigarettes, drugs of any kind. I hated the 'maggots' as I called those who sat around and smoked hash. I despised people who ran to an aspirin bottle when they had a headache, like my mother always did. I had never given in to my needs for comfort and hated others who were able to.

But for me, acid was different. In acid, I found a private

therapist. I travelled further, quicker, alone on acid than in weeks of sessions. It put me in touch with my body — I did not go on 'head trips'.

The first time I took acid had been with Jerry and Becky. That time, the dose was far too huge for me to cope with: I discovered that I didn't have a middle, that I couldn't stand anything made of metal, that my caravan was a cardboard box, that the countryside was made of plastic, that kittens were very serious indeed when they were 'playing' and, above all, that I didn't have 'a place': I kept asking, 'Where do I live? Where do I sleep? Where is my place?' I also caused my daughter some amusement and exasperation by constantly asking: 'Do I want to go to the toilet?' To which she answered, 'How do *I* know, it's your bum!' Becky knew where she began and I ended. I had no such sense of self.

The second time I took acid, I spent most of the time alone, and wrote this to Jerry afterwards:

I am writing during the gentle come-down from a trip. My eyes are still like saucers and I'm dripping sweat, but I want to tell you what a good letter yours was, so simple, like a slap in the face, down-to-earth and I saw you suddenly, so direct and uncomplicated and no-nonsense and I like the bit about me being a genius at creating problems. Right. But I got rid of some of them today, lying on the bathroom floor looking at the water cistern with my feet in the basin, smelling Becky's weed-up nappies and digging the cold floor. So I looked in the mirror and saw, yes, she's ugly, and I had a two-hour long think about that and decided, 'OK, so do you live in that skin and like it, or not?' And that was so tiring I had to curl up again on the bathroom floor and decide. Well, I thought a lot about what you said last time, that you can make the trip what you like. And I came across a piece of truth, a peaceful truth and I kept repeating it, and started to smile. It was: USE THE HIGH, DON'T LET THE HIGH USE YOU. So I stood up (I also collapsed again a few times) and I shook the life back into my body and decided, 'OK, so this is me, I lie down and let me get on top of myself, or I just dig being me.' I kept asking, 'How can I make myself comfortable?', that is, nice to be me, and I saw that that's all there ever is, that's the only problem anyone can have.

Now I know it's wrong to sit and wait to be warmly loved; you either go get or sit quiet and feel your loneliness, but whatever happens, not blame anyone, and that's what I was doing. I was tight, strung up, screwed up, desperate for contact, hating myself and my skin and my face and my body, but needing people and not knowing how to make contact, and blaming you for not giving me the togetherness I needed to feel, watching for the letters, waiting for a Jerrydaddy that doesn't exist, running to nothing from nothing.

Acid is strange, you open your eyes big and wide, and you stare and you look people straight in the face and you forget you're ugly and you feel high and silly and a bit crazy, but you feel full of joy and that you want others to be there and you feel gay and floppy and sloppy and the world slows down, it's not all so bad, you love others because you feel great yourself, not that kind of love I usually love, desperate sucking-clinging-fuck-some-warmth-in-to-me-please, join-me-up-with-myself, with-you, with-the-world, be-my-bridge, help-me, stop-me-drowning, let-me-take-a-peep-out-of-the-womb-without-coming-out, without-standing-on-my-feet.

And to David I wrote a few days later:

Dear David,

I haven't written to you up till now because I felt I had only banalities and repetitions to tell you — a lot of depression and constant refuge into suicidal feelings. Always the same business of not being able to exist contentedly except via a male.

I spent a very blind, pleasurable week with a German boy of twenty here, and I took an LSD trip, my happiest day here I think. This young guy was so obviously a stranger that even I couldn't fool myself that he was my lost breast, so I simply had to stand up and take care of myself. So after some quiet tears of realization of my separateness, I got up and shut myself in the bathroom for a couple of hours and tried to sort a few things out.

I tried to discover why, under acid, the world becomes so plastic and two-dimensional for me, why so un-fleshy and un-soft. I lay down on the cold floor and tried to relax. Things slowly began to get good, it was good being there alone. The thing for me, for a hysteric, seemed to be not to be swamped and drowned by rushing energies, but to harness them and use them, greedily, to enjoy. When I got to this, the world started to open up, and the bathroom stopped being two-dimensional and started to expand. I moved my body to get some life into it and then embarked gleefully on a new world exploration, and left the bathroom.

I'd like to have stayed feeling like that forever, but there I was the next day, pretty much my despondent self. But I know the trip wasn't wasted, because that whole thing happened, the music and the lollipops, the laughter, Becky, and feeling beautiful.

But now I'm still back to looking for that magic god who's going to open my eyes, dust my brain and drag the sickness out of my stomach. I know now that my wanting a lover is simply wanting to be cuddled, and to have someone to play with. My sex obsession has melted away.

I'm glad enough if I can get through the day just feeling nice about something for a couple of minutes. Most of the time, my body is cut off from me, I am stiff all over and move through the world stiffly. No blood flows through me and I'm sure my stomach and bowels are full of nascent cancer-seeds. My head is full of gunpowder and my jaw is the trigger. I wake each morning with my jaws cemented together and my hands, if I don't oil them soon, will wither away with arthritis. Spain's a good place for showing up sickness in glaring colours, no watercolour landscapes, escapes, here.

The German boy I met on holiday came to stay with me in England. This hurt Jerry terribly. One of my escapes from the huge feelings I couldn't cope with when I related closely to someone was always to run to another lover, a faery figure, a secret, safe and stimulating daddy, someone it would be totally unrealistic to relate to on an everyday basis. I recognized this at times, but couldn't yet stop a pattern so deeply embedded. Jerry and I tried to help one another. Now when I look back on those times, I shudder at the chaos, the confusion we were in. But we were alive and determined to stay alive, fighting so hard to breathe.

On 7th November, I wrote to David:

David, I am ready to break down and it's only a question of time and space. So many realizations, coming in so fast, each one illuminated and clear in the moment, so difficult to recapture the next. I'm tired of fighting, I want to sink completely, see the lot.

After Dieter went back and I was still on my hysterical love cloud about him and not caring about Jerry at all, just kind of being with him in a disdainful way, orgasm was so easy it frightened me out of my skin, I didn't know myself, I went into fits of horror saying 'this isn't me'.

Then when I let myself feel my need for Jerry again, I stopped being able to have orgasm. I could not open up so completely to someone so close. I wrote to David:

This really terrible thing happened on Thursday. About an hour before he was off to therapy, Jerry said something to me that really woke me up, I could feel life flowing in me, the first time for so long, and I dared to let it flow and felt incredible need, all over me, my chest and hands and head, a real good cracking-up, just letting my need flow, such a relief, and I had a short vision of Jerry and me being very well able to give one another therapy and was feeling how safe and good it was. But my good feelings lasted only a very short time — Jerry obviously wanted to get away, he was into making cups of tea and getting ready and didn't want to make love. I tried not to notice he didn't want me, but I did notice and I was cracking up, I needed to cry, to be touched. My world was coming to blackness. I went downstairs to tell Jerry what I felt and when I saw him making tea when I was hanging over a precipice, I broke and threw the kettle round the kitchen and ran and locked myself in my room. I was panting with anger and freak, but I felt good now, the block was broken, and I needed very badly to cry. I needed just to lie there and go through with it alone, because there's only yourself anyway in the end.

But there was Jerry knocking at my locked door, so I got up and broke the spell of knowing what I felt. I stopped the deep hurt angry breathing because there was Jerry, aggressive and puzzled and trying to shout solutions out of me. And when he was gone, all I felt was pain, I had a terrible time, so split and helpless and had to go and teach at evening school.

So how do I integrate all the bits now that you've helped me wake them all up? I've experienced hate and aggression and I accept them and am not frightened. But I *am* frightened of need: I know now how to be angry healthily and have felt its healing effects. But how do you go into need curatively? My need is still in the quagmire, unclear, nuclear, unthought-out, unaware. I need while hating, I need while denying it, while hating to need. How do I need cleanly? That will only happen when I have two feet to stand on and not just half a foot and a shaky crutch.

In the autumn of 1970, I had noticed adverts. for an organization called Quaesitor. They were offering encounter groups at monstrous prices. I was angry. I knew from my experience that ordinary people could get together and run a group, there was nothing to pay anyone for. So I put an ad. for free groups in International Times. The response was immediate: a small group of us met in my house and began to find out what you can do with nothing but a room, and some bodies. This experiment was to prove the most important adjunct to my therapy with David. Jerry and me, Laszlo, Sylvia, John, Terry, Marie and Jackie, a nucleus that stayed together for a year, while dozens more stayed awhile and then passed on. These groups became my new world where I could integrate all that David had helped me feel about myself. No leaders, no techniques, no expertise: we worked from what we had, our bodies and our hangups about them.

In one group, Laszlo suggested that, one by one, we take our clothes off and find out what we felt about being seen, touched, described, by the rest of the group, and also to tell the others about our own body-image. I wrote afterwards:

And they all said to me, friendly, not knowing about my scarred stomach, 'Come on, Jenny, you be first.' I stood there, completely stuck, terrified, and them all smiling at me, a bit puzzled. I burst into tears. I showed them my butchered stomach and lay down. They looked at me caringly and talked to me and told me beautiful things and then they laid down with me and touched me and stroked me and were so loving, I couldn't believe it.

Later the whole group found a space in my small room to lie flat in, close together. We all relaxed and breathed. And because it was safe, and I was happy, and I loved some of the people, I started deep breathing, and I didn't stop. I wasn't frightened, like in the sessions. I went up to where I've been with you, David, when I start to tense and freak, and then beyond, I just kept going, because there was nothing to be afraid of, there was a room full of people I trusted and it was so warm and safe and there wasn't an inch of my room without a body on it. So I kept going and charged the whole of my body with energy: porcupine pins and needles everywhere, I got higher and higher, I went deeper and deeper, till my teeth were chattering crazily. And then all I know is, I was surrounded, there were Jerry and all the others I know so well, all looking down at me, gentle and concerned. I was deep in it, I had absolutely no feeling of apology or embarrassment any more, I was far too involved to feel any of that. My ugliness feelings about my stomach were forgotten. What shone out beyond all else was my total intouchness: I could feel every knot and block in me. I kept moaning, 'my knees, my knees'. They were tight. Fumbling hands loosened them, and judders were set off immediately all over my body. The tension in my hands I could ease out for myself, but my mouth was hopeless, there was nothing that could be done about it. Derek tried leaning on it, but my shivering continued and my jaw was locked.

I kept going into fits of giggles when I felt how clumsy they all were, how they didn't know how to let me let things happen and were all so busy 'doing'. And later, when they rocked me in the air, I was giggling then too, for pure joy and love and pleasure.

At one point, I opened my eyes: my room had the hottest, deepest colours, it was a wild acid dream of beauty. I had to close my eyes. After the rocking, I lay back, and Jerry said, 'Let's give her space', and they sat back. But I felt as if their hands were still on me and that I was floating near the ceiling. The whole thing was a gentle love-trip, but my teeth kept on juddering, and my eyes were full of the terror of so much feeling for a long time.

The flood

At Christmas, 1970, I went back to Germany and the past. I visited Vicky's mother, slept in my dead friend's bed. I wrote to Jerry:

Vicky's mother gave me a hot bath, towels, the world and a dressing-gown and a German feather bed, and fussed and clucked and my identity started seeping into the floor and I felt so happy I could cry. She said she couldn't take me to see Vicky's grandparents, because I was so like Vicky, they'd have a heart attack.

I felt so in love with Vicky, like after she died, I just wanted to touch her and kiss the pillow, but she's been dead four years now. Her mother says she was 'shining and triumphant' in her coffin, as if saying, 'ich hab's geschafft' — 'I did it'. Vicky won, yes, but I'd rather she'd lost and was in bed with me here now.

As I walked to her bedroom, I grew several inches taller and became bonier and my face changed and I was on the brink of fear but it didn't come, ecstasy instead as I became Vicky.

But then a bad night full of nightmares. I was hanging on a cliff, sheer rock beneath me, hanging on to a cracking branch and wishing to be safe in a warm bed, and promising myself if I ever got to a warm bed again, I wouldn't climb any more cliffs.

Then a second night in Vicky's bed and such terrible dreams. woke up stiff after a terrible, terrible quarrel with you in the night. I wanted to kill you and woke up chewing over and over Vicky's death with 'if onlys' and thinking how much more healthy murder is than suicide.

Then I went back to sleep this morning and had another dream which made me feel sick and disgusted. I was in the school gym, being particularly stroppy, refusing to do anything the others did and doing what I liked. Then this Thing, a female Thing, wispy and ghostly as if she didn't have a proper body, started advancing towards me. She was sticky and tricky, not monstrously frightening, but like fog or mist, I didn't know how to fight back. So I started to run for my life, and the rest of the dream was one of those life-and-death chases, with this thin female being always just behind me, and the feeling of her tentacles almost on me, a weak, pitiful creature, but none-the-less revolting. I ran through doors which would never shut properly behind me, I was always trying to bolt inefficient bolts, and always had the feeling she could seep through the cracks. Once I was struggling to bolt a door and realized I was bolting it on to thin air; panic and terror and a feeling of impotence, a sensation that any strength I had was leaving me and that there was no-one in the world who would save me from this creature.

It ended in the bathroom. I locked the door behind me, but it made no difference: a great long thin arm got in and was stroking me in a slimy fashion from behind; the whole essence of this creature was seeping through the cracks. I grabbed hold of a strange ugly soft doll that this creature had been carrying and had squeezed through the door. I put the dead limp doll in the toilet and pulled the chain, though without hope because I thought it would never go down, but that the water would overflow and I would be lost. It did start to overflow, but then the doll disappeared, and the dream was over.

But the feelings weren't. It was as if I had those clammy hands all over me.

You know, Vicky's mother is so like mine, only worse. She's more educated, more snobbish if that's possible, less humourous, and she's suffered more. But really, basically, identical: she doesn't let you breathe or move, she's got her own ritual for washing up, for everything. I feel her tyranny even as far as the toilet. She would never understand how obvious it is that she built Vicky's suicide step by step and day by day. This house is horrific. There is horror in every room behind the shine.

So I went home to England, to my own warm bed, and to Jerry. We felt ready to move in together, so he came and lived at PNP house. I wrote to David, 12th January, 1971:

Dear David,

At midnight, I set myself this impossible task, to tell you and myself what is happening. My head is full of incoherence, it is getting dangerous, maybe it's been as bad as this before, but at least then I couldn't see the full extent of the horror. But there's no hiding now.

I came back from Germany so relatively 'clear', I came back knowing the sense of my relationship with Jerry, the one factor that remains constant, that allows these further delvings into horror. I came back a week early because I wanted Jerry and because I had a longing for my Becky, and because to be in Germany made no sense: everyone so sweet to me, but everything so empty. I have a home and feel best there.

I took mescaline in Germany, so different from acid, you stay in contact with the world around you, in magical contact, the world so fascinating, and people so transparent, lovable in their weakness, sitting around they were like chimpanzees and birds. Everything was so clear, I could see all the rules and moves and whose go is it next? and where's the referee? and did someone go over the line?

But when I got home from watching this game in all its beauty and boredom, there was the mirror, and I have never seen anything so ugly in all my life. I was shocked, mesmerized. So old, David, how did I get so old, and my skin like the face of the moon, so ugly, David, unbelievable. I cried, just hot water flowing, because I knew my body had had it, dead, no healing possible and I knew this body will never feel good in the world.

Jerry and I had both grown through being apart a couple of weeks and we are ready to be together. I felt my full height for a few days, and twice I had baby orgasms, so easy, only whispers, but so easy.

But now, David, I am bad again, I'm so sick it's unbelievable. Maybe it's because I've got Jerry that I've allowed myself to feel this sick. David, this is no fun, just wanting to die because you're dead already anyway so you might as well not have the tension of life flaunting itself before your eyes and you can't participate. Plenty of understanding, oh yes, and so what? The same cul-de-sac as Freudian therapy as I see it and I hope you can convince me otherwise, David, because I don't want to be right. I just see circles and two years of therapy, all very cosy, and I'd pay you just to spend a couple of hours chatting with you, but what's it all got to do with therapy?

David, I am very insane, I didn't know it, and if you did, then you've been kidding me up very kindly, but it's a shock when I find out, like giving birth to a thalidomide kid and no chance to kill it.

And I'm wearing Jerry down, it's no fun being 24-hour-a-day therapist to a real nut with a lot of power and no thanks. I beat him up last night, I've never done that before to a man, I felt a little relief afterwards, but it didn't last long because I soon split off the half of me that did it. I'm a real head case, I didn't realize, I always thought it was the body. But how can you heal a mad head, the body's there, you can get at it, but where's the head? All those tubes, so complicated, you get lost in it.

I woke up crying my eyes out in the middle of the night, having tried to kill Jerry in my dream; and I went to sleep and woke up crying my eyes out, having tried to kill him in another dream. And in the afternoon, I slept for ten minutes and woke up crying, and you can believe it's getting us both down. I don't even believe in my own spring-ups any more.

But therapy continued, and I didn't kill myself. One hour a fortnight, later two hours, kept all the beads of my energy trips threaded together, kept me connected with what was happening to me. David didn't interpret, but he got excited: he got excited when I found my own insights; he would pounce on them and hold them up to the light for me to see; he wouldn't let me smother them over in more words. And he only let me talk when there was energy and movement behind my words. When I got confused or ran away with myself, he would lie me down, shut me up, have me breathe myself back into my senses. And one day, he broke a great taboo. My therapist wrote me, his patient, a poem.

Hysteric

Women's lib means doing your own thing,
Setting your teeth at the world's wind
Steeling your skin
Against the black
Horror of being
Woman and outcast.

It would take an axe to chop up the ice
In your head, but they cut your body
Instead,
Took out one twin alive and one dead,
They left the terrible wild man
Of your rage inside, crying to kick out,
But the only sound was a scream in the dark.

No wonder you felt for the blacks, the beaten,
All that hunger and thirst
After humanness.
When they stood rebels against the last wall
and shot them, the sun turned black
As a hanged girl,
So what right had you to your own skin?

All cats were you,
Soft fur, pent claws, cut glass,
A hiss in the spitting dark,
And tigerish dreams.

When you shut your eyes
And shuddered to be you
Your teeth rattled like knives
But no sound came
Only a green smell of ether
The vast hunt of the mind in outer
Space
Forever.

Every emotion was like a spell
You could not break.
At Salem they would have burnt you
At the stake
For sorcery,
And for your soft cat's eyes,
That saw too much.

Outcast girl,
In the middle of the rain, in the middle of the night,
With your half-mad mum in your skull,
        and your half-dead dad
On your back,
How did you get home again,
Get back in a warm room,
By the fire, set your eyes straight
At a human face
Come into your own skin at last,
In spite of the world's ache?

David
February, 1971

○   ○   ○

In March 1971, I took another acid trip and wrote:

The first thing I had to do was say 'goodbye' to Vicky.
Everybody thinks that's a picture of me on my wall, but it's

Vicky. I looked at her and knew that all that united us was our suicides, and so I had to say goodbye to her, for that is no longer my way. The parting was like any other, tears, and a certain relief.

I lock my door, and that is a very good feeling, the peace is immediate. I have a long discussion with myself as to whether this time and space are really mine, whether I really can be alone like this for myself. I go anxiously through all the people I may be shutting out.

Then I let the shivering take me over, it joins me up and it is good to allow myself to shiver. I discover that clothes are strange things, separating one part of my body from the other parts, and that although I want to be covered, I want all my body together in one place, wrapped around by something big. I experience taking off my clothes *for me* for the first time. I am very sorry for my chest, it is so tiny and thin. But my hands are big and strong and they decide to look after my chest and I bring all of myself together with my hands and I am sorry we have been kept apart so long.

It is such a peaceful world to sort things out in, here in this room. Then suddenly I switch into the outside world: can I live when car accidents and fires and bombs and pain are happening? Can I let them happen and still allow myself to live? I think into these horrors and realize I can't bear them, I can't carry them all, it is too much for me, one pain at a time is enough. I think of hungriness and cold and no bed and wonder, can it all be true? Is it really true that there are people out there organizing wars? It doesn't feel possible. I am seeing heads of government and bombs falling all in ugly modern comic-strip colours and harsh, two-dimensional pictures. Then I know that I can do nothing unless I am sure of myself. And I know it is right to take advantage of these white colonial sheets around me and of the middle-class acid. I am only one, and I will carry a lot, but it is too heavy for me all at once.

The peace is enormous. But interruptions keep coming. Jerry keeps calling on me. The pineapple he brings is wonderful. I am very grateful to be fed, it is very good to be fed. Then I am back in my world once more. But there is this voice! Jerry is playing back a tape he has made. His voice is huge, unnatural, it is in my floor and in my room. I try to shut it out and get tangled up with trying. I go to the door and listen, and my paranoia explodes in a burst of energy and I yell and scream at Jerry to turn it off. I think he is playing back a tape where he is saying very intimate things about me. I crash back into my room and I am trembling all over with mad rushing energy and I sit down with myself and ask, 'what happened?' And then I write down: PARANOIA IS NEVER BEING PRIVATE.

It is Sunday and our group arrives. I am acutely aware of how awkward we all are together. I usually try to block this out.

Jack Lewis works with me, using Gestalt, my first experience of this method.

I am feeling really ugly. He asks me what part of me I feel to be especially ugly. 'The skin on my face.' He asks if there is any part of me I feel to be beautiful. 'The skin on my thighs, it is soft and smooth'. He gets me to have a dialogue between the skin on my face, which I feel to be ancient, prehistoric, hideous, and my 'new' skin. I feel my way into first one, then the other. At first, I can only become 'old skin' with ease. Old Skin says to Young Skin: 'I hate you, I want to kill you.' Then I be Young Skin, frightened and trying to pacify Old Skin. I am stuck, so Jack gets me to look very closely in my mind at Old Skin and see if anything happens. Soon I see it drying up, it is so thirsty and dead; I see it cracking, shrivelling. And underneath, red, moist softness is showing through. Then I become Young Skin, not even skin yet, just flesh. I am suspended somewhere between the two, Old Skin is dying, flaking away, and Young Skin is not yet formed. Jack says, 'Stay with Young Skin.' I am just a blob, very alive, but formless. Then soon I make out a huge head, with a tiny, curled up body, obviously a foetus. I don't have any arms and legs yet, just buds. But I have a smile, not a smile on lips and mouth, but the Potential of a smile, a smile hidden in the middle of the warmest part of me, with one big eye peeping upwards. And the more I peep and glance around, the bigger my smile gets, a naughty smile, full of anticipation and pleasure and curiosity. Then I take a deep breath, and another one, and each time I take a breath, my body gets bigger and each time I feel myself puffing up bigger, my smile gets bigger with pleasure, until I feel the enclosure too small and begin to wriggle. I am wriggling and grinning and breathing deeper; and as I wriggle, I get a budding feeling, and the budding becomes a reaching out, and the buds are about to become arms and legs, but someone comes in and interrupts.

Old Skin says to Young Skin: 'Why should you have any pleasure? I never did.' And Young Skin freezes and stops growing and is very cold.

On 28th March 1971, I wrote to David:

I would like to record these times too. Previously I have invented that I may only bring you magnificent improvements or occasionally catastrophic depressions. But this ordinariness, this blocked-but-in-touch-with-the-blockedness and this just-under-the-surface-excitement I want to tell you about too. David, there is joy just around the corner. The joy of doing things for myself and for my body, the joy of yoga and dancing and swimming, all timid and stiff, but full of potential; the joy of our groups, still tense and nervous, but excitement and fullness there for the taking; the wonder of my therapy with you and the therapy I feel so nearly-ready to offer others; the quiet joy of knowing soon I can look at people and the world and not mind my age because now is forever.

I am reading Fritz Perls' 'Gestalt Therapy Verbatim' and I would like to keep every word written in the air before my eyes, I'd like to make it all a part of my way of living. I feel that everything is coming together and that I can bear it; I am frightened often, yes, but no longer need to run. The house is quiet. I am nervous, but no longer hope-less.

Pick the pieces up

There was this hope
blowing through a hole in the sky
that things could be made right.

If the wind would turn
so they could carry the dead back alive
out of snow,
if only the clock had stopped
before the fuse ran out on the time bomb,
if grey flesh would mend
or the drowned child swim home
from the sea.

There is a thin flame, in our time,
licking for warmth round the roots of the heart.
The cold eye kills it,
the dead hand of reason
knocks its life out.
So only a ghost still plays in the dream.

There is so much force
in a human cry:
a scream can crack open rocks,
but not stone men.
A baby's howl echoes to the roots of the earth,
but not in the next room.
People's throats become graves nothing bursts from,
so even grief has no healing.

David

It was shortly after this that I had to cope with one of those
setbacks that comes to nearly everyone in therapy: a visit to my
mother's house. I went there for a couple of days with Jerry
and wrote afterwards to David:

After two evenings of television, Jerry and I went into the
kitchen, gently, to escape. The storm broke. My mother
howled and screamed about politeness and how she does all she
can to make us welcome and when she comes to us there's not
even a proper chair to sit on. I sat silently 'like a sullen teenager'
Jerry told me later, and let her storm on. It was a very heavy

experience for me, because before I've always been busy hardening myself to what's coming at me and haven't been able to listen to what is really going on. But now I have new ears.

Here was this obviously hurt, out-of-touch old woman whom I didn't really know, sitting in an armchair informing me, Jerry and the cat with all the catastrophic energy I have inherited that I had a wonderful childhood. What a happy, united family we had been! and what dear little children we were, until of course it 'became the fashion for children to rebel' whereupon I followed the fashion, only I was in a ridiculous position because I 'didn't have anything to rebel against'. I had had all the freedom anyone could wish for and a mother who was so 'with it' she had let my long-haired boyfriends play guitars in her drawing-room while she supplied us with Espresso coffee. Jerry had it impressed upon him what 'wonderful powers of imagination' I had and how I should have been an actress because I was so good at over-dramatising my life. These powers were then illustrated from letters and diaries of mine my mother confidently admitted to having read 'in my own interest'.

I was stunned. Not because it was new: I had heard it all a thousand times before; but because my ears were new and I could hear clearly each Catch 22. But still I couldn't react: I felt that if I let anger or tears show, she would have 'won'.

So I was left with my feelings of injustice and fury and misery at the twenty-odd years of life I'd wasted as a monster born to a monster who had been born to another monster and wasted sixty-odd years of *her* life.

The pressure in my chest and head, David, is still there. It's not something I can deal with alone. I need to sob and rant and rage and cry and kick and have someone there to help me pick up the pieces.

A week or so later, Jerry and I went to Spain. I wrote to David, 15th April, 1971:

I have not come out of a non-living state ever since that scene with my mother. The only thing I'm clear about is how the mechanism works: if aggression or sorrow are suppressed, everything else is too. I'm living in a twilight world, knowing the answers, but as stuck as anyone who doesn't. I glide through the days, not dead or alive, not happy or unhappy, just a stupid being-in-the-world through a glass box.

So then I did something I'd never done before. I tried to write my mother a real letter.

Dear Mum,

   I am going to try something I have always held to be impossible, to end a twenty-year-old game and to start perhaps a relationship which could be something more than just biological accident.

   I have very little awareness of who I'm writing to, and only a very shaky, new-born trust in my own existence. Let me first tell you all that I know objectively about you. I know that you were born into an unlucky sex at a bad time in history. I know you had to fight for your life to escape the trap you were born into. I know you were a very sad child and that you didn't have any of the aids and opportunities I have had to understand your sadness and the things that were done to you. I know that you tried to find happiness, and to give it, in a marriage to a very cold, sad man who became my father. I know you had no help or understanding from him and I respect your second attempt to find happiness for yourself by breaking with him. From then on, I am not so clear, because then I am in the world, and anything you did was coloured for me by how I experienced it. That you always did what you thought right and best is not in doubt.

   No-one can really know your life and suffering and happinesses except you, and I want you to admit just this one thing: that I am the only person who can tell you how *my* life has been. You can tell me how you imagined my life to be, you can tell me how *you* saw things, but you can never tell me how *I* experienced *my* life.

   The thing is, for whatever reasons, I grew up to be a suicidal, neurotic wreck. And now the time has come to respect myself enough to tell you that I no longer intend to sit silently by while you tell me what a happy childhood I had and how much freedom you 'gave' me (I see freedom as something that can only be taken away, not given).

I went on to tell my mother in great detail about my life, my sexual experiences and my feelings towards her. I ended:

What you remember and what I remember of all these years just don't tally. I felt you were trying to control my life and ideas and feelings and perception of the world. I have no doubt that you were very miserable to see your daughter grow up in anything but your own image, but maybe the alternative of having me give up, submit, and end up a schizophrenic in Bexley Mental Hospital might not have appealed to you either.

Now half my life is over and I am still unable to live because I have to spend all my time trying to undo the mess that was done. Far from the 'loving mother' image you have of yourself, I felt you had a basic underlying hatred of me, a hatred of anything in me you couldn't control, as if you were saying *you* hadn't been happy, so why should *I* be? You hadn't been free, so why should I be? I know this from being a mother myself: I am an emotional cripple. I cannot love Becky properly, and she feels it. It doesn't matter how much I do for her, give her, I cannot flow towards her, because I myself feel bitter and deprived. I feel I had a cramped childhood, and although I try not to cramp her freedom in any way, I cannot yet spontaneously put my arms out to her. I know you were able to do this when we were babies, but what happened when you noticed I started wanting to walk and breathe alone?

Dream, 2nd May, 1971
I am in a flat with a blond woman I don't recognize; she is about thirty and famous. I have the feeling she has given up on men, she is disappointed; she seems sad and calm, soft. We don't speak, but there is a gentle unspoken attachment between us. I go over to her. There is consent in her manner and I feel very much her equal, though we are worlds apart. I feel I can help her by giving her a little love. I touch her; everything is very

*smooth and gentle, visually sexual, but without genital feelings.
I start to take off her bra and touch her chest. She has very
small round, hard breasts and her skin is white. My pleasure
comes from the feeling of acceptance and consent.*

*On waking, I remember the dream with pleasure, especially
because it was a woman. To love a woman would be to love
myself and to have done with the hatred and fear of my mother
which separates me from loving and respecting a female body. I
can't yet identify with this open, accepting, mature woman, but
she must be there somewhere in me or I couldn't dream about
her.*

Nightmare, 3rd May, 1971
*I am flying high in the sky which is dark and troubled. Jerry is
with me. We have to keep flying around and must not come
down low. There is a foreboding atmosphere. I have to fly over
a forest which frightens me. Jerry keeps flying near me,
grinning, coaxing and goading me to fly down over the forest. I
accept this until suddenly the horror comes over me that this
person who is flying with me is maybe my real enemy. I try
weakly to fly away from him and wake up in cold electric
terror. The feeling was that we had been fighting together
against some outside evil when suddenly I fear I am being
tricked and he is the real evil.*

Jerry worked with me on this dream, using Fritz Perls' method.
First I talk to 'the power of flying': You are a strain; you are a
pleasure, but a tyranny. You keep me going, you won't let me
relax, give in, fall down.'

Then I talk to the force of gravity which is constantly pulling
me down and which I have to fight. I discover through talking
to it that it is fire and energy, the devil, laughing and playful,
mischievous and amoral.

Then I become Devil-Fire myself; but I daren't use the voice
I hear in my ears: it is chuckling and witch-like. *Dignity* is
stopping me using this voice. So I get a picture of Dignity. He is
a cold, stiff statue which stops at the waist and is shrouded in
mist below that point. He never moves his mouth, never smiles

or cries, and yet he is not cruel — that would be beneath his dignity. He makes anyone who comes near him feel good, but doesn't have to do anything to spread this feeling. He is eternally calm and untouchable. Only death can bring him down, but death itself is Dignified.

Jerry tries to get me to bring Dignity down to have a look at the Devil. But there is always the mist surrounding Dignity's lower half which prevents him from descending. He won't *speak* about the Devil, but this is what he thinks: 'You poor creature, so evil and dirty and enslaved, so undignified and ugly and hateful. But it's not your fault, you were born like that. I pity you. But you must be destroyed, people must be protected from you, you cannot be allowed to spread your destruction and contamination around.'

Then the Devil looks at Dignity and cackles and laughs and dances in his everlasting fire, which is himself, and taunts: 'Oh, you poor fool, you pity me and yet you are the sad one, you are dead, you will never know the warmth of my fire or the fun of my dance.'

○   ○   ○

While I was in Spain, David sent me back some of my very early letters to have a look at. I hated them. David wrote:

Your old letters were horrifying to you because you have changed so much you hardly recognize yourself. At the same time, I think you fear you could be plucked back into that maelstrom. I know it is hard, but one of the things you will learn as you get better is that it is still possible to have bad times, very bad times, but you now have so much more resilience and intactness that you will be able to spring back up into hope and warmth again. Guard those back letters well. I want them back one day. I enjoyed the poem to Jerry. How many more poems have you got hidden away in drawers, or inside you?

Then I sent David this dream:

*I am sicking up broken glass, like the glass when a car wind-
screen has shattered. My throat feels raw, just as it would if I
really did sick up glass. I am glad this stuff is coming out and
feel there's more to come, but sicking makes me feel terrible.*

David wrote back:

The dream, and what you felt from it, are all part of learning
to feel the hurts that were done to you. Cutting people out,
being cut out, cutting off, all spare the pain of the real cuts in
childhood. Being in a glass box was preferable to the glass
shattering or the glass inside being spat out. Perhaps you are at
last ready to let some real bitchiness and pain be expressed,
instead of suffering in silence, in the cold.

Dear David,
Got back a few hours ago from a calamitous cold and
cockroachy week on the Isles of Formentera and Ibiza where I
learned to love baths, beds and industrial pollution. I was sad
and bad, I've been down so long, since the unepisode with my
mother, and now I have become twenty-nine and I was back to
giving up completely.
I took acid to try and shift out of the rut and had a Horrible
time, on a dark beach with all the horrors of my childhood
returning. I was just a frozen head lying there, my body
destroyed and to breathe a most unthinkable thing. And
Paranoia such as never before, though probably it's always
there: Jerry would sniff and I'd hear him laughing, the breeze
was people whispering, the wild creatures were coming to get
me. I was exposed and abandoned on an island, and islands are
terrible. I kept feel-seeing Jerry's face laughing or smirking,
making faces, or I felt him disappearing. I had such a horrible
time, David, it was an intensification of the awful reality I've
been trying to see through and change. And Confusion — all
through, I never got clear, I woke the next morning in the same
state and couldn't feel out what I had learnt, like after the other
times.
But maybe now I've got your letter — David, it made me so

happy, just the right time, just the right words, and on top of the happiness of seeing Pepe and Becky and living in a real house with water and lights and dinners to cook. Christ, what's with me, such weediness would have shamed me a year ago. I have become a big blob and retired from youth with a big sigh of relief. I lived nearly all the week without a mirror, I have never done that before; I know I was hideous, sun-fried to lobsterdom, yet that was a relief, just to be ugly and not to have to be anything else. The rest of my life has been an unrealistic competition, trying to join the Miss Worlds for reasons obscure and always a painful game.

And now I'm playing the one I always do with you, and I enjoy it so much, there's something you do to my energy even through a typewriter ribbon. It's called finding Clarity in Chaos and the Promising in the Hopeless. So, well, at one point, Jerry (Christ, he was trying so hard and me stalling him at every point) said, 'Become discomfort'. So I did: I was twisted tubes, mangled up so no blood or air could get through, a labyrinth of squeezed-up pipes, bent into a space far too small. For a blessed moment, it worked: I became the thing, understood it, and knew the outlet, to stretch and breathe, and I did and was calm for a while. But then egolessness came back. I was trying to control Jerry, trying to force him to be me because it was too much horrorful effort to be myself. I kept asking him out-of-touch questions: What are we frightened of? Why are you frightened of being alone? Why are people so scared not to exist? I kept pressuring him, trying to squeeze answers out of him, and every time they weren't jewels of clarity, I became impatient and wiped him out, and with him my own only chance of existing.

I became disgusted with what our relationship had become: me eternally frustrated and disappointed, because what I want cannot be had: someone to mould me and hold me the whole time, someone to boss me and coax me into doing what I want to do anyway, someone to do the living for me, to wait on my ego hand and foot and yet, impossible bind, to be themselves, separate and strong so that I can respect and lean and trust and sink. I am a spineless corseted jellyfish that has lost its ooze.

David, it is so good to read your letter. I don't even care if you've been blinded by seeing me only in my character party-dress, I don't care if it's all lies and illusions, I just know it makes me alive again to read that I have changed and that there is hope when all I feel is that I am a parasitic nothing who is wasting a very beautiful world. David, there are so many things I want to do in the therapy with you, I want a zillion hours non-stop. I want to beat the hell out of my mother-cushion, Christ it's about time, twenty-nine and still fighting madly for a breast which was a snare and a delusion and hung me up for life. A quote from the birthday card my mother sent me — there is a key in the picture — 'I don't know what the key is for — let's pretend you're twenty-one — not that *you* ever had a key — the door was never locked!' Lies and damned lies, there were never any bloody doors, just an eternity-high brick wall.

David, a huge hug for all the ones that shrivelled frightened inside me.

Jenny

Dear David,

I am in a strange state. All I know is, I'm not a hysteric any more, and this leaves me in a strange limbo. I feel dead and depressed but it's different; I feel stupid and unclear and I can't define the difference. My feelings and my thoughts are really clogged up, I'm so armoured, my body feels sore. Mostly I feel I haven't moved for three years, that here I am in stupid Spain for no reason and that I'm the same as all the other stupid times I've been here. I constantly put myself down, but not in a whirling hysterical confusion. I'm like a centipede that's lost its legs, really helpless and dead. I've been producing nightmares at the rate of about one every two nights. And I can't settle to anything — I used to have these enormous powers of sticking at a thing, however uncomfortable, but now I'm like a bored, sulky child, fidgeting around, moaning constantly, not staying with anything for more than half an hour, full of guilt and discomfort and never ever breathing. All so vague, the days floating by.

The last two days, I just sat and tears started coming, once —

when Jerry said how awful I'd looked in England with my spots (he was saying it to say how nice I look now, which I don't feel) — I felt so sorry for myself, but I wouldn't let myself cry properly. I am so full of pride, I just can't let go. Then yesterday evening I kept feeling I wanted my father and just to let myself think that made the tears flow, but I still wouldn't let the sobbing come, though it is a tremendous job to keep it in. Jerry helps a lot, but I won't let it go too far, as soon as I feel I'm going to cry my heart out, I hate him and me. There's masses of tears inside and my head clogs up, just like when I was a child. I grizzle and moan but I feel if I let go, I'd drown and break into pieces. My resistance is enormous to all the psychodrama, encounter and Perls techniques, because I know they work. I'm nearly bursting as I write this; I'm going to suffocate through holding my chest so hard. Sometimes it's real agony and all so formless. I know so well that you would say a couple of magic words and clarity would beam down on the whole situation, but I'm pretty scared of you too because I've really suppressed letting myself see you as a person all these years; I feel so confused about all the secret shoulds and shouldn'ts I've put on the therapy. Christ, I'm really fed up with being a slave to everyone else's interpretations and approval of me. I feel angry with myself about it but then that goes in a circle too. Maybe I'm experiencing hysteria in slow motion without the energy of it taking me over.

On the last day before going back to England, I took an LSD trip to unclog myself.

I felt it would be bad, but I wanted no-one with me. Previously when it's been bad, I've clung to the other person to take away my pain. I went to bed to try and make myself comfortable. My whole body was wracked with tension and pain, as if I were blown up hard and couldn't relieve the pressure, and yet also as if I were being squashed flat from above, so that my bones all jumbled up and there was no flesh in between to stop them hurting one another. I tried to find a way to lie on my bed. I tossed and turned; I tried to breathe and relax but couldn't. 'Head' crying broke out because of my hurt, but never reached my chest. I kept saying, 'They're crushing me, they won't let me breathe, they won't let me live, I'm dying, I'm dead, there's nothing left of me, I don't know if I can fight, the weight is too much, I don't know if I'll pull through.'

I was amazed and shocked at what had been done to me, I couldn't believe it was so bad. It was like a steamroller had run over me, my bones were crushed, my stomach mangled. I struggled and struggled, very weak, as if something were pushing me down into the bed.

Suddenly, I saw my father's face and my mother's face, and I felt them very separate from me, I saw them objectively, like strangers, and *they slipped off me*. I could feel them slipping away. I cried with relief, again only a very shallow crying. I kept saying, 'About time, about bloody time, twenty-nine years, about time, it's been so long, so bloody long.' And gradually, I lost a lot of other people too: Vicky's family were the first to go. I realized with a shock that far from keeping faithful to Vicky by going back to her life, I was betraying her and myself by pandering to her aunt and mother, the very people that created a Vicky who would commit suicide. And Pepe. I'd clung to him and chased him so Becky would 'keep her father'. Now I determined not to write unless moved to: he could keep the relationship going for a change. It was such a relief to slip all these people off me, even if I wouldn't be able to keep it up. I went through the rest of my disapproving relatives, relinquishing each one of them, and had a big think about Jerry too.

My physical discomfort continued, but I found a way of letting the street noises come into my body and that helped a bit. After a few hours, I found myself lying quietly and remembered what had gone before as a storm in a nightmare.

Later, I took a look at my body. I was very brown and I found a way of looking so that my eyes were gentle and did not criticize. I would suddenly switch back to seeing just wounds and scars, but they didn't matter nearly so much now. I laughed a bitter laugh when I thought how irrelevant it is how I look to the outside world: what does it matter what my face or stomach look like as long as I am wracked with pain? The only thing that matters is to feel good inside.

Quite suddenly, I saw my body as very sexual, and that shocked me. I could actually feel the seductiveness of my own body. I went very stiff when I felt this and looked around me, overcome by paranoia. I carefully explored what was going on: I'd look at my body, changing the way I looked, so that one minute I'd see myself as forty, flabby, decadent, yet still very seductive. Then I'd see me as slim and firm, young and brown. I could switch back and forth at will. My pubic hair took me on the strangest trip. I looked at it, and it started to move, pulsate and grow, and there was a beautiful light on it; it looked like dancing spiders' legs, horrific no more. But as my pleasurable feelings grew, as I got absorbed in watching the movement and energy, suddenly I would be seized with fear and my hair would shrink again and become still. The paranoia was amazing. I could hear my name being whispered, suddenly the room would be crowded, I felt as if people were pressing aginst the windows and doors and walls. Then I'd go back to letting in excitement again: I could feel the beginnings of a joining-up between my eye and my pubic hair, as if a faint energy line were drawn directly from one to the other, across my 'dead' lower stomach which normally feels nothing. I felt a sort of melting and tingling, very tentative, but definitely there.

Much later, after many hours alone, I went for a walk along the beach with Jerry. The evening sun was shining brightly. I had a long dress on, no pants under it, and no shoes. It was warm and the beach was deserted. There had been tremendous seastorms for days but now the sea was quieter. The sand was warm under my feet. I played in the waves. I sat down for a long time and thought through a great many things and sometimes tears came. Lying on the sand, I felt a great peace in my body. Wet sand is so clean. I felt my own age, and very long and brown and beautiful within myself. I was very happy, a deep, quiet, sad happiness. I felt I had worked very hard to gain my peace.

David wrote me a poem about this trip.

Journey

Bad dreams
Can twist from a strange sky
It seems
As soon as the sun's set,
Scorching the mind
Black as a struck tree.
But mostly we forget
What sleep can spill
In the half-light,
Waking to the whiteness of a new cold day.

Yet,
though looks, like lightning, sometimes kill,
Nightmares can blast the blind back into sight.

Daytrips carry an acid truth
Too terrible to bear
For most, cutting beneath the skin
Until bones scream.
So how do you dare
To lie down and swim
In the lake of pain that is locked
Inside you? How can your blocked
Body be scared awake?

As you come near
You start to shake,
Warmed by the loosened fear,
Feeling the birth sweat break.

Some tortures are curative.

David

In June 1971, I went to work in Malta for a fortnight. I received a troubled letter from Jerry, and wrote to him:

I know the pain can feel like death, but you know it isn't death; only the pangs of birth in a body that has been numbed so long the blood now flowing is an agony. Stay with it, my Jerry, I am in it too, and we will come home to one another and we will lick our wounds back to life. Jerry, get for yourself the two books which have helped me here to be more pain-full: *Pleasure* by Lowen, and especially *The Primal Scream* by Janov. They will give you hell, but they will help you to stay with what you feel and never ever want to run away again.

I had long days of being alone with myself in Malta. It was a period of intense learning for me. When I got back to England, I wrote to David:

I can no longer pretend needs which have fallen away from me. I like to sleep alone, to have my room to myself. I like to express my affection and sexuality to other people. I do not like to have to feel cold or hostile towards Jerry because he acts like my policeman mother when I could like him so much. I want to go out without leave, and come home without announcement. I like having baths alone. I like to walk around naked. I do not want to hide my body because someone else owns it. My caring for others is strong and flows freely without compulsion. People are no longer a threat and a duty, I can enjoy them, help them, leave them, or ask them for help.

David, how can I express a difference that is so subtle I cannot get hold of it? I am not draining outwards. The world does not bombard me. Things do not shock me. I am content. I am ordinary. I still get stomachache and truncate my sexuality. I bite my mouth. But what's come back is cheek: not the 'high' outrageousness that shields my shyness, but the cheek of knowing what I am not willing to do and what I want. There is a strange quietness about not being a hysteric. No drama. I'm just the same you know, without all the appendages.

At this stage, Jerry and I would give each other therapy sessions at home, sometimes every day. One morning, after an encounter group the night before, I was feeling very aggressive and used a pillow to bite on. Something gave way in my stomach and I felt relaxed and could breathe. Then Jerry got a big mirror and held it in front of me as I was lying there, flushed with exertion. I caught my breath at what I saw and jumped out of bed. I had been shocked to see a face I hardly knew. My eyes and teeth shocked me most, my eyes because they were green and I didn't know I had green eyes, my teeth because, although they are uneven, suddenly I saw them as attractive. Jerry helped me to stay with what I was feeling, and I realized I couldn't conceive of myself as being anything other than the sum of my mother and father. My mother has brown eyes, my father blue. I realized I had never simply looked into a mirror expecting nothing and let come out at me whatever was there. I had always looked hating, or trying to see a stereotyped beauty that I could never be. What I saw now was a face that was in no way like my ideal, but was alive and very much an individual. This word took me a long time to say, as if I were breaking an age-old taboo.

○   ○   ○

It was summertime. Our encounter group had reached a peak of integration and warmth. On 15th July, 1971, I wrote to David:

The whole group spent the weekend at a nudist camp five minutes from my mother's house. I think I have never felt so close to freedom and happiness. I couldn't bear the thought of coming away. All those families, ugly men and women, happy in their natural ugliness! And a dance, can you imagine it, an old-age pensioners' dance in the nude?

As a child, I was afraid to move my body through space. I hated sport at school, it filled me with rage. Now, at the camp, I learnt to play table tennis, in the evening, in the nude and all those middle-aged, middle-class people looking on, the ones I would normally find so boring; everyone so easy with everyone else, all so accepting. And you know, I'm not really ugly at all, it's just that I hadn't seen anyone else's ugliness.

That night, Jerry and I slept at my mother's. Here, a long over-due confrontation took place. I wrote to David:

It took three hours. At one point, I could feel my anger reaching such a pitch at my Mum's sarcasm, that I nearly walked out. My anger brought her down a bit and we talked to exhaustion. Once, when she managed to say something about herself, she started to cry, but wouldn't let herself. When the subject of sex came round, she suddenly got worried that Jerry hadn't had any breakfast.

It was a long, uphill grind, but I felt in a way she was very brave (Jerry says I was very brave), because she was taking a lot of knocks and shocks, yet she held her ground and didn't leave. Most of the time she kept very cool and occasionally delivered little gems of information such as: 'I never let you kiddies out of my sight for one moment. I was your only friend. I took the place of friends. You were always with me so you didn't need friends to play with, we were so close, in the streets you would clutch tightly on to me.' At another point, she said, 'Well, if it makes you feel any better, in fact I didn't love you much, you were always a little brat.'

Later, I talked quietly alone in the kitchen with my mother. I invited her once more to come and see my life. I was looking her straight in the eyes and I felt for the first time that she was a human being, not just a disastrous energy mechanism destroying my life. Something moved in my chest and I went over and hugged her tight for the first time in twenty years.

But this morning, I woke up bad again. I wanted my mother to die and my father to be alive. I couldn't stand her face; I kept seeing it across the room, the face when I was talking to her about her violence and her saying how she would cry at night with the injustice of what I'd said, and me starting to doubt my own memories, but hanging on to them for dear life.

So here am I giving others great therapy sessions while I myself am back to feeling thoroughly destroyed and blocked. So many marvellous things are happening, but I've got a huge hurdle to jump and I don't know how to, or even what it is.

Dream 16th July, 1971

*I am on a flimsy boat being taken across a grey sea to my death
by a man I don't know who is just doing his job, polite because
I'm a girl and it's the right thing to feel a bit off about
executing a young girl. I have been convicted of a couple of
murders. I am to be hung. In the sea, there is a huge wobbly
construction from which the man has to hang me and cut the
rope to break my neck. I plead with him weakly and desperately
not to kill me, I can't bear to think I am going to die. He is
matter-of-fact and business-like.*

*There is a break in the dream. Somehow, the wooden
structure falls with me into the sea before he can cut the rope.
It is a wooden cross. I think I have a chance to get away but
don't feel much energy for saving myself. I hear chanting on
shore and realize a Catholic festival is going on. I think maybe
they will help save me, especially as I am carrying a cross. I get
to shore and make my way to the local priest. I realize my
mistake as soon as I enter his door. The executioner has already
got there before me and has explained my 'case'. The priest is
saying, 'Oh, well, if it's like that . .' meaning, of course, I must
die.*

*Instead of fleeing as soon as I see the trap, I stand stubbornly
and proudly at the door in defiance, believing that my obvious
innocence will see me through.*

Then I wake up, fall asleep again, and *dream it all over again*,
this time with Jerry and other people I know all on the side of
the executioner.

I felt I was back at the beginning of therapy, unapproachable,
mouth-biting, stubborn against explosion, so at the end of July,
I took some more acid, to give myself therapy.

Letter to David

I locked myself in my room to try to do it alone. For two
hours I writhed. I made faces, I stretched and stretched my
mouth wide open to try and release the tension around it. My
whole body was wracked and trembling with tension. I realized
the face I was making was one of screaming, but no noise came.

When I tried to make a noise, all that came out was the timidest of squeaks. The kids were laughing in another room, the house was full of the sounds of people living, yet I in the silence of my room was too afraid to make the slightest sound 'in case someone heard and came'.

I decided I needed Jerry to help me through this noise block. He was giving someone else therapy next door. I felt my tension streaming towards its new-found object: Jerry was unavailable. I wanted him NOW. I was a bundle of energy draining out under my door to his room. I noted this, but couldn't contain it. I called to ask how long he'd be. He said ten minutes. My raging tension made this sound like a lifetime. Soon I realized I'd forgotten what I wanted him for, I was so busy being frustrated that I couldn't have him immediately.

See opposite page for Jenny's writings while waiting.

When he came in, I asked him to help unstick me by frightening me into yelling. He made a sudden movement. I freaked completely. I went into hysterics, crying my guts out and screaming for him please not to frighten me, please not to make any more faces. I grabbed hold of him, pleading and crying. But because of the enormous amount of energy set free by the acid, even when Jerry said, OK, he wouldn't deliberately frighten me any more, I couldn't come down, I couldn't stop the terror. This was the most horrific experience of my therapy: a living nightmare of the worst kind. Every way Jerry sat, every look on his face, the tiniest movement of his lips or fingers, and I felt my life in danger. I was shaking all over with fear; the whole room was coming at me. If I looked at Jerry, he became a threatening monster. I was in a most terrible trap. I felt very clearly in my stomach a life-or-death scream, but was too scared to let it out, too terrified finally to feel that absolute terror of death. I landed myself instead with half an hour of continuous horror. I tried to bring myself down by going into the bathroom on my own, but some big bumble-flies buzzing around sent me into another wave of terror. Jerry kept saying I should make a noise to frighten him, but I was too terrified of retaliation to do that.

By since is telling me

I am running myself through mine back to
reality.

I am earning myself a hole in space where
I'm allowed to exist
because I take up space in space.

I am not nothing

I give up / I return to
the silence

having the life kicked out of
you / as something to scream
about.

tension demands
the entire life force
of a living organism
to keep it going

there is no energy left
over for living

The test of how real you are
is how real a noise can you
make

When you're already real, there's nothing more
no be scared of because nothing's
more scary than reality.

I am a listener
        for disapproval

tension is waiting for approval.

testing out reality
is finding out how much power
you have to make other people
do things for you.

I am enough
to be silent when you
are dead

tension is waiting for
permission to exist

It doesn't matter what they did to
you

take a bite of reality

Don't sort it out with them

THEY'RE NOT REAL

nor I am till I make
this noise

All dreams are an
excuse for the noise.

All dreams are holding on a

small noises are an excuse
for the big noise

I DO NOT NEED PERMISSION

Scream
        yourself through to
                reality

even the queen would get
        Mad if she screamed

I'll try
get someone-else to try to
letter because to believe I

I DONT

Don't make a sound
Don't let me hear you make a sound
One more sound from you   + I'll ..

Quiet as a mouse
        even mice make sounds
                when they're scared

The giraffe or the camel,   I can't remember which,
    is the only known animal that can make no ~~soom~~ vocal noise
                                                            whatever

I am not a giraffe or a camel,   I can't remember which

I am listening for someone to make me real

I laugh
then I listen
after someone to make me believe in my laugh

I am not real
so how can my laugh be

I spend my life listening

   listening for others

   listening is tension
listening is not making a sound
listening for others to live for me
   listening for the permission to live
          that never comes.

listening & looking
     watching
Watching is tension, watching every move
  watching every move
  pouncing with my eyes

     lest anyone make a move
     I haven't planned
controlling myself
  controlling others
   controlling others to help me
     keep a hold on.

Slowly I simmered down, though the effects of the terror lasted another hour or so, so that I still couldn't cope with sudden movement. Jerry helped me to come down by lying very still and letting me slowly move my hands and feel the blanket. I made tiny movements and gradually nursed myself to recovery. With Jerry lying at arm's length, I softly reached out my hands to him. I felt my hands were at an age when the finger-joints are not co-ordinated so the fingers just dab. I was sucking one thumb the whole time. I would dab Jerry's face and get a play-reaction from him and this would send me into giggles that sounded like a fifteen-month-old baby. The giggles would subside and turn into tears, because it was so good to be safe. The pleasure of being allowed to dab his face with wet fingers and have him softly nibble them or make 'frightening' faces that weren't frightening was the most beautiful thing I have felt. Now and again, he would really frighten me, and I would dissolve into sobs again, but after a while, I got naughtier and naughtier and more and more daring as I discovered I was safe, until I got to a stage where I used my foot, putting it to his face, and he made 'pooh' faces which delighted me so much I felt I could never get bored with the game. At one point, having been bonked by me, Jerry rose up and pretended to be a monster, making monster noises. I wasn't at all frightened: I knew who he was, and I was safe. It just made me laugh till my tummy hurt.

David, I never felt so alive in all my life, I feel like crying with joy even now. I felt I needed hours and hours of this kind of healing so that I could get to know all the other parts of my body and what they can do.

A few days after this experience, we held a 12-hour encounter group and I worked on the terror inside me again. Laszlo let me use his face and he was a marvellous actor and extremely effective. He had me completely in his power: a Donald Duck face and I was a mass of two-year-old giggles, a monster-face, scowling and forbidding, and I was yelling in terror. Rhoda helped me. Gradually, over a period of an hour, I worked through fear into frightened anger into angry anger. At one point, I slapped Laszlo round the face and was so shocked, I flipped back into the present and said 'sorry' in a grown-up voice, and then went back in again. I kept sobbing, 'Your face is so big, too big, too near, you're too big for me, I can't fight you you.' I got more and more exhausted, but I felt I couldn't relax and sleep because I didn't know what this face would do next. I used my feet and legs to push him away, they seemed the strongest part of me, and eventually I got to a stage where he couldn't surprise and frighten me any more, because I was ready to push him off. I felt clean and happy and tired afterwards.

Then in August, another big setback, again through a visit 'home', this time to my sister in Lancaster. But this time, instead of Jerry being able to help with my feelings, our relationship nearly broke up. It seemed my execution dream had come true.

To David I wrote:
When my sister got married, I would visit her now and again but always came away hurt and confused and angry. She and her husband used me as the family clown. Once, when I told them of getting my head bashed in by my boyfriend, they both laughed. She has said during this visit, in explanation, that 'it never occurred to her I had any feelings', it was 'just Jenny', nothing real or painful about it. I could never get her or her boyfriends to take me seriously, but I never understood what was going on. I seemed to be fighting against phantoms and cobwebs, just like when I was a child, with Mum leading the show and my stepfather and sister joining in the chorus.

Well, we had an encounter group up here and I brought up these things that have hurt me. My growing health and Jerry's presence (our relationship was at a very beautiful stage) lulled me to the trap I was in. I found myself in a snakepit. My sister, her boyfriend, and her husband all started attacking me. I had a feeling I know so well: 'What on earth's going on?' There's a line-up, like in my execution dreams where I'm going to be killed and I don't know why. It got too much for me, I turned and asked Jerry for help.

Jerry said, 'I'm tired, I'm going to bed', and got up to leave.

I couldn't believe it. I was standing at a precipice and he was pushing me off. I was finished, but I couldn't show it. I made the mistake of keeping cool and sniping at Jerry for his 'lethargy'. Then I became more desperate and said he was destroying me by leaving me. For his own reasons, he then let rip. He shouted and screamed at me, he said he wanted to kill me. I was in a swirling nightmare. I started to put my shoes on to leave. And then Alan hit me. I was stunned. Evidently, he'd offered help, and I'd pushed him away. I was crazy with confusion and I wanted Jerry.

I cried all night, without noise, except for choking and coughing like when a child. I told Jerry I was leaving him, we were finished. He was then so preoccupied with his own feelings about this that there was no chance of him helping me. The whole of the next day passed in confusion and pain. The following night I woke up again after about half an hour, choking and coughing and crying; I cried for about an hour.

The next day, I asked for a session. It was brief, but good. I went into being stifled by my family, them not being able to stand the life in me. Alan held my throat and this brought up deep crying and yelling. I felt my fear of things 'coming at me'. I lay with closed eyes and could feel a thousand wavy spiders' legs weaving around me, never quite touching me, me never knowing when they were going to attack. Jerry threw a cushion at me, and I screamed and broke into crying again. Then I got into yelling at them to fuck off and leave me alone and let me live. I shouted, 'I'm different, I'm not like you, I don't want to be like you.' When I'd finished, I was laughing and felt clean and bouncy.

I ran a marvellous children's encounter group afterwards and felt very confident and quite happy to face any further attacks in a more gut way.

But the night ended badly because Jerry, who'd been refusing to work on himself though he'd been helping everyone else, told me he was being the 'good boy' with me. He said he wanted to give up fighting his urge to be that. But he also said that when he finally lets it all out, it would 'really hurt me'. Of course that made me freeze. I said I wasn't going to play along

with any game of his if I was going to have to pay for it afterwards, that I'd give him all the help and support he wanted in
therapy, but I wasn't going to cut my own throat.

This morning I felt very vulnerable again. I felt awful about
Jerry, it cracks me up to be without a friend and I know I can't
stand alone in this state, I see no virtue in forcing myself to be
hard and alone again.

Letter to my friend Jackie, 24th August, 1971
Dearest Jackie,

I look forward to talking to you, but I don't know if I'll be
able to say anything very clear; this month has been total
confusion, a terrible regression to times I thought I'd left
behind me. I am still too close to know what has been going on,
but a lot of it is to do with being with my sister. It seems part
of my neurosis was still to believe in the possibility of an ideal
loving relationship with her where we would lick each other's
wounds. I was hurt badly in Lancaster, and was shocked to
discover I was still unable to deal with it — it discouraged me to
find I was further back than I thought. I looked to Jerry for
support, my expectations were too much for him, and
consequently my feelings for him cooled off tremendously.
Ever since, we have been quarrelling daily about seemingly
ridiculous things and our relationship seems to have come to a
full stop. My feelings for him alternate between extreme
affection and remorse, especially when I wake up at night, and
then feeling that we both need some fresh air. He doesn't seem
strong enough to bring me through to any kind of clarity and
his extreme dependence annoys me. And I certainly can't help
him, I feel I am doing him harm, lashing out at him every
minute because he is not the strong person I want. I'm very
selfish when I'm unclear, I can't just 'snap out of it' and help or
encourage him. He absorbs all the tension I discharge on to him
instead of smacking it right back at me so I have to deal with it
myself.

So really the only good thing I have to report is my relationship with the children — I have been able to love and be with
Becky and Anna, my niece, constantly. I can identify with

all their needs instead of seeing them as demands on my energy.

I think the main hangup with my sister is the fact that after a lifetime of being put down by her and my mother, I am looking for recognition — of the things I have accomplished with myself and my life. I have expected her to relate to me as an adult, but find instead she is still my competitive sibling.

Jackie, it's a cesspit. I don't know if any good comes of swimming in a cesspit . . . .

Things were bad for a long time. In September, I went for a session with Rhoda Edwards and wrote this:

For more weeks and months than I can remember, I have stagnated. My bones and muscles and organs have ached. I have awoken each morning older and tireder, despairing, unable to breathe, my jaw locked; I couldn't cry or play or give or let things come into me. For a week, I slept separately from Jerry, getting tighter and tighter, wanting so much to burst, but hating everyone so much there was no place to get opened up. On my own, once, I made noise, and that helped me to stop dying completely. I knew all the answers, applied them to my patients, but not to me. I was stiff, my chin spots came back, there was no feeling at all in my genitals, my stomach was a tight balloon. I felt my therapy had failed, I was nowhere.

So I asked Rhoda, 'Can you unlock my jaw?' and Rhoda began to touch me.

As soon as she started on my feet, I felt something on the top of my head. As she moved up my legs, my stomach was gurgling. To my thighs, and peace overcame me, a peace that was gentle enough to bear. The part of me that wriggles and overreacts was asleep. Rhoda's energy and gentle firmness enabled me to stay at a level of soft excitation which I could bear quietly. I breathed gently throughout and made gentle noises for a whole hour. I never got bored, my thoughts never wandered. The cat jumped on me, but it seemed part of what was happening, a cat was not out-of-place. The small of my back flooded with wet heat, like hot water being poured inside my skin. For fleeting seconds, I felt a pouring in my genitals, for longer down the front of my body. My hands and feet stayed cold.

One tear fell out, a tear for pleasure missed. Later, a couple more tears, and couple of small sobs, for my life that had come back, and for pleasure to come.

Rhoda moved further up my body. Awareness of my jaw tension became acute. My mouth pouted in an 'I won't' expression, my frown got tight. I yelled louder. I started to get chaotic. Rhoda quietened me and continued working on my body with firm and gentle fingers.

I got hungry. Tiny sucking noises came from my mouth. I wanted juice. Rhoda got me three plums. The feel of them in my hand gave me so much pleasure, I didn't eat them at first, just kept them there. Rhoda finished, I emerged as from a long sleep. She told me to rest, and covered me up. She left me alone and I ate my plums. The cat was staring at me; I felt it was saying things to me and I laughed.

When I stood up, I felt as weak as after a fortnight in hospital. I was giddy and vibrating.

Next morning when I woke up, I didn't know who I was. I felt completely relaxed, nothing in my body hurt me.

Around this time, I wrote a poem one day in the bath:

> I am digging deep to reach a little girl
> buried beneath the scars
> of a lifetime of dying
> starved
> lying paralysed
> by the knotted tubes
> trapped
> beneath the rock-hard twisted muscles
> and the frozen bones.
>
> I'm screaming out to you little girl
> wait for me!
> I'm digging deep to reach you
> deep where you fight to breathe

in the foul air locked
in my blocked body

baby girl child
wait for me!

Jenny

A few days later, I took another trip.

I went to my room, but almost immediately felt stuffy. I wanted to be outside. I collected Becky from school and went to the park with her. I lay in my coat near the tennis courts. I felt a bit ill, but relaxed into it and became one with the grass and the ground, just let my body melt into the world around me. Becky lay with me and sensed something different about me. She was tense. I felt so good I was able to listen to her and love her and not try and push her and her bad feelings away. She was able to get closer and closer, tell me about little worries of hers, like wanting to come home to dinner from school. I felt a shock in my body to know that she had come from me, that she was someone different from me.

I would have been content to lie there forever on the grass with Becky, watching the people around me, but Becky wanted to go home and I wanted to do what she wanted.

When I left the park, the horror began. Instead of clean air and cool grass — black dust and screeching metal, monsters rushing at us, fighting for space, barely missing mowing each other down, big eyes glaring blindly, teeth bared. I was terrified of crossing the road. Becky helped me. The noise and fury shook me to the roots. I looked at a wooden fence; it was alive, it seemed to reach out towards me. It was trapped there, in the city, pining for its home, for the forest. I felt its warmth and my life streamed towards it and my tears flowed hot and free. I felt Becky's hot little hand in mind and the contrast between that and the metal streaking by cut me up, I cried through the streets. I imagined that metal cutting into living flesh.

When we reached home, I went straight in to Jackie. She put her arms round me and I sobbed and sobbed with relief to feel alive and safe. It was the sweetest crying; I was happy and told her through my sobs, 'It's so difficult to come alive, Jackie, so difficult to feel again.'

I went up to my room and walked round it with my jacket on. My whole body had come alive, my teeth were chattering, I hung my limbs loose and cried my eyes out with relief and sorrow for lost life. Vicky's picture made more tears pour, because I wasn't her any more. Becky came in and played, Jerry came in and played with her. They didn't interfere with me. I felt more separate than ever in my life before, and this made me feel completely with them. I lay on the floor and my teeth chattered on and on, releasing tension all over my body. Each new outbreak of trembling usually ended in more tears, but my laughter came soon too: I looked at Becky eating her banana and she looked like a chimpanzee and I laughed and laughed, until it changed into crying again.

We've got fleas in the house at the moment from the cats. Fleas became tension for me. I would relax, then suddenly seize up in case a flea jumped on me: I would watch for them and become absorbed in the tension of watching. Then I'd realize what I was doing, let my jaw go, my teeth would start to chatter, I'd let the shivering go all through my body and then I could sink once more into whatever I was lying on. I felt thoroughly alive. Then I was seized with a longing to see Pepe, to have him there with us. I wanted to say sorry for all the heart-break, I wanted to see him without cobwebs and have him really see me, and to know my tears weren't directed against him. I sobbed and sobbed for him and for the distance between us.

I looked at Jerry to see if I could open up to the one who *was* there. I felt a tight tension. I looked at Becky and felt fine. Jerry touched me and I seized up again. Looking at him, I felt a terrible tight atmosphere around us. I felt there was immense dishonesty in our relationship — my dishonesty certainly — and I started twisting myself up trying to work out why I got such bad feelings looking at him. Then everything went foggy and it wasn't until hours later that I unravelled the knot and discovered where the haziness led back to. Jerry had said, joking, that he would walk out if I didn't stop my continuous stream of giggles and weeping. I had swallowed this, and clammed up.

I was dashed into confusion. Jerry tried in vain to help me, then left to make dinner. I lay with Becky and started melting into her flesh and feeling how she had come from me. Then suddenly, I felt fear come creeping up from around the corners of my eyes and I tried to keep it away for a bit. But it still came bristling, things in the room were beginning to move. I called for Jerry to come back. His face was starting to change and I knew I was going to have a really bad fear session like last time if I let it continue. I got up, switched more light on and jumped around. Gradually it came clear to me that my ungrounding had been caused by accepting Jerry's playful 'no crying' prohibition. So I thumped around and yelled at Jerry in a playful but energetic way for taking away my pleasure, and the bad time was over.

Jerry, Alan and I went off to Holland Park at midnight. We were all frightened: of police dogs, of guards, of ourselves. But the air was cutting clean and cool, my body was warm from the day's experiences. I left the other two and wandered alone through the pitch-black wood. I was not afraid, only mildly anxious at what I would do if Fear came. The air was very good and so was my moving body.

My footsteps turned leaden heavy as we made our way home. I didn't want to go back to a cardboard box in a dirty street, no air, cramped, fleas, tension.

But as I walked into my room, there was another fairyland, like in the park: my sleeping child beautiful, bathed in red light.

My own bed was small and bony, the sheets wrong, not enough space. I started to feel bitter at the loss of good feelings, at the flea-bites all over me. But now I have known hot thick blood flowing freely through my once-glass body and that I will not lose.

At the nudist camp one day, I wrote:

> the city's screeching metal
> slowly fades away
>> my skin is greedy
>> sucking up the heat
>> till my body melts
>> and fuses with the grass.

At the beginning of October, I wrote to David:

Three hours giving therapy a day, and the groups and the phone, and hours with Gerda taking dictation, and the tension of the screams reaching eviction-pitch, make a very weary Jenny.

So I decided Saturday was for me. The park was good in the morning, I kept dozing and felt my body so delicate, the aeroplanes groaning overhead flew right through me. There was space there, so I wanted to hand myself the world for the day and let my body find a way of joining up with it. So I went home and took some acid. Too many children and people, the phone, someone knocking out a cupboard and putting in a fridge; so I escaped, I thought, back to the sun and the green.

But what had happened to the park? The roads to it had become longer, dirtier, more frightening. Paranoia came creeping, but you can't scream in the streets. The cars were coming at me; I held on to a Belisha beacon and moved when there was a space. A man passed by, I tensed, avoided his face, he might jump at me. I kept it all down: I had to get to the park; everything would be alright, Jackie was in the park. My legs were weak, I needed to collapse.

But what had happened to the park? My body had run out of strength, I had to let myself sink down. But the first part of the park had turned into Brighton Beach. I had to get to the big, quiet field.

In the big, quiet field where we lie, there was a football match. And the rest of the park was littered with bodies. Not only I wanted the green.

There was enough of me left to laugh a little. I traced out a body-sized space and lay down in it. The sun was strong, I opened my face to it. Where would I find Jackie on Brighton Beach? I knew I couldn't get back home, and anyway, the house was worse. Good god, overpopulation is for real, we're crawling over one another; when will we start to eat one another?

I needed to shiver all over. But people don't shiver in the hot sun without being taken away and handed over to kind people in white coats and sprayed with evil smells. So I daren't shiver. I couldn't laugh or cry either. People don't laugh or cry lying alone in the park. If I concentrate on my breathing, I'll be alright. Maybe then the sick feeling will go away.

Oh god, I've really done it this time, stuck in this fucking park, prowling with fuzz. Christ, my body feels awful, falling to pieces; my mind is a mass of unconnected, flying atoms. I have only my lungs, they're still there. Keep still, don't start wriggling and fighting, that leads to chaos, sink into the ground, let it all come.

The sun is good, but oh christ! I can't see, my vision's splintered, everything's flickering with energy fighting to get out, I daren't look.

Becky! It's Becky, she's suddenly here, now I'll be alright. Hold my hand, Becky, sit with me. I don't feel well.

But she's forgotten already, she's off with her little friend. It's boring lying here with me; it's balls and bats she wants. Becky! Come back! Those boys are looking at me. Beck — could you possibly — fetch Jerry?

How long will it take Jerry to arrive? Better not think about it. How can a body that doesn't exist feel so ill? This is like being dead while conscious. Becky's friend has gone for Jerry. Becky's hand is warm. Oh, it's so beautiful when you stroke me, Becky, that makes me feel so good; yes, please keep doing that.

People will think we're weird, lying here like lovers. But it feels good, it helps me till Jerry comes. It'll be alright when Jerry comes.

Something's wrong, it's not how I expected. Jerry's here, but I can't feel him. He hasn't come into me. He might as well not be there. Jerry, help me! He doesn't hand me the answers, it's not better. There's no contact. I can't feel anything. Jerry, hold me, can't you come closer? Oh god, this is the end, now what do we do? Go home! But I can't. I can't walk. I'll be sick. I can't face the cars. I'll have hysterics.

Jerry, this is the most terrible time of my life. I lean on you but I don't feel you. How come your voice is so many miles away? I can't feel anything. I CAN'T FEEL ME. Are the people looking? I'm going to collapse.

Jerry, why am I walking home when I just spent so many hours getting here? I wanted the green.

Everybody did. This is the longest journey of my life.

Home is terrible: that dirty, nasty little box, all those people. In my room, on my bed, I twist and turn. Jackie comes. Jerry and Jackie are with me, and I still don't feel better. What have I done to myself? Why doesn't anything you say make sense? Hit the bed?! What for? I want to feel nice. Jackie, am I usually like this? I usually laugh and cry? There's nothing coming out of me, my cells are dry and closed. There's nothing for anything to come out of, no me. I'm dead. I killed myself in the park and now I'm going to be like this for ever.

Jackie goes. Jerry's getting fed up. I'm lost, I can't feel, I'm just whirling twisted atoms, unrelated, each in pain, separate, dried up.

WHAT WAS THAT? Why are you dropping cold water on me? I am shocked back to life. I *can* feel. That cold water is so warm. A soft feeling on my neck. More? A whole cupful! Why are you pouring cupfuls of water on me? What do you mean, don't I like it? Well, yes, I suppose I do. It's lovely. And I can feel my leg where you rub it, and my back.

A bubble of colour, the world becomes three-dimensional for a few seconds, then it's gone again, I've lost it. Jerry tells me, don't worry, it'll come back again, and each time it'll stay a little longer.

I sink into it. I believe Jerry. And it happens. It takes a long time. I move my hands. They can feel. I lick. I lick Jerry's hands and face.\I suck his tummy where it's soft; he curls up, hysterical with ticklishness; he tries to get me off. The more he fights, the harder I hang on. It's marvellous, lick, lick, suck; I have a mouth! I can feel my mouth. The coldness is going away. Big areas of me are still dead, it takes a long time.

It's good fighting, struggling, moving. It's good lying and being held. Why didn't you make it like this all the time for me? It's like it now. Yes, I know; alright, I won't think. I've got skin.

Grapes! Where did you get grapes from? How could I have eaten them so many times before and never felt them like this!

I'm alone in here now, and it's good. I'm so warm, my skin is marvellous. Wht a beautiful room mine is, flooded in red light. Where have I been? I'm *here now*.

The children arrive. Marion and Becky. Marion is a fairy filled with starlight magic. She's got a rubber face and is making me laugh. She's pretending to answer the phone. Is Jenny here? I'll see. Jenny, are you here or not here? Jenny's here, but she's laughing her head off. Goodbye.

The room's in riot. The kids are building a world, and I'm in it. I've got a part. A tennis racquet now is a TV screen for Marion: she switches herself off and on. My sides are aching. Becky says, 'Jen, why does your jaw shiver like that?' I have been asleep for a hundred years, Becky; now you have to kiss me, and I come alive.

○   ○   ○

This was a period of great melting for me. My body was getting younger and younger. One morning, in bed with Jerry, I had an urgent feeling in my mouth, and started stuffing the sheet into it. More and more urgency was awakened, until I was stuffing my own fists into my mouth; and this immediately broke me out into soft crying. I felt like a hungry, left baby.

At the weekend group, these feelings developed further: my mouth was curious; I wanted to feel out the world with my mouth. I wanted to put hard objects of various shapes into it. At the same time, I got an urgent sensation in the centre of each palm: I had to hold round objects to satisfy the feeling. My fingers were stretching out a little, but still unco-ordinated, not fully awake.

In my next session with David, I was feeling out how my feet are dead and cold. I moved my ankles and felt the stiffness and pain in them and in my legs, sharp pain in my unused legs. I started pushing down with my heels. I was a baby, pushing down, feeling out my own strength, growing and feeling myself out. Now my mouth, hands and heels were all the same age. I hugged David, because I was happy.

My growing was affecting my daughter. I wrote to David:

All the black layers are surfacing in her; it is bad between us sometimes. But there are sunny spots between the clouds when she suddenly gives in to herself; then she will come to me and get the cuddling she never got. One morning, the day of her birthday party, in a black mood, all dressed up in her new clothes and miserable as hell, she was stuck in her cloud. I wanted to bring it to a head. I held her and she struggled to get away, screaming, crying and yelling, kicking at me. Finally, I gave up and she stormed out. Quite soon, she came back and sat sadly in my lap. I held her and rocked her.

Although it was not so clear at the time, looking back over my therapy, I see how a period of melting would make way for the next layer of ice in me to surface. At the beginning of November, I wrote this after a therapy session with David:

I felt a fascination for David's eye and stared deep into it. Letting myself be drawn by the energy and shape of it, connections started flooding in: eye equals vagina, the lips, the lashes, the bony brow, the soft, fathomless interior, the power to stream or withdraw energy, to be cold and dry or weep with warm emotion. David suggested I do a Gestalt, that is, speak as if I were my vagina. At the time, I was feeling kind and gentle and sad towards myself. Writing now, I am in a cold mood, and this is how it comes out:

'I have no name. I never had a name. I didn't even know I existed. I was told I didn't exist, and that I had no feeling. I was not allowed to look at myself; I grew up thinking I was ugly. I am angry and cold because I have been made to hate myself. I have no teeth, but I bite and grab because I do not know how to receive, how to take gently, because all feeling was taken away from me. I am very old; I was never young, I have hurt myself all my life; I have never touched myself with love. I am too embarrassed to look at the world; I am neither male nor female: I am too big to be female, too small to be male. I am awkward and ugly and ungainly. I am dirty and must revolt anyone who comes near me. I must cover myself up and hide. I must tense myself up, hold myself together and keep control of myself. There is something wrong with anyone who wants me.'

Mouse

Mouse
is excitable,
can pounce
on your breath,
make rooms hum
with vitality.

Mouse has fur
smelling of musk,
stays hidden usually
until dusk.
There is an animal
in this room you could almost
stroke.

Mouse
can lie still
as a bird in your hand,
watching and waiting.
Sometimes even
mice with electric eyes
sleep.

Mouse
has sensitive whiskers,
delicate as an eyelash

with instant communication.
Can play mouse games,
will travel.

Mouse
runs up some people's legs
goes tapping
through the body
like a pulse,
makes tired people
jump into hot life.

Mouse
is witch-like
can cast spells.
The pricking of a thumb
tells
there's mouse in the house
to be routed out.

Mouse
is caught in a man-trap
as quick as a car-crash.
The screaming is over,
don't let the children see.
Someone will clean up
The mess of blood and tissue
quiet as a mouse.

David

The next day, at our Sunday group, I felt suddenly tense and
angry when some uninvited strangers walked in. I sat apart
feeling bad inside with pent-up aggression swirling around, but
also with good feelings for Julie and Sharon (I had given them
both sessions today and felt a lot of love for them). Julie asked
me what was up and whether there was anything I'd like to do.
I said I'd like the group to surround me closely and that I'd like
to keep my eyes shut so I didn't know who was touching me.

Almost immediately, I broke down, sobbing and crying for a long time with Julie holding me. I felt very good to be able to let my feelings come through like that, and was amazed once more to see how once feelings are flowing, all paranoia disappears: no need for approval, no need to know or bother about what anyone was thinking of me.

I curled up small, and when my sobbing was over, my jaw began to judder and I started making playful shivering noises and the group joined in. Then I started giggling and enjoying the noise and the fuss I was making, and others started giggling too until we were just a heap.

But then the week started sliding downwards, in tune with my monthly cycle. By Thursday, things were bad with me. I hated the group and most of the people in it. On Friday, I took some space for myself, moved around doing yoga in my room, anything to get life back into my body. I started to breathe and feel better. Lying face downwards on the bed, I began to hum and covered my head to be completely private in my own world. Suddenly, hysterical fear, and I yelled out: 'They're going to cut my head off!' I didn't know where the words or the feeling were coming from, but I could feel a definite physical threat to my head, that it would be hit or struck off, just because I was being with myself and enjoying it. I began to cry, but Jerry was in the room sending out hostile vibes, so I didn't let my crying come. It turned to mucous and I kept coughing and my nose filled up. The feelings went up into my head and I felt ill and stuffy like when a child; I had held back my sobbing so many times. I felt wretched and ill after this. I was obsessed with a thought that I dared not speak out; it was, 'I can't bear to know I came from her.' Even to write the word 'her' was difficult.

I will continue not to exist as long as I won't admit where I come from.

I've had a long run of good health, but now I'm really contaminated again.

One morning soon after this I woke up moaning and groaning having had a dream of a man's arms around me. I told Jerry the dream and said it wasn't specifically sexual: I imagine a man opening his arms to me, and he is wearing a baggy overcoat and a baggy warm jumper and he holds me very close and tight and is taller than me. Jerry asked me what my father used to wear. I burst into tears; I felt my heart would break if I really let go into the crying. I felt a terrible war in my chest, two sides tearing each other apart.

In our group that same evening, I was lying on the floor with everyone round me. People's eyes and faces looked soft, and the energy of their soft caring was too much for me; I couldn't look. I felt terror. To accept softness is to melt, and to melt is to lose my character, because I am unmeltable; I am hard and immovable. Jerry asked, 'What is the hardest part of you? ' I answered, 'My jaw', and he got people to stroke it. Immediately, crying welled and surged out from somewhere inside me, but still I couldn't let my heart really break, and I ended up with a terrible headache.

A couple of days later, after a session with David, I wrote to him:

I realize how I can't take from you when you're available. When you've gone, I'll let myself feel a little of the warmth and joy of having someone there just for me, but only when you've gone home. When I'm with you, I see you as a brittle head-master who can snap. I have an image of myself as a Spanish gypsy, primitive inside, a side I have to hide from you and keep on a lead. If I flow too freely, I might overstep hidden barriers. One of my mother's regular sayings was 'don't go too far', or 'that's gone far enough'.

If I catch myself thinking of you, I have to shudder and shake off the pleasure of it. I feel uneasy and uncomfortable when you seem very interested in me, when you start getting excited about a session, or enthusiastic about the therapy. I'm trying to stay cool and observant. Whenever you get high, I go stiff. When you come very near and start getting bouncy and clever, I shrink your face with my eyes. I can feel myself demoisturizing your face so that it becomes dry and brittle, just like any Englishman on any tube. I won't let your life come through; I can make you look mean.

David had told me to let my good side show when I got home. But I couldn't, I was offhand and rejecting as ever with Jerry. But next morning, when we had sex, it was like never before, everything happened inside, nothing on the outside, and I felt orgasm beginning in such a smooth way that nothing inside me said no and my whole body moved from within and afterwards I was calm and could open my eyes and I didn't talk or try to wipe out what had happened; there was no conflict inside me.

David's answering letter came soon:

I get your message: I am not to get excited if you come to life. It would be better if I switched myself off. This is where we collide, Jenny, against this barrier, the hidden barrier. It's alright for you to be warm — on your own. It's alright for someone else to be warm — but not about you. Every good thing that has happened in the therapy has happened in spite of this barrier. Every blockage and hold-up is because of this barrier. Well, I have to report that the barrier is breaking down. It is letting too much through. You are going too far! Can you hear me gloating? Can you hear me rubbing my hands in schoolboy enthusiasm? Be careful — what might slip out through the barricades next? So when you open up from inside, and nothing freaks, and nothing says no — what am I supposed to feel, a clinical interest?

The barrier is all that is left of your neurosis, all that is left of your pride. The barrier has receded greatly. You let people get much closer. You are a much warmer person. Your eyes hide so much less. But not too close, or too warm, or the eyes will sharpen to make the distance come back. The pride and the stubbornness are beginning to fight to survive within you, their last footholds are threatened. There is a smell of danger in the air. This man David must be watched. He is getting too near the centre of it all, I can feel your hackles rising.

What is the most difficult thing in the world for you to admit? That you can be moved by someone else. You can be moved alright, from within, by your own feelings. You can be moved *for* someone else, as a therapist, as a protester, as a comrade-in-arms. But to be moved *by* someone else, that is the ground you want to retain behind your barrier, that is where you start to squirm, to go stiff, where you are afraid to go too far. That is where you call out your cool reserves, and put on your rejecting front, even when beneath that you cry out for contact.

To be moved by someone else is to function with the last split gone. That is frightening. That removes your age-old protection against hurt, against the person who moves you going away. If you really love someone, really care for someone, they will go away, you will be cut off from them. So you cut yourself off first, it hurts less that way, and after a while you get used to it.

That is why if someone gets too nice, you will hate them. That is why the pleas to the therapist to give you pain, although it has a rational side to it, plays into your defence. For you the deepest pain is risked when somebody enjoys you, or when you enjoy someone. That is taboo. Anything else. Screams of pain, streaming of pleasure, these you will open to as long as they don't get *personalized*.

That is why the moments when Jerry's face becomes so beautiful it makes you cry, are rare ones. That is why the words stuck in your throat when you told me how you felt about your undemonstrative Englishman of a therapist.

The crime of crimes is to hang on, and to hang on tight. For Jenny there is death in the air if she squeezes too tight, the other will push her away. Unable to cling, unable to want, to reach out, to squeeze anyone so tight they could never escape, she tightens her grip on herself, she is squeezed in the vice of her own body.

So I will play your game. I will be nonchalant about your experience in bed. So what? Just some silly cow having an orgasm. Who wants to get excited or pleased about that? Shrink it down to size, it has nothing to do with therapy: a fluke in the weather, or an odd coincidence very likely. Orgasms have nothing to do with people. If you give happiness a name, it will turn round and bite your head off.

If the process of helping you come alive did not move me, did not make me high, did not charge the room, I would be a corpse, and you still in your ice-box.

Primal

Go back.
Go back taut through the blood of dreams
to the jungle room where the tigers roar,
murder your way through a thousand screams
in the cut-throat night to the empty door:
go back.

Lie down. Lie down now if you can't be fed
in a clench of pain in a screwed up sheet,
clutch the pillow and play at dead,
freeze your head and tense your feet:
lie down.

Let go.
Let go your chin if you need to shake
kick out your legs if you want a fight,
hang on my neck until you break.
Close your eyes, and they still look bright:
let's go.

David

My daughter, Becky; nine years old

In mid-November, I held a weekend therapy-training group. The
highlight was Sunday afternoon. I was tired, so I said to Becky,
OK you take over.

She led a brilliant session. She got us to lie down and do
various stretching and tensing exercises and deep breathing. She
got us sniffing each other round the room, then standing up and
jumping, collapsing and resting again. What was beautiful was
the un-uptightness about doing 'silly' things because a child was
ordering us about.

She got us into an inner and outer circle, facing a partner to
express various emotions — 'be a monster', 'be shy', then she
said, 'Look and look at each other and get angrier and angrier,

then do the opposite.' We asked her what the opposite was. 'Look and look and get kinder and kinder and then do a dance together.'

When we were finally exhausted by an exhilarating game of Simple Simon, Becky brought on The Entertainment: quite spontaneously, she became each of us in turn, taking us off, copying our unconscious tics and mannerisms, our fossilized miseries. We had to guess who she was being. Then she went through people we knew well who were absent. It was one of the most brilliant pieces of theatre I have ever seen; she had us in hysterics.

Then came the Sunday night group. Becky, having expended oceans of happy energy in the afternoon, began to snivel in a frustrated, held-back way. I wanted to provoke her to come out more, so I wrapped a blanket around her whilst she yelled her protests and started to cry loudly. I asked the group for help. We held the edges of the blanket so that she was safe and cradled, yet could kick and fight and yell. She screamed blue murder and finally managed to split a hole in the blanket and escape out of the bottom. We all cheered her, but she was far from finished. She sobbed and cried from the pit of her stomach, and kicked, but would not allow anyone to touch or comfort her; she just went on and on. When she had quietened, she whispered to me that she felt a scream in her stomach but couldn't let it out. I said, 'Don't force it, it'll come when it wants to', but she wasn't satisfied and soon turned her aggression towards Jerry, hitting him with pillows. He collected the pillows, sat on them, and wouldn't fight back. So Julie and I broke the impasse by attacking him too and there was a general pillow fight. But Becky got hit twice too hard. She whispered to me that she wanted the group to help her get her bad feelings out by rocking her in the blanket again.

We held her for ages in an open sleeping bag whilst she went through everything from laughing to yelling anger and bitter crying. She said she felt a bomb had burst in her and that, 'This is only the beginning.' At one point, she just kept crying miserably, 'Hands, hands!' I put mine in front of her face and her crying deepened. 'What do hands do? ' I asked 'They hurt me'. She cried and cried, finally saying, 'I want my Daddy.' I asked her what she'd say if he were there. She answered, 'I love him.'

Her eye contact, whenever her mood allowed it, was marvellous. She didn't just look up, but looked carefully at each person in the group; and when she was yelling to be put down, she yelled at each person individually to let go of the blanket.

I was so pleased and proud and shocked that this all worked so smoothly, even though she complained, 'I didn't get anything I wanted from the group, all I got was violence, violence, violence.' I was too newly-born myself at the time to see that 'the group' meant me.

Nightmare about Becky, 20th November, 1971.

I am in my caravan. There is a wobbly ladder leaning up against the side of it and Becky is playing on it.

Suddenly, the ladder falls and there is a terrible moment when I imagine Becky to be crushed and broken, but my own legs won't work properly so it seems to take me ages to rush round the side of the 'van. I am calling to other people to help. but they are all very unconcerned and unresponsive. I can't find Becky anywhere. I go up to everyone, begging them to let me know what has happened to her. No-one answers. My voice is weak — the more urgent I feel, the less comes out of me. There is one woman that I am sure knows about Becky, but is deliberately withholding information to punish me. Then she points over to the fireplace, where there is a brown paper bag. I lift it up and see Becky. She is smiling and radiant as if she's just had orgasm. She says to me: 'Wait a minute, till this stuff wears off', meaning she can't speak properly yet because someone's stuck a needle full of anaesthetic into her. I desperately try to get Jerry to react to this terrible thing which has been done, but nothing comes out of him, he just ignores me. I start to beat him up, trying to tear him to pieces, and I wake with electric nightmare energy all over me.

Another dream, the same night

I am in a scruffy old house, being introduced to a young schizophrenic boy whom I find attractive. They tell me he is uncontactable now. I feel a liaison with him.

I am alone with him in the kitchen. I don't believe he can't feel. We put our arms round each other and there is tremendous charge between us. We have intercourse standing up and I wake up with terrific positive energy charge all over me and feeling extremely sexual.

What stood out for me after this night was the similarity of the body charge which affected every part of me, yet in the nightmare the energy is cold and horrific, in the other the charge is hot and deeply pleasurable.

Scream Cat Nightmare, 21st November 1971.

I come home late one evening, it is dark and damp. Home is a scruffy hotel. Two people have been killed, and no-one knows how it happened.

It is I who discover what is going on: I see a brown paper bag. It is big and moving; there is a flurry and a homosexual guy gets knocked down. Confusion, a dreadful scream, and he is dead. I capture the bundle and throw it in a room and try to close the door. A whole series of attempts to close doors follows, like in so many of my nightmares: none of them quite close, there are no latches and always very wide gaps under the doors.

I have captured the Scream Cat. It is an evil creature with a mean-looking mouth and wicked teeth. One bite and the victim dies. It does not kill to eat, it kills to kill, and goes out looking for people to kill.

I can't get anyone else to take the situation seriously. I yell at people to get the police, because I can't move myself, I am holding on to the door of the room where the scream cat is. I am not sure whether the cat can make itself small and get under the door. I peep in and see it friendziedly biting and clawing at the barred windows. I can see that its fury and energy will

ensure that it gets out one way or another very soon. Three
people have died already.

I give up holding the door and rush to telephone the police,
who keep asking me whether it's really important. I'm so
annoyed with everyone's attitude that I no longer take proper
care and people's lives are in danger. I lock myself in a room to
await help in a given-up sort of way. I see the cat escape from
its room. It rushes down the hallway away from me and up the
curtains.

I wake up once more with nightmare electricity all over me.

Letter from David, 24th November 1971
Dear Jenny,

I feel strongly you are in a healing crisis which will open the
way for much more pleasure and contentment. Stay with it.
Orgasms compete with scream cats. The wild-cat in the bag is
the cat of wanting, the cat who will fight back when it is shut
out of the warmth, and not freeze. Your scream cat wants
stroking, but no-one is allowed near it. 'Going too far' equals
letting the cat out of the bag.

There is a lot to keep in touch with just now, many miracles
have happened and there are more round the corner. Waiting is
like dying, but only by waiting for your body to find its own
pathways can you live. The temptation is to take short cuts, to
break a way out of the explosive trapped feeling. But if you can
be in your death layer without hating yourself, if you feel the
cold horror and give in to the shudders, then the death layer
will invert like it did after acid in the park.

Space to breathe is the big need all the time, and having time,
and believing that your body is not a dead duck, or someone
else's object, or a frozen cage, but something which protests
because it wants your permission to live, to breathe, to melt, to
speak, — and it can be so easy.

Love to you, over 300 miles.

David

The Scream Cat

The scream cat
is everyone's victim,
a black shape
haunting a dream,
the dark clot
of blood Dr. Seuss
never put in his book.

Everyone wants to drown it,
everyone wants to cut its head off,
everyone wants to claw at its throat-strings,
everyone wants to treat it like a foetus.

So the scream cat is silenced,
and laps no more liquids,
its purr is put out,
its ghost shape looms like a paralysis.

From its knot of grief
big as a fist, a sound comes tearing,
sharp enough to slit a throat
and get out.

For the cat of pain
never dies
until you have murdered
the last of its nine lives,
throwing grey ash
on even the white fires that spit
from its caged eyes.

David

A letter to David, 14th December, 1971
    David, I felt last session was one of the best ever. It was such
a relief to break through my anti-crying taboo. I realize to cry

like that with only one person present is really dangerous for me: in a group it's easier, it's safe.

I am sad to be going away to Germany now, missing two sessions.

I want to talk to you about a feeling I don't trust — as if there is an illusion in me that keeps me going, that still believes I will 'get' you in the end, whatever that means. I am hanging on, never really letting it come to me that you are just a man in the street. And then there is this other fear: what'll I do if I do win, I wouldn't know what to do, I'm afraid somehow you will be seduced by my need. David, I am so unclear about all this, I'll have to have a lot more sessions like last one before I understand. I feel out of touch, slightly disgusted, as if I'm putting my hands into hysterical shit and covering myself with it.

David wrote back:

Dear Jenny,

You are right about last session, and it is a shame there is a gap now. But the threads are all there waiting to be picked up again. This whole question of your needs, expectations, is pretty crucial. It can, as you see it, go in one of two ways. If you expect to 'get' me in the sense I think you mean, then you fall into the disappointment pit. Fear of this pit has led you until recently, to ward me off, to skewer me with your eyes, to make me an unperson, to freeze me into a role. If you hang on, you will have to let go and will fall into the pit. If you kill the need to hang on, you dry up in your wilderness. This is the trap you see yourself in.

The truth is that I *am* a man in the street, but not 'just' a man in the street. There *are* bonds between us, the bonds forged out of need, pain and warmth. Therapy is a bridge that can carry the weight of your need. You doubt this, but the only way to test it is to stand on the bridge. The further you get from dry land, the scarier it gets: the disappointment pit looms beneath. If I am seduced by your need, the bridge breaks. If your fear wins — you step back off the bridge, on the wrong side, the contactless side.

In your despairing moments, you doubt such a bridge can support you. You yell at me through your tears that I am a man who fell out of the sky. You want to go home: that means off the bridge quick, home is the old known shore. On the bridge is the man out of the street who is both involved and not involved in your life. He is not involved because he can go away from it all, he can go back to his own life and forget you. He is involved because he is committed to seeing you through to the other side, because helping you is more than a job, because he has come to really care what happens to you. It is about this man, this stranger who tugs at your feelings, that you begin to have longings, doubts, confusions. Does he block your way? Will you pull him down? Will he drop his hands and let you drown on the way? Everything is stacked against him: he is male, middle class and English. But at the moment, you can't see beyond him. His face seems to fill the near horizon.

It's all about this slow business of trust, and about letting yourself crack up, like last time, while the bridge remains firm. It's all about daring, as you are now doing, to let your stiff pride right down, into *expressing* the longing — into going with the melting. It will be stormy, because your need is very strong. You still fight the hunger. On the bridge, strange things happen: people's faces change shape and colour; eyes light up, or become monstrous. 'I don't know who you are!' you shout in the darkness.

I will tell you who I am. I am not a magician and I am not your father. Nor will you trap me into being your lover. Roles again, into which you would cast me. Or else I am a stranger? You see it one way or the other: I am your all, or your nothing. I see myself as someone travelling with you on a unique journey.

Jenny, it is also to do with control. With me as a stranger, or as a lover, you still keep the control. I am not even the doctor, who can make it better. It has to grow better as you open up. To cross the bridge, you have to give up the control, to trust those feelings, those fantasies, those longings. You have to be swept off your feet by the sorrow of loss, the terror of falling, and the joy of getting the lights back in your eyes, and the melting back in your loins.

To be paranoid is to know you will be pushed off. To be hysterical is to push other people off. To be human is last session and what we are building: a way of relating that breaks through the roles, defies expectations, and therefore can create new things, even at times miracles. All this lies deeper than any seduction.

Love,

David

I wrote to David from Germany:

Dear David,

It's like now the oldest bad and the newest good are there side by side. Therapy is never as I imagined: the speed, the flash of lightning, the sloughing of the skin and the cracking of shells. Really, it's morning after morning of silent despair, aching bones, a cramped spine, a knotted stomach, tightness and a huge silent scream inside. And then, sometimes, strange things at night, dreams that feel real and whole, dreams that tap me on the shoulder and say, 'hey, look, this is how it was, take a look', and with every look the past is allowed a little more elbow-room in the present, and when it's no longer being elbowed out of existence, it sits there quietly and is accepted.

And then, strange things happen in the night. Sex is the strangest thing. It's just like everything else, you breathe and it happens; if you do what you don't want to do, it's not good, and if you give your cells a chance to breathe and speak, it's just like sliding down a slide, something I never dared do as a child.

When I got your last letter, I felt like someone was punching me gently in the stomach as I read it. You are reaching me. I went out that day at twilight; just Becky, me and a huge empty park. Becky lent me her rollerskates. I never had rollerskates as a child. Everything physical was dangerous. Becky helped me to my feet, held my hand and took me over that concrete square again and again, laughing hugely when it seemed I would do the splits, leaving me at last to find my own way. Then we went to the playing apparatus. Becky was on a thing that whizzed round and round, you just stand on an iron bar and hang on and hope. She went much too fast for me, I just shut my eyes and died. And when she stopped, I lay down in the sand. When the trees had stopped swirling, my blood still carried on. I let the whirlwind continue, for half an hour it seemed. When all was quiet, I stood up. Becky was high up on the iron skeleton of a ship, right up at the mast. I let the hot-shit feeling fall through the bottom of my stomach and collapse my knees. OK, so she likes it, well let's find out. I climbed up the first few rungs till I had to stop. Up just one more rung, a few minutes' rest to let the sick subside, and on again and again, each step like an operation, each step to be breathed through my whole body and assimilated. The top rung I left for another day.

When it was dark and we were very tired, we walked home, Becky under my cape; we were a four-legged monster that felt warm and good. Becky was hugging me and enjoying the trust of walking blindfold, and she didn't fall.

And last night, another rung in a smooth ladder of strange newness in the night. Sex like a swing that you just let rock; if you breathe deep, there is no paranoia, no-one jumps out at you; the world is quiet except for your breathing. And a light touch on the head travels all over, down and out, there is no separation any more in the body, no inside and outside, everything is one.

David, the peace seems endless stretching before me, a gentle excitement at doing nothing, time 'to waste time', wasting means, it seems, feeling good, playing cards because Becky wants to, knitting with no Dad there to say it's a 'cow-like occupation', Being nice to Jerry because I've run out of reasons not to be.

David wrote back:

Dear Jenny,
    So you really are on holiday!
    The feeling I get from your letter is that there is something in you deeper and stronger than all the pain. When you feel

contentment, quietness,\melting, that open feeling, it comes
from inside, not from outside. What I hear in your letter is feet
that aren't running. I experience the feelings in your letter not
as something that blew on to you temporarily out of the trees,
but as *you*. This magic that starts melting is Jenny-magic, you
are not bewitched. Only hysterics get bewitched; and in a sense,
you have always hidden yourself behind a kind of witch image:
witches have aching bones, and cramped spines; witches are
tight, with knotted stomachs and can see only their own hate.
Witches look at themselves in the mirror and find themselves
ugly. Witches have cold eyes that root you to the spot. Witches
never never melt. Witches are hooked by their own spells.
Witches seduce people and break them in half. Witches are
proud.

So what is the opposite of a witch? For you I think the
opposite is a cow. I think of cows as animals with a lot of space
inside them: they move quietly, they have time, they don't run
unless someone panics them, except when they feel like it and
go charging through the fields because it is fun. Cows have soft
shudderly currents in their udders and wombs. Cows are alive,
whereas witches are found only in dreams.

Your letter tells me that in spite of all you went through as a
child, in spite of all you had put on you, in spite of all the life
you unlived, you have this restfulness inside you — and it is very
powerful and very deep. But you thought it was never there,
you thought this had been stolen away, that any kind of
sweet feeling was in some other universe you were shut out
from. This means you always had it but dared never show it:
if you relax for a minute, if you get under the skin, into the
flesh of an experience, if you become three-dimensional, if
you for one minute stop watching *them* and how they react
to you, then the world comes tumbling down. Well, that was
then.

So now it is pain that has to become secondary, a gap in
the flow of good feelings, instead of how you have always
seen it: that pain is your essence, and pleasure a brief diversion
you are allowed to taste occasionally.

You thought you were dry inside. All dry, nothing else. You

thought the juice of life was something over there: you might attract it towards you if you 'played young'. But the juice of life is not over there. Even deserts have moisture in them, under the ground. Aries, your days are numbered. Life for you meant being on fire, but fire-heat is dry heat, it parches the skin, and makes bones crack. What I hear in your letter is the sound of running water. The dryness in you is making way for the real Jenny to claim her own.

Witches are coming back

If you think a witch
is a hag on a stick
in October, remember
a dark girl, on the beach,
on an island, scratching her magic
in the sand. Witches
are crazy with life,
it throws them in spasms,
there is a fire inside
huge as hunger.

The witch is transfixed:
like a child in a dream
She gets hooked on her own spells.
She may seduce you
but you cannot reduce her,
her black her electric eyes
conjure with darkness in you.
The body
becomes a tunnel
through which the winds rush
and even bones start melting.

But not hers,
she is unmeltable.
When a fever of witches is afoot
and men go glassy to contain their terror,
they will try anything to put a witch out:
bring fire to fire and burn her,
slaughter with water,
or break her neck, a dry stick.
If you try to knock her senseless
she proves tough as a commando,
even ECT only blows one or two of her fuses,
so making love to a witch is still deadly.

Behind the black magic of skin
the wild fires,
behind the wild fires
the stone wall,
behind the stone wall
the huge hurt,
like a hole in space.
Go through the hole
and the spell is broken.

David

Riding
the
waves

Germany, 4th January, 1972.
Dear David,
   Who is this person who keeps sending me poetry in letters
which talk about me from an inside I lost twenty-five years ago,
this person who trusts me so much more than I trust myself?
People like you don't exist. I know they don't because I've been
all round the world and back, looking. With my eyes closed.
   I started to cry in bed last night. I suddenly saw you sitting
in that chair with a blanket round you, dying of cancer. You
might die like my father did, just when I'd found a way of
getting on with him.
   I feel so uncomfortable that you find so much time to write
to me, David, I keep thinking, where's the trick? How *can* this
man be so nice, there's got to be something wrong with you.
But you haven't even got the fault of perfection, you've got
your isms and tics too.

6th January, 1972.
Dear Miss James,
   I thank you for your letter of the 4th inst. Its contents have
been noted.

                                        Yours distantly
                                        Dr. Boadella

Sorry, you've got yourself the wrong therapist. He is making you too uncomfortable. He isn't doctor enough. Next time I see you, I'll wear a white coat, and try to look like Elsworth Baker.

I'm glad I've got my isms and tics. I won't accept your saint-image. I'll accept the ordinariness, yes, I have clay feet, and if I don't blow myself up like a bicycle tyre, it's perhaps because I learnt that the best sessions are the spontaneous ones and the best poems write themselves.

10th January, 1972.
Dear David,

Your 'Dear Miss James letter' had me rolling around. It's good sitting here writing to you, David. I've got someone to write to, and it's so satisfying bouncing a ball when there's someone bouncy to bounce it back again.

I'm not OK enough within myself yet simply to feel good without occasional pushes from the outside world: all I need is to meet someone that responds to me as me without roles, someone interested in the same things, or just someone it's easy to be with, to be honest with. Then movement inside me just happens, I start to tremble and feel nervous and high, everything inside me starts to go runny. It's not that then I'm marvellously healthy, it's that energy is rushing all over me and even if the high is slightly hysterical, at least I know now exactly what's going on and can watch it and feel it.

David, I'm embarrassed when I see your envelopes arrive, and happy and pleased and excited. I'm shy when I read what you say, scared of being shocked by you, holding back in case you say something completely outrageous. Something in me closes up at the power of what you write, at your energy and honesty. David, I know who you are, you're Tigger in Winnie-the-Pooh, you're who everyone thought I was, only you do it better, you don't put me off, you get through. Some stars came together when you answered my letter four summers ago.

Robot-dream, January 1972.
I am in a flimsy, empty modern building. There is a group of rather weedy people with me. A mechanical man has got us all

trapped there. He is ordering us about and has got all the others lined up against the wall. He grins sarcastically and says: 'Yes, we'll have a bit of trouble with her', meaning he knows I won't give in right away. I stand stubbornly in the middle of the room, sure that resistance will mean getting physically hurt, but determined not to give in without at least the show of a fight. He pulls my hair, almost playfully, not really trying very hard because he knows his power and is not in a hurry. I think how if he was clever enough, he'd pull thin strands of hair which would hurt more, instead of great handfuls of it.

A great space-ship is coming in very fast from the sky; it's a gigantic metal construction, flat and huge, all flashing lights and coming straight for the house. The spaceman will contact it and it will come and get us all. Someone says, no one of us is strong enough to fight him. I say 'No, no one of us is, but all together we can stop him', and immediately I go for him, praying the others will have the sense to help. I grab hold of the spaceman's neck and squeeze. His head is a light bulb and it goes misty as I strangle him. The others do help, but rather weakly, but at least enough for me to be able to hold him down and start dismantling and unplugging him. I have no idea how he ticks, but he seems to work electrically. I pull out as many plugs as I can see, each disconnection making him a bit weaker, but he doesn't die completely. I pull out a sparking plug between his legs, vaguely surprised at this electrical version of a little penis. I keep finding more and more connections, it seems the more plugs I unplug, the more there are. I feel violent and horrible doing this, as if I am a murderer, but it's my survival or his. All this is done in a desperate hurry, under great pressure, because the space contraption is right above the house. I drag the machine man round a corner, trying to keep him out of direct visual contact with his space-ship, because I feel he may still have some way of getting a message to them and guiding them. The lights from the ship are flashing on and off and lighting up the house. I hope the other people will have the sense to stand around unpreoccupied by the windows to fool the space-ship and make out everything's all right, nothing's happening. I still need all my strength to keep the spaceman under control, because he just won't die, although he is completely helpless now. Still, I don't trust him and think he may have some trick up his sleeve. He is somehow getting softer and more insinuating the more I bang him with metal bars and unplug him. He is dressed in leather and the further I uncover him, tearing away his props, the warmer he gets. He seems to be made of flesh underneath. He has a loose, floppy mouth, which I try to cover with my hand to stop him making any contact with the space people. I put my hand between his legs and am surprised by how warm he is there, soft and floppy. I start to stroke and rub him, whether to keep his mind off contacting the ship, or to comfort him for what I have had to do to him, or just because I like it, I don't know. I start to get warm too. I am lying beside him and starting to feel very sexual and melty. But then I realize if I start to go unconscious, I won't be on guard against the danger and it may be fatal, so I come out of it.

I wake up full of bad electricity and lie awake terrified and uncomfortable, totally immobile.

David wrote to me:

It's marvellous to have you dismembering a robot and finding flesh and blood underneath. So many dreams, nightmares, before, where *you* were frozen by something so terrible only someone outside, who never came, could rescue you. Control, control — your control of others, the others controlling you, a world of sparking electricity. But something different here, the dream shifts, the metal starts falling away, you start off as a murderer banging at his iron skull, then you shift, the warmth starts to take you over, you begin humanising him. You melt, and even the robot stiffie begins to soften and lose his threat.

So when you wake up full of bad electricity and lie terrified, it carries a simple message: that was too nice, that was too warm, that was frighteningly alive. The bad electricity in you is the good electricity switched off. Who the hell makes love to a robot, better stop! When people start flowing, they flow all over the place, all sorts of boundaries are threatened.

To recognize that you become terrified *because* you like it, that the biggest danger is that you will get hurt if you move, if you make sounds, if you become terrifyingly alive, all this helps even the terror to start to loosen its grip. In so many dreams, nightmares, you are cornered, caught, there is no way of escaping doom. In spite of the threat from the space-ship, this dream does not come across as a doom dream.

There is still some kind of war going on, but you are not losing it.

17th January 1972
Dear David,

I got back from Germany on Saturday, took one look at my overcrowded house and left. I went with Becky to my mother's and slept there. Or tried to: my mother sat in my room and held a monologue for hours on end about how the human race is made up of 'good, superior beings' and 'evil, inferior people' and how the good ones are descended from space travellers. The only bit about Reich that interests her is the fact that he thought he was descended from space people, because she thinks she is. I just lay there, going deader and deader, not because of the content of what she was saying, but because there was no room for me; she pretended it was a conversation with me agreeing, yet when at one point I tried to point out that I thought differently, she brushed me aside with a 'Oh but you *must* agree, it's obvious.'

Next morning, I couldn't leave the house quick enough. I couldn't hate my mother or be angry, I was deadened with a feeling of hopelessness. When I got home, I lay on my bed, my energy locked away. Jerry came in and chatted and I started to talk a bit. Then I felt it all welling up: the impossibility of facing where I came from (a spacewoman!); I felt if I let the knowledge come into me, my body would crush and the roof would fall in. I cannot live knowing I come from nothing, from insanity, and yet I cannot walk around with the heavy weight of pretence upon me, looking at people and hiding from the enormity of that place I come from, that Woolworths house with cardboard people and tinsel decorations and furniture more important than children.

I cried and cried, but most of my energy went into holding back; it was a really bad trip, I was scared stiff, and I didn't give in. I'd glimpsed the pit and backed up and felt annoyed at myself for this, but at least the shivers had returned to my body, I could feel hot and cold, and I could feel my genitals from inside again.

Session with David, 5th February, 1972

I was already crying as I sat on the stairs of the hotel, waiting to go in for my session. I was crying with the relief, perhaps, of being somewhere, at David's, where I could finally wallow in my own feelings. A girl I had tried to help for a very brief time had hung herself in a mental hospital nearby. She was twenty and she was German. I don't know what it is about this suicide that makes me cry. It certainly isn't identification like with Vicky; it wasn't love for the girl, for I found her terribly unlovable; it wasn't guilt, though I know I could have done more. I think I was crying because I can't cry, because I can't feel, because there is a cloud in me, over my mind, that prevents me from knowing this girl really killed herself, prevents me from realizing that that dead white face was the same as the agonized one I had talked to so often. Something is blocking my feelings.

So there I sat on the stairs, already crying. Something my sister had said made me want to cry more. She'd said, 'I really like David'. I felt as if he were being taken away from me. I felt the nearest thing to jealousy since my childhood, a real threat to my existence. It's OK for my sister to have therapy with David and for them to get on well, but it was the simple clarity of her feelings that suddenly threatened me. Because I can't say that. David is far too important to me for me to say that; his image is too highly charged for me to even think too much about him.

I started to hate the girl who was having her session before me. I thought of saying fierce words to David about having to wait so long. And then I went on a very vivid trip: I felt as if I were coming to a prostitute. I couldn't get what I needed at home, so I had to come to some hotel and pay to get warmth for a couple of hours from someone who already had so many children. This made me feel like dirt, like nothing, like some poor little waif, and it made me see therapy as obscene.

When I got in to David, I was already exploding. I'd been neatly packed away for so long, but now it was all coming out unasked for. I can't even remember what happened, whether we spoke, how it came about, but suddenly I was cracking wide open. It was the most dreadful feeling, like breaking through a plate-glass window or being dragged back from death when you're in pain. I was sobbing, resisting like hell and trying to drag myself out of the flood. It went on and on, and there was that strange light like under acid or when you suddenly come out of anaesthetic. There was too much energy in the upper half of my body and I was semi-hysterical. I kept yelling I hated David, I didn't want to come back, I wanted to stay where I was, I was too old and tired to come back to life, it hurt too much.

The feelings got very bad when I looked away from David, his face changed into a monster with long teeth, laughing, and when I looked back at him, he seemed to be composing his face quickly and smiling. If I looked away, he would change again; total terror was just a second away. I sobbed myself to exhaustion and felt myself closing off again, the terror is too terrible to go into.

Where do you come from?

From a space
dark as the back of the skull,
from a race
stranger than human,
across the fissure
between this world and that,
I come, like a ghost who has not given up,

with my bursting head
to be born.

I did not ask to come
into your white world of walls;
I did not ask to live
with the vanishing tricks of flesh;
I did not ask to touch
the glass in front of the skin;
I did not ask to look
at demonic eyes that devour me;
I did not ask to face
the hallucination of people.

All I ask is, now I am here,
to cry myself real,
not to fall
forever
out of my body.

Spare me the white scream
and the final Mouth
huge as the sky
closing over me.
I have not yet asked to die.

David

Acid Trip, 6th February, 1972

The dog shat on the rug and it was a good feeling to have other
people clear it up. The kids were rushing in and out, the house
was crowded as usual, but I just stayed on my bed and let it all
happen. I felt warm and friendly.

When the group started, I discovered I had lost all previous
knowledge: when they started working on Marie, and she was

yelling, and they were all huddled round her, I thought they were tormenting her. I got very confused; my impulse was to jump up and help her, tear them all off her. I called Julie over from across the room, I wanted to hold her hand. I curled up next to her, sucked my thumb and hung on to her with the other hand. Every time I got frightened by something in the group, I warded off the terror by sucking more strongly on my thumb and hanging tighter on to Julie. She said I was radiating heat and I felt pleased. I kept asking her questions — what groups were for and whether they were always like this and what I was usually like. I asked, 'Why is everyone so serious? Mustn't we laugh? ' Julie said, 'It's all supposed to be terribly solemn, people take themselves very seriously,' and her face was so nice and funny that I went into a fit of giggles.

Julie and Marie and I settled in another room. Julie stroked my skin and I felt marvellous. I told her I was frightened of my sister and she asked me if she reminded me of anyone. I said she and mum used to gang up on me and Julie and Marie both said, 'Ahh!' and I felt they knew something I didn't. They seemed to keep talking about mothers. I shuddered and said, 'I wouldn't like my mother to walk in now; I wouldn't like to see her face' and Julie and Marie kept nodding and umming and looking wise and I got mildly paranoid, as if they were trying to make me think of something I didn't want to think about. They chatted together a lot, in quiet, sad voices, weary with a kind of wisdom. I didn't understand what was going on because there I was, small and being looked after, with a tight tummy and a strange thirsty mouth, and no other world existed.

My dress had slipped down and I saw my bare breast. I asked Julie why we wear clothes and she said again in that wise, half-amused way, 'Well, for one thing it's cold...' and she and Marie laughed gently together, and I felt there was something mysterious about clothes. Julie asked me if I'd like to take my clothes off, but some kind of inhibition filtered through. I asked more questions. They told me about people not liking bodies and covering them up and it all sounded like a fairy-tale. And when I heard them talking about the things their mothers had done to them, I couldn't believe it and asked, 'Why? ' and they said, 'Ah!' and sighed, and I kept having this feeling there was something huge going on I didn't know about. Then Julie told me I'm usually the one who tries to answer other people's questions; and they told me about being a therapist and that was strange to hear, like something from the future. They seemed to be saying the whole world was full of evil people hurting their babies, hurting anything that lived and laughed, and I couldn't believe it. I thought we were probably just three exceptions, accident victims, and that we had gathered together to look after one another and make us better. Then as it dawned on me that the whole world really was hostile, I huddled closer and closer and felt we were on a little island, secretly grabbing some warmth and light and lying and laughing together.

Later on, all the kids piled in: Kate, incredibly beautiful, Anna, so thirsty for affection, and my own Becky, the most beautiful creature in the world. They huddled and cuddled up with us and made us laugh. We were all girls, three big and sore and three small and still living, so precious; and I was so happy and proud.

Late in the evening, we traipsed back into the group, the kids dressed in flowing clothes, their hair all over the place, all of us rosy and high and hot. There was a stony reception. I squeezed on to my bed and went subdued and the three babies huddled up to me for warmth and I felt homeless. We were 'good' till the group ended. Then I said, 'Now we can play? ' and paradise returned.

Kate and Becky, with their beautiful pre-adolescent bodies and flowing hair and robes, Murray doing his marvellous face and voice acts. The kids played and danced and fought. I watched the most exquisite encounter group, the kids working through rivalry, playing out their death fears, their terror of being killed or injured by huge grown-ups, and getting comfort from one another when they needed it. The room was swirling with energy. I was breathtaken by the beauty of the creature that had come from my body. I saw Becky as delicate and slightly injured, yet starting to stand up, fighting back, learning to laugh and live and get what she wants. I lay feeling like a mother who has created and brought forth and now lies back to

watch and admire and to wallow in pride and enjoyment. I
didn't need to move myself; I let their wonderful healing
energy come at me, flow over me, and felt so clearly the
curing power of healthy young animal energy and the contrast
with the sick, constipated, glassy vibes of some of the young
men in our groups. I also felt my mother in me: how I cringed
and flinched thinking the children would fall against the mirror
and cut themselves. I felt the 'stop!' climbing up to my throat,
but I didn't let it out; it had no right there in that room. My
pictures came flying off the walls, the room got messier and
messier, more and more what it should be: a place where the
living live. I felt clearly how I had never moved as a child, never
shrieked with joy, never hit a grown-up with a pillow, never
stayed up till one o'clock in the morning.

Murray and the kids put on a wonderful circus for me, each
taking it in turn to be in the centre. Jerry came in a bit growly,
but soon relaxed into it. Later, one by one, the babies fell
asleep. In the end, I was the only one left awake. I lifted the
soft sleeping bodies so that I could get up. I got down my
mirror from the wall and sat down in front of it. I had work to
do. I looked at the photos of me on the wall, photos of me as a
child. I saw a sad, grey, injured little face, deep black rings
under my eyes and a mouth always smiling, no matter what
they did, always grinning. I looked in the mirror and saw criss-
crossed lines all over my face, cuts of hurts, my mouth looked
shrunken and withdrawn, the lips too thin. Nothing in my face
looked whole or right. Then I opened my mouth wide, I stared
down my own throat. I looked at my fat juicy tongue, at my
wet mouth, and I knew: 'there I am, that's me, that's what's
left of me.'

I sat naked in front of the mirror. I thought my thighs and
breasts looked slim and young and beautiful. I didn't try to
make my damaged stomach look nice like I used to. I liked
myself. I sat with my legs open wide and kept looking back at
the photos. I felt I'd just been born. I pressed the knots of
tension in my stomach and felt a ghastly nauseous feeling. I
kept on pressing, timidly, but determined. Something broke and
I was back to the very first session with David when he said,

'Well, now you've got someone you can let it all out on without being hit.' I had cried a little then and now I cried again, 'I've come home, I've come home!' I've got a home; I'm nearly thirty, but now I have a warm place in the world with people who love me.

I finally fell asleep at six o'clock in the morning, resting my hand on the puppy's hot tummy.

A very important group, 2nd March 1972

When it was my turn, I started crying almost immediately. I said how tired I was of carrying around other people's images of me. I said I felt I let people come to within a few inches of my skin and then there was an impermeable wall of glass round me. I might seem warm and receptive towards people, but really I wouldn't let anyone in and I was tired of being like that.

I said to John and Murray and Martin how warm I felt about them because they kept coming back to the groups, they had a trust I felt I was learning from. I broke down in sobs when I talked about trusting. This was the Thursday group, the group I run for the 'others', and to break down in it was to break through a great barrier, I felt I was giving away my most secret parts. I cried about how long it takes to destroy a child's trust, how it doesn't take just a few days of coldness and blows, but that you have to push that child away day after day, month after month, year after year before it is finally killed.

That night after the group, Jerry wanted to make love with me, but it hurt me and I broke out crying and said, 'I want my Mummy' and for the first time I felt that 'Mummy' was just a feeling, a need, a warm safe thing, a connection long before her anger and hate had made the word 'Mummy' repugnant. Jerry responded immediately and held me and the next thing I knew, it was morning.

Out of Reach

Why are you always just out of reach,
flinching from warmth like a crushed thing
in case it melts you,
collecting yourself like a prisoner
to speak through glass
no words ever shatter?

Your body's a bomb that may one day go off,
its fuse ticks away under the skin
too easily bruisable.
I try to follow your eyes as they skip
like hot stones, and wonder
is it hunger that gnaws at you
like a tumour?

Only in dreams,
sometimes yours, sometimes mine,
can lips be liquid,
the body flow towards fire,
a face contain and hold you,
can touch no longer torture.

David
March, 1972

Session with David, 11th March 1972

I went to the session determined to stop David from pouncing
all over me. I lay down and started to shiver. David jumped,
eager to make suggestions. I stared at him, fierce words passing
through my brain but not coming out of my mouth, confusion
mounting as I blocked my hostility. He said my lip had snarled;
that threw me, as I hadn't been aware of it. A wild silent
turmoil as David got caught up in my silence and kept making
more suggestions. Somehow, I cooled down the whirl in my
brain and managed to speak.

I told him how resentful I felt when I came home, how annoyed with him I was when away from him, but how I couldn't face him with my criticisms. I said there was no space for me to feel with him reacting so quickly to me all the time. Just like my mother, answering before I've finished speaking, so I had to become a quick clever talker to compete, to get a word in, to put myself in the picture, to stop her suffocating me. (Later she was to say that she couldn't breathe when I was around, as I 'used up all the oxygen').

I said, 'It's your nice kind face and bright eyes and friendly smile that paralyze me. How can I be nasty in the face of such niceness? ' I am suffocated with niceness, there is not room for me to be 'bad' because everyone is so busy being nice. We are such a happy family. So I told David I wanted space and silence; I know myself a bit now and I can feel how to work with myself. Sometimes I need help, but I will ask for it. I don't want suggestions and more suggestions, I wanted him to stop diving at me.

David moved and sat away from me. I looked at him and suddenly burst into tears, half of joy, half shock and fear. I tried to crawl into the wall, it was just like the other time when I felt the pain of passing through thick, shattering glass. I sobbed for a while, and unfortunately David came and sat too near again. What had happened was that by daring to push David away, I had for a moment truly let him in. I had been unguarded, just for a second, my eyes and mind had opened, I was unwatchful, and David had sprung out from space, become suddenly four-dimensional — he had become absolutely present too, he really was here, now. With him threateningly close, I had had to protect myself, consign him to two-dimensional flatness, keep him at bay. Now I was seeing him for the first time, or so it felt. The sensation of letting him come into me was so shattering that I said, 'God, now I know why I block it off.'

I don't know who you are

said the scarred girl
to the man who fell out of the sky.
I want to go home, I want to die,
and yet this bond between us,
tell me why?

I have my hands,
he said, a little rough
to touch your skin,
a bit too dry for your cold head,
I have my arms,
he said, a bit too tough
to hold you in
when you feel dead,
I have my eyes,
he said, not warm enough
for yours to swim.

I have been looking
for you
all the years, she said,
all the dark years.
Too blue, too blue, your eyes,
she told him,
through the cold tears.

When her cry came,
it was like a sheet being torn open to let the air in,
and she was breathing again.

David

Dream next day, 12th March, 1972.
I dreamt my mother-cat was suckling some babies. But
they weren't her babies, they were jerbils. I found them
under some hay in the cage, sorely neglected; some of

them hadn't been able to fight their way to get a teat to suck. I found one little jerbil so tiny and fragile, it didn't look as though it had had a drop of milk in its life. It was about half an inch long, and very weak, I was almost scared to touch it.

I put it to one of mama-cat's teats and immediately it sucked enthusiastically; then I found another about an inch long, and I saved it too. I was very wary of mama-cat. I had to put the baby jerbils to her with great care. I felt if she got a whiff of the fact that they weren't kittens, but mice-creatures, she'd eat them instead of feeding them. If they didn't move too quickly, I felt she might be fooled.

Telling this dream the next day, I suddenly saw its meaning: my mother suckled me only on condition that I did not grow different from her. I must not make a move out of place, I must grow up identical to her; if I grow into a different creature, she will pounce and eat me up.

○   ○   ○

One Sunday, overinterference from someone in the group who was trying to help brought me out of my feelings. I got confused and tight and went into a depression which I didn't shift for about a fortnight. I wrote to David when it was over:

I didn't cut off from my bad body feelings. I felt I was eating cotton wool, my head was a balloon, my intestines dry and sandscraped, the pores of my skin like inturned nipples. Jerry sometimes tried to help, but I was proud, stubborn, impenetrable. I was a silently screaming frustrated child who has finally had to face the inability of its parents to make anything feel nice.

One Monday morning, with the kitchen full of my sister and the kids and mess and noise, I thought I'd go crazy. I hated Jerry for reading, for doing anything when I was in such pain. I wanted to kill him in the car. I hated myself more and more. At midday, I was supposed to help him with a session. It was all too much, and in my room I flopped on my bed and started to cry softly, hopelessly. Jerry came in, and I let him see how I was. He came over and picked me up and put me on his lap. I cried some more and I knew it was alright. The knot was broken.

And then I could live ordinarily again. I could enjoy little things, like crocheting and cleaning up, like having lots of children and people around. I started sitting for hours at night in the scruffy kitchen talking to Sharon and Martin. I could never have done that a year ago. Martin says when I first spent time with him that it was 'like having an audience with the Queen'.

Many little things came together at this time: I gave up taking the pill after six years on it during which I'd hardly had a period; now I wanted life to move in me again, and blood is part of life. I fostered a beautiful six-month-old Brazilian baby; in fact, I only had it for two weeks as his mother came back. I started relating in a teenage-like way to Jerry's eighteen-year-old sister Sharon.

I went to my next session with David feeling beautiful. David said as I walked in that I looked as though I'd had a session already. I said I was afraid that if I was soft in front of him, I might look beautiful. He said I did. I said how I found it terribly dangerous to see David as touchable. When I had felt this out, looking at him and talking and breathing, I put my arms out to him, and he held me for a long time. My fear of something 'sexual', whatever that is, disappeared: what I felt were relaxed arms, a warm chest, tuned breathing, and that was the whole world. And in that instant, I knew I had felt this closeness before: I *had* been held as a child. David said, 'I know you have, because if you hadn't, it would have been far more difficult to reach you.' I cried for those who can't be reached and for myself because I nearly wasn't. David said that the person he'd been writing to for so long, that I maintained didn't exist, was lying on the bed next to him.

I had a vision then of a mother looking down at her baby and being so overwhelmed with love for it that she would cry. And I felt that that baby, looking into her eyes, would explode with joy and that this would be echoed in later life by sexual explosion.

David, I love you very much and it's starting not to matter 'who you are'.

David wrote me a poem about this session:

Foundling

Suddenly
she was washed up on solid ground
uncrushed
and there was this stillness
as of a survivor
like someone left
   for one or two hours
the blood waking from the shock of its stunned sleep
   hours broken by weeks
the trembling starting to ease
   weeks aching like years
a torrent of words slowed to a single stream
   years opening at last to make room for her eyes.

So pain drained, of a wound exhausted,
a vast bruise cleared from the face of the sun
as she lay in herself
in the cold room, empty
of furniture, bare
of the last obstacle,
warm as a hug from another life

and ordinary tears
shone like a blessing.

David

○   ○   ○

At the end of May, I went to Spain, just me and Becky and a girlfriend. Almost every night for the first two weeks, I was beset with bad dreams and nightmares. I wrote to Jerry:

I am very jealous that you are there and I am here. It is difficult to accept that what I have here is all I have, myself, my daughter, occasionally Pepe. When I am at home and everybody is wanting me, calling for me, it is so easy to feel I am more, I have more. Here I have only me and the sounds inside me. I feel as alone as ever before in my life; the difference is I have stopped 'looking'. I go to bed with the sun and do not walk the streets looking for warmth when the sun has gone. When I am too full of sadness or confusion, I go to bed and curl up and think or sleep and dream.

I have little faith that I will pull out of this shadowy pain enough to live fully. I can only light up when someone else puts a match to me. Only my dreams seem real. For brief moments, a walk with Pepe on the beach, the sun at five in the morning, my body when I touch it, I come alive. But mainly I feel I am waiting to join my father. And then I feel there is nothing I can do but stay in London and help patch up a few more people and pretend there is hope. Hope there is of clearing the confusion, I know that now, but what hope ever of bringing the scars back to life? Just the sight of a messy noisy table at breakfast here brings tears to my eyes to remember the regimental perfection of a perfectly laid dead table every day of my childhood.

Maybe time and tide will bring new waves, but this is me today, and it would take more warmth than this sun to reach me.

Trip, 2nd June, 1972

I woke up very early after another bad night and a bad dream about Jerry. I needed to punch and kick the bed. I knew I couldn't wait any longer to do something about these feelings, they were right on the surface. I got all the mattresses on the floor, I took some acid, lay down and immediately started working on myself.

I needed to cry, and this was the thing I was most scared of doing, because I didn't want anyone to come and comfort me and take it away. My crying was strangled and the mucus went to my head; I could feel all my channels blocking up and knew very clearly in that moment what illness is and how we get ill, and the misery of the feeling. All illness is blocked-up channels; I was with my Dad again when he died of cancer.

I got to feeling so bad, I called for help. No-one heard and I realized how if you need something badly enough, you really have to yell for it. Sue came in. My jaw was juddering and my whole body too, and that felt good, to shake life back into me. I was very warm. But it was a mistake to get Sue: I wasn't ready to face my feelings about her. There were criss-crossed cobwebs and lines veiling my sight when I looked at her which prevented any energy from passing between our eyes. I felt she was very much like me, guarded, and with no confidence in her own feelings. Her two-year-old son helped me though. A two-year-old says all the right things, like 'fuck-off Jenny' so I could get into a dialogue with some energy in it, which is what I needed.

Sue asked me what she could do to help. I found it so difficult to say I needed help, I needed someone. Finally I said I wanted to be held, and I lay in her lap, but it was all wrong. I wasn't admitting in my feelings that I wanted contact, and so I felt our skins as dry and cold with no energy passing between us. I was hiding the fact that I wanted Jerry, and this secret was cutting off all my electricity.

When Sue left me alone, I managed at last to let go. There was so much pleasure in my pain. I started crying, 'I want Jerry, I want him to come', and I soon realized how scared I was that Sue would hear. So I pushed myself further: 'Yes, I *do* want him, I do!' and suddenly there I was, facing one of my most basic splits: I was not allowed to tell Mum I wanted Dad. All those years of 'We'll be happy when Dad leaves', never a question of what I felt about him. And then the taboo on crying: always being threatened or comforted, usually the first, anything to get me to stop crying. All these things came together, and I felt my chest breaking. I lay on my front with my arms spread out and my crying turned to despair and exasperation at all those years of pain because of something so simple: my whole life gone because I wasn't allowed to tell my Mum how much I wanted Dad.

I exhausted myself crying, but I knew that this feeling has to come back again and again, it is so deep: now I understand my longing for Martin when I am with Jerry, my longing for Jerry when I am with Sue, why I miss Pepe when we're separated, my anxiety when 'one of the group' is missing. I thought, thank god that I separated from Jerry and took acid out here and that everything has come together for me. But now, with such want inside me released, I didn't know what to do with it. I burst out crying again and again, I just wanted Jerry and everything seemed empty if I couldn't have him. I was trying to resign myself, but then I realized, 'NO! no more waiting.' If a baby is 'sensible' and waits, it dies. Waiting is dying, waiting is giving up life. No more resigning, I will get angry if I can't have what I want; I am not going to wait to live any more, I will not be consoled.

Then there was Nicky, giving me lollipops and playing with me. I came up for air, laughed with him, until the quietness came down on me again. I felt need in every cell of my body and I started crying again.

The day was getting older and Sue said she was going out. I did not want to be left alone to go into my head: I'd gone off several times already, into prisons and Vietnam and cars and into my own death. (Can death also be a sensuous shriek?).

So I said to Sue, 'Take me too.' I could hardly stand up, I was trembling all over. But I was proud of the vibrating, proud to be alive: this trembling is what my mother did not manage to kill. Sue brushed my hair. That was such a beautiful feeling, I wanted her to go on forever. I asked her if there was anything left to enjoy in the world if I could not have Jerry. She said, 'Yes' in a very definite, playful voice. I said, 'WHAT? '

Sue was right.

I didn't want to put clothes on, but it was a big fiesta day in Spain, and I compromised. I put on a loose shirt and no shoes and felt naked and brown and good. Sitges had turned to bedlam, every inch of ground covered with people in ridiculous stiff clothes; and hundreds of cars, sitting on the earth and not a part of it.

I felt so good in myself, I even enjoyed the people staring. We were barefoot and simply dressed and the Spaniards stared in amazement.

The ground felt so good underfoot, sandy stony unmade-up roads, warm pavements and stone walls. We found a stone seat and lay there, our backs against the cliff behind. I loved the feel of everything my body touched. Nicky ran around naked. Amazed passers-by couldn't hide their pleasure at seeing him. We were very different from the people there that day and I felt that the only way to spread health is to be healthy.

A book I am reading, Malinowski's 'Sexual Life of Savages' was affecting me, causing me to see my surroundings in terms of tribal families and adventures with nature. I longed to roll naked in the sand. I felt the need for water on my skin. The beach was like a tin of sardines, but I knew I could make my world with just a few feet of space. We lay at the water's edge. I could feel the sand even through my shirt and I watched the Catalans play on their day off. The ill bodies were frightening, especially the two-year-old ones, still being killed. But there were beautiful ones too: a plump young woman near us lit up brightly, laughed in confidence at her own loveliness, looked over to us, half-shy, half-flirtatiously. Most family groupings on the beach contained three generations; the Spaniards are still tribal.

Sue asked me what the fiesta was about, and I said, 'it's the day the saints come out on broomsticks.'

In the evening, I went running along the water's edge like last year with Jerry. Marion was with me and we sat and screamed out to sea all the names of the people we wanted to appear.

Another day in Spain, I wrote to David:

I do not feel the same with you since my sister came to you for therapy. I am standing in the shadows asleep. I will not compete. I used to feel you were mine, I was fierce about it. But now you have been spread so thinly over so much of my family, I have turned my face away. I can't tell you I love you any more because now you're not my secret. Something is lost. I will see you soon to find out what it is.

David wrote back:

I have noticed the shift in you since Snowy was on the scene. It's almost as though you're testing me: if you drop back several steps, will she take your place? All part of the jealousy thing which you got very close to in the trip. Jealousy is when you want one person and no-one else will do in place.

Snowy coming to me for therapy was a jolt — you took a step back, expecting desertion. You are away, Snowy takes your hour. A stand-in for Jenny? *No-one* stood in for Jenny that day. There was a Jenny-absence, Jenny was away, she was missing, she was in her shadows asleep or running in her dreams, or waking up somewhere to realize home is a hole in the heart. But for me, people do not replace each other. There are no stand-ins.

Now you've written, I think I can admit your silence was a pain. I want to see your face again. Therapy isn't jam, you can't spread it, thinly or thickly. Therapy is coming close with someone and not twisting them up. Therapy is not letting a face turn away. Therapy means being there, forever, until the trip is finished.

Jenny, come back, a letter can't stand in for a session. Goodnight,

Love, David

14th June, 1972

It was yesterday your letter came, David. I sobbed my way through it, I felt I was going to drown.

Today I am high and happy and warm so it is more difficult to conjure back the dambusting effect of your letter. I had felt deserted, rejected, unhelped, unseen, because of things that have been happening here. Then Pepe sought me out, cared for me, talked to me and cried. And then comes your letter telling me I exist.

I felt, 'this man has gone crazy'. I was crying your name and thinking, 'this is a love-letter, the man's taken leave of his senses.' I felt you were seducing me, calling me, that you were being special and talking as if there was no-one else in the world to take account of, to account to. It was a lover's letter; I sobbed because such a need and a passion were opened up in me, and behind it an anger because you can't be what you seem to be, we are not two young people together. I was confused reading it, you calling me, calling me, telling me to come, you can't do that, and using my name, that gets right through, and talking about my face as if I've got one, and about holes in the therapy, in that room, because I'm not there. I'm used to being missed because someone wants me to do something for them, but your letter was a seduction. Your letter becomes sexual because it is full of red blood and is frighteningly illogical and passionate. You cannot call me, I AM A PATIENT, David, and I bet you wear a tie at breakfast.

I've lost the feeling today, David, but it was an aching pleasurable pain. I liked the passion I felt raging around in me when I accepted your letter into myself and let my need splurge out. How much I want just to give in to my father, to forget all the taboos against loving him and let myself drown in hot tears and urine and flooding in my chest.

Who is this man David who sees me as a separate speck of dust amongst the millions when no-one else does?

My god, it's difficult knowing you, I don't know what I've let myself in for, and there's no backing out now. I feel so mistrustful, wanting the pleasure, wanting to be seduced into feeling, but knowing somehow you're not really real, not really there, just some really good guy in a hotel room saying strange things to me.

Maybe Jerry and I can learn to be for each other what you are for me. But if I really love you, then that will be the end of the therapy, and I will lose you, you will die on me, like Dad did before I ever really had him.

I am having simple moments of great happiness out here: when I play ball for hours on end not caring any more what I look like; when I dance and I am really with the music and all the faces are fun not threat; when I can make playful contact with people; when my body feels peaceful in the sun and does not hurt except for the pleasant ache of lots of movement.

Times are only bad when I am outside myself, when I am lonely and looking, looking to be loved in a way no-one can because it is the sort of love that comes through a lifetime together that I want.

16th June, 1972

OK, Jenny, so I write these daft impossible letters, call them love if you like. I don't want sex from you, I don't want to eat you up, I just want you to live. To seduce you, yes, to call you, towards those pleasure-pain feelings of being alive, when the split begins to break down, like it broke down on your trip. Therapy has to be more than warm soup at a hostel, a plateful for everyone. Next please. All the structure of therapy pushes it towards this, hours, payment, all the dead skin of therapy. But the energy of therapy has to be 'special', it has to be specific. Therapy is a calling. It has to find you behind all the disguises or it is meaningless. Things have to push towards growth, be called into growth, behind the dead skin. You have to be found while you're alive, Jenny, it's no use finding you when you're dead.

I had another love-letter in Spain, from my sister; a gentle bombshell considering the life-time of hostility that lay behind us.

Dear Jen,

Needed to write to you before I went to sleep although the dawn is coming up. Had another encounter group tonight and just now I don't feel afraid to say I love you. I wish you were near so I could hold you. Jen, I feel we talk the same language. I know what you're on about and your life makes sense. There's some people who are so confused they make me feel small-minded and crude but I'm sure really we've got things straight and they just make their confusion sound intellectual because that's all they've got. What matters is loving people and being loved and breathing and not being afraid. I feel like crying. There are lots and lots of people in the world but so few when you take a really good close look. You're one of them, Jen.

Love, Sno.

First session with David after Spain, July 1st, 1972

I went expecting nothing, expecting still to be blocked as I have been in the groups this week after feeling no welcome from Jerry, and receiving a basinful of shit from Alex in the Thursday group about dreading me coming home and not wanting me in the groups.

I went in to David, and found there was another world, a magical one. All the world outside was putting me down, sneering, not believing in me, seeing me as I know I am not. Suddenly, David, gentle, receptive, allseeing, the father my illusions believed in and here he is. He is sitting looking at me, I exist. He is wanting nothing from me, only wanting me to live, be warm and feel good. David is not trying to kill me, he accepts that I should move and he is not frightened of me; he has nothing to gain from being cruel to me.

I start to talk, feeling that I would not be allowed to do that in the groups. I would have to 'say it with feeling', there would be a way to and a way not to. I start to say things about Jerry, and very soon I am in anger and tears. I am angry about the methods of our groups, the lack of warmth now, the new expertise and expectations, the streamlining, taking away caring and relating. Then David put his hand out to me; he seemed moved. I yelled it away, I turned away. I couldn't bear anything I did or said to move him. I wanted no movement from his side; I have to keep him cool and distant or I will no longer know myself. I will be swimming in a new, warm sea not knowing where the current will take me. I keep myself cool by knowing always that David is not mine; he belongs to another woman, he has other babies and other duties, I cannot go home with him and he cannot come home with me. I must not love a man, I must not reach out my arms to a man because I am a girl, and little girls love their mothers and not their fathers. I must stay eternally wild eyes watching and waiting. I have not a leg to stand on, no legs to stamp, kick, push out my angry longing. I have to stay cool lest I turn him on; I must not let him see passion in me in case he gets swept along on the tide.

The next day was our Sunday group. What had happened was that while I was in Spain, some people had come to our house who had trained with Janov in the States, and some of their methods had been absorbed into our ways of working. I wrote this about the group:

The group, god how I hated it, half a dozen people moaning and yelling and screaming all at once, and I hated all of them, I didn't believe them. I had been having such a good time in my room in the nude with beads and fruit and Terry taking pictures of me and Marie. That was fun, like in the old kind of Sunday groups we had. I resented Julie's screaming, resented the group starting when all I wanted was to play. I forced myself to stay in the group. I hated it. I felt such anger, I couldn't bear them all yelling at once. It was obscene. I felt close only to the ones who seemed out of it. I was like Martin, seeing it all as crazy, barmy, weird. I was seething. I was saying how furious I was, and somehow suddenly the attention was on me. I said, 'Fuck you' to Jerry over and over again; I can't remember what he was saying. The others were sitting in a semi-circle round me, telling me to say it with feeling. Fucking idiots. I remember Jerry throwing me a cushion because I was hitting the wrong thing. I threw it back to him and screamed. Julie provoked me more and I screamed at her and then I was deep in it.

I went on and on and on. The door was wide open inside me and my whole past was laid before me and I had to do nothing except travel along it. As long as I had the energy, the journey was simple. I needed the people round me to stay put and not break the spell. They did stay, but they kept interfering, using blasted techniques when I was already deep in the thing the techniques are destined to provoke. Jerry kept doubting me, people tried to bring me down and out, but I'd climbed solidly enough into myself not to be waylaid. I said, 'I'm special, I'm different, I'm not like you.' This is a vital feeling to me, and Jerry was trying to kill it, saying 'how did I use it?' Alan kept asking what was special about me and Alex was sneering at me. I had to fight. But I was right, and it was good; I felt my difference, I am not like anyone else; I am separate; I exist. My chest was flooding, I was soaked in sweat. I went in, deep into myself, again and again, carrying on for over an hour. It was a self-assertion trip, weathering any storm of opposition to my being as I am, noisy, big, annoying, and very much alive.

A couple of days later, I was sitting in the kitchen, waiting to go to Ireland, talking to Jerry. I had slept two nights with Martin and had felt a body flow which blew my mind right away. Jerry was in terrible pain and I felt a lot for him. I was sad to hurt him, but knew I couldn't lie any more to my own needs, my own body. As I was listening to Jerry's hurt, the picture of Martin got uglier and uglier in my head. I started to see him as someone weak and worthless sucking off me. The more I listened to Jerry, the worse my image of Martin became, as if it were his fault. In the middle of this, Martin walked into the kitchen, stopped dead, and left.

I burst into tears. I was so shocked by the contrast between how I had started to see him in my mind, and what he looked like really: he was strong and beautiful, and I wanted him. The conflict was laid out plainly before me by this chance encounter: I wanted his strength and protection, but I was terrified of losing Jerry. Martin wasn't enough on his own. I did not want to live with my father. Mummy, I have to tell you, I need to tell you, I love Daddy, I need him. I feel terror at her anger: 'OK, you go and live with him then.' NO! I know how horrible his empty morgue is, I would not want to live with Dad's deadness, can hardly bear one day a month of boredom in his perfectly sterile cage.

I wanted so much in that moment to see my mother in the present, to tell her, explain to her, the hatred of all those years, how I'd killed myself inside for fear of her leaving me if I cried out my feelings for Dad; and then how ever after I'd wanted to kill her because she had me trapped. Now I was suddenly free; I could yell: MUMMY I WANT DADDY: I want his body; I need him, I burn inside for him. But I do not want to live with him. I need you too, Mummy.

The next day, travelling by road through the countryside, I wrote to Jerry:

Jerry, please hear me, I am someone who cares what happens to you, but I am English and different from you and I have a different life behind me and in front of me. I hope it will be near your life, but it will be separate, I will not be you.

We are driving through an England I didn't know existed, of thatched cottages and green so green everywhere, and my eyes are opening. My body is swimming with sexuality, opened up to a sensuousness somehow I always knew was there in me.

Guy said, 'Look, a White Horse on the hillside'. He stopped the van and we climbed the steep hill to look at the ancient figure. We are English. I feel there must be Hobbits living nearby. The wind is high and warm and I am dressed in wild warm colours, layers and layers of cotton, trousers and shirts and skirts and an orange bandana. I am 30, supple and brown. I am in myself and not surging towards Guy. He is there, it is good to have company; but I have found my sexuality through not being sexual. I know I do not want Guy, he does not have my kind of vibes. He has the right vibes for striding across an English hillside to see a white horse, to talk charmingly to old ladies, to surge happily over the unaccustomed humanness of Welsh shopkeepers, to dig bees and birds and motorcar engines and the happiness of a new morning. We are totally separate, as comfortable as brother and sister, no looking, no trying, no urging. What I am in love with is my feelings, my rushing blood and surging liquids, the freedom of feeling without brakes on. Something has come back to me from a long time in the past.

Yesterday morning with you in the kitchen, I wanted so much to tell my mother in the present, 'Mummy, as surely as I have your eyes and lips and skin, I have your pain in my veins; but now I can talk to you and I want to say, I loved my Daddy with all the passion of a little child. Mummy, I wanted the manness of him, his rough chin and heavy hands, the smell of his pullover and his pipe, the feel of his thick army overcoat, the sound of his Lambeth backstreet laugh. Mummy, I was frightened you would go or send me to stay with his cold, so I shut up, and I remained a shadow ever since.'

Jerry, you have stayed with me through affair after affair with all my faery fathers, and I have stayed around whilst you waded through your morass, broke my door down and destroyed my peace, yelled at my life and clawed at my warmth. We have both eaten each other's shit and will probably eat a lot more. But the connection is there, the moments of health as well as the seas of poison connect us. I will try to scream out my jealousy and hurt when it is my turn, and I will try to brave the storms of your hurt turned against me, Jerry, because I cannot lie to my body, and I don't want to lie to yours.

At the moment, where I'm at is 'finding Daddy and telling Mummy'. And that means I am asserting Body over sentimentality. I am yelling: I am Hot, I am Rough, I know what I want and that is a man. Jerry, if my projection on to you as my mother is too much for your life, then you must say, 'I will not suffer for your mother's trips, get the hell out of it.' I will try to accept you doing that without rejecting *you*. I, in my turn, want the right to scream, 'NO! I will not feed you at the breast, unless my breasts are full and willing.' I have to see these feelings through, Jerry, and you have to protect yourself from me as you see fit.

Believe it or not, we are both on the same side.

Jen.

On the boat to Ireland, 5th July, 1972

I thought I would go mad, all the nightmares of a life-time come true, and it's happening all around me. Children being killed, hit, threatened for not sitting still. Don't move, don't fidget. Escalation. Higher and higher, the threats becoming more and more violent. The children, refusing to be killed, their instinct strong, look for a way out, disobey, get hit, brutalized, deaden themselves, their faces are getting ugly, their bodies bruised and hate-filled. Sullen young mothers, younger than me, with spiteful eyes, murderous hands and miserable, mean mouths, — spanked children themselves once. Hideous fathers, fat at thirty, big paunches and bums and baggy trousers, harsh, murderous faces, muscles a hundred times more terrifying than their harsh wives' hard hands. These men threaten with the unsubtle violence of a police-state, more dangerous to life and limb, but less confusing than the half-hidden cajoling threats of a bad-tempered democracy; no tactical softness here to unbalance and split their offspring.

I bore it and bore it, trapped energy lifting me further and further from the ground. And suddenly, there I was, standing in front of her made-up face, young under the hate. 'Please don't, please don't hit him. Let him sit by me.' 'I BEG YOUR PARDON? Do you mind, he's *my* son!' Outraged self-righteousness. 'Yes, I know he is, but you're beating him up for nothing.' 'I AM NOT. You can mind your own business.' 'Kids are everyone's business' . . . feeble, impotent, I go away, dying.

Northern accents, Irish accents, London accents, words echoing in my brain from Germany and Spain, 'Sei ruhig! No te muevas! ' Words that kill, sit still, don't move, do that again and I'll . . . I felt the paralysis in my own body and a frenzy to save the children, to get them away, to give sanctuary. I cried, but no relief. Then dreams in the night, on the hard ship floor, we are all in a gas chamber, I awake in the morning to death, and as we dock, watch the children staring out blankly as they are driven away in the padded backseats of nice shiny cars; unreachable.

Dream about my Father (disguised as Martin), 8th July, 1972
I come home and find Martin has hung himself just inside the front door. Sobbing rises in me, but I can't really feel my loss. I ask, 'How long has he been there?' My mother answers, 'Oh, he's only just done it.' 'What? Then he might still be alive!' I rush to the front door, several people rush with me, and we cut him down. His body is still warm, and as soon as the rope is cut, he starts to breathe. We hold him, like in an encounter group, so that life can come back into him. Then he comes out in typically Martin-fashion with some comment like, 'Well, hold me properly then.' I feel a mixture of wanting to smack him and wanting to hug him.

Another dream about my father, 10th July, 1972
My father still goes to work, not knowing that he is dying of cancer. I decide to try and get him to give up work, even at the risk of him guessing he is ill. I get him to sit down on my bed

and say 'Considering he had had that head tumour out (when I was seventeen), didn't he think he ought to have a good time, give up work, in case he got ill again and never enjoyed his leisure?'

He is looking at me, he is very close to me. I break down and tell him how much I love him, and how frightened I am for him, and suddenly he gives in. He flops forward on my bed, and his body heaves with sobbing. It's as if he has given in to me, all his stiffness and pretence has fallen away and he can't hold on any longer. He is letting his love show. My pleasure is huge, but as I sit there stroking him, his head in my lap, I start to fantasy about my own face. Because I have 'won', because I am getting what I want, I imagine that my teeth are growing, like a Vampire's teeth, and that my face is changing, becoming evil.

Session with David, 22nd July, 1972

I am confused between pleasure and guilt. This session, I asked David questions, and some of his answers made me zing with good feelings, especially when he said I am absolutely nothing like my sister, that it is difficult to imagine in fact that we are sisters; and when he said he is very strongly affected emotionally by my sessions.

I discovered it was almost impossible for me to stand up straight and walk round the room with David sitting there. I felt my standing up as a provocation, as if I was trying to 'lead him on' (my mother's phrase). I was being a teenager, a gypsy, I was showing off, trying to seduce him. I had to walk carefully like an invalid in case I felt or looked good, in case I enjoyed being a girl, in case I had any effect on David. I had to put on a troubled and preoccupied and closed look and hide it if I felt gay and boisterous and beautiful.

Then I felt out what happened if David stood against the wall. I felt I had him cornered, that I was threatening him. I had to step carefully, tread lightly, breathe gently in case I frightened or surprised or provoked him ('Don't do that dear, you *know* the effect it has on boys.').

When David of his own accord sat behind me and touched my

back and neck, my stormy looks broke suddenly to reveal a wide grin. I felt naughty, and very good inside. I had what I wanted, I had a man behind me, someone to hold me up, someone gentle and loving and firm. To have a man behind me is somehow more personal than having him face me. It means he knows I exist and I don't have to do or be anything, he is just there loving me.

Group the next day

Jerry's probing questions forced me to realize that if I didn't have someone to think about when I went to sleep, I couldn't go to sleep. If I wasn't in love with someone, if I stopped myself fantasying about David, then the world seemed empty. When I am not in love, everything is flat and dull and mundane, like living with my mother: just restrictions, no emotions, no excitement. I need to be in love to feel alive. There must be *two* because there never were two. I must have someone to run to when I am on bad terms with the other. I can only be two-dimensional as long as I have to stay with only one.

Letter to David, 24th July, 1972
Dear David,

Please help me with your clarity because I feel our relation-ship is in danger. I feel I am walking round you in circles, not looking at you, because I am hiding something. I am hiding One Big Question, which is where all my fantasies lead: 'If your wife died, would you marry me?'

When I saw Dad so sad and lonely, I thought I could make him happy if I was his wife. I want to know if I am good enough for you (him), whether I am just a freak patient, freaky little girl, or a real woman. The pleasure of the ensnaring game is so great, I fear I am ensnared in it for ever. As long as you give me pleasure by your responsiveness, what incentive is there to move on, to feel bad, to lose Dad when I can have him, even just a little bit? If you were to get killed tomorrow, there would be no-one who could *see* me; the world would be barren and I unseen. I would have to go back to my mother and a life of angry, sullen frustration. I am fighting hard not to give up the most beautiful part of my neurosis.

Dear Jenny,

Your One Big Question sums up the trap, and also contains the way out. If I say, 'Yes, I would marry you', you are hung up forever on me, waiting for my wife to die, and other men are not good enough. If I say, 'No, I would not marry you,' you are rejected, the old cold hurt is there more bitter than ever, the crunch has come, the play is over, and your impulse could be to throw me off like a discarded lover.

Becoming real and three-dimensional doesn't mean you get the therapist in the end. It doesn't mean he says 'yes' and starts to live with you. It means you dare to want to, it means you give up your long hard fight to hold back the hot flush of warmth which is where sex and love can no longer be separated. Because if you could really get through your fear of the strength of the love feelings for me, you would overcome the 'fixation'. The fixation is being caught between those feelings, which would melt you down, and the fear you will get rejected, despised, laughed at or taken advantage of. Seduction is alright, if your heart is not in it. Loving me is alright, if there isn't a hint of sexuality in it, if it's puritan Jenny. So, usually, you keep your One Big Question out of your mind, and the One Big Answer out of your body. The answer does not come from me, it comes from your body. The answer is going in to your pleasure and your guilt, at daring to feel what your pride desperately tries to stop you feeling.

Has the therapy become neurotic? Yes, the battle between having sexual feelings and having to shut them off because you mustn't have sexual feelings for someone you love, yes, that is neurotic. If I touch you, you must tense, or freeze. If I look at you, you must harden your eyes. So you preserve yourself and stay fixed. Your fear is that if you melt, you become the gypsy, the seductress; I will despise you and you will despise yourself. If you lead me on, I will suddenly turn and become a cold man, or a hot split man who will pounce and suck you into himself. The sickness of your therapy is acting the invalid because it is safer than not acting, and letting your body express its honesty, and that honesty includes, in fact is built out of, the ability to stay with good feelings; your body knows that sexual seductive feelings can be good too. Your terror is that as soon as you slide from virgin into gypsy, you cease to be good enough, you become the slut, the harlot.

What is the ensnaring game? Surely it is living your role of attracting and repelling at the same time. Your high energy pulls people towards you. You hook your therapist too. The repelling is the shell you build to keep people away so you always feel alone. You opened your heart to Jerry in Spain, but he was far away, and it was safer. The repelling of me is in all the troubled and closed looks you put on to hide your good feeling which might threaten me and so us, you protect our 'precious' relationship by keeping out anything that could make you swell with *real* pride, glow with real body warmth. You won't let me, or anyone, inside; you keep everyone controlled and therefore locked out, in case of what they might discover if they really got inside you — that you were a nobody, a wraith, a nothing, a freaked-out ghost of a person.

Are you good enough for me (him, any man)? What is goodness? Is it being the good mummy to a cold hard man, thawing out your dead babies? That way you are always safe; you can believe you are exciting if you can bring excitement into someone else's life, but the cold babies warming up don't *see* you. In the end, nothing comes back from the line of dead fathers, except dismissal, contempt, they stay wrapped in their own misery, even if you turned them on for a bit, even if for them, no-one else can be as good as you.

You don't mean that. You mean 'Am I good enough when I stop all the games?' Am I good enough when energy just pours where it has to pour and you get carried on the tide? Are you good enough when you dissolve in a rush of feeling and hot urine?

So how do I see you? As freaky little girl or as a real woman? To begin with, you were a freaky patient who wrote me from Germany and complained of nymphomania, who put me on a doctor-pedestal and wouldn't look me in the eye. You were also a body whose muscles I pushed. Then I began to see Jenny, at first only hurt Jenny, who was also doing quite a lot of hurting. In the early part of the therapy, you would block the connection between sessions. I felt you were never there, you could never face anything. That was my freaky patient. In the gaps I began to get glimpses, somebody looked back who looked clear instead of clouded, who dared to feel beautiful instead of ugly, who could begin to laugh or cry without being torn apart. There were times when you would just lie down and be with yourself, and stop running from ghosts, times when your body allowed you to breathe and your mind allowed you to let people in. That Jenny was real as real and reached my heart, but she has such a time getting out from under all that crushing weight of the dead hands of control and the dead eyes of the past. You say you are fighting hard not to give up the most beautiful part of your neurosis. If the most beautiful part of your neurosis is being moved, is beginning to melt with good feelings, to surrender to what is for a while, then which is the neurosis, the good feelings or the fighting against them? When I picture you fighting hard, I feel your neck knot in my hand, see eyes that don't see me, hear your breathing die. If you asked me what is the most beautiful part — not of the neurosis but of the work to undo the neurosis — it is when you let yourself surrender more, when womb feelings start to bubble under your scars, when you let your eyes soften, when hot feelings burst from you and you own your body for a while.

So 'where do we go from here?' you ask. Here is Jenny adrift in pleasure and guilt; does she back away, or cast off and go with the tide? Which means being fixated? Fixated means stuck, and if you hide the guilt, and switch off or ration the pleasure, then that would mean stuck. To let your fantasies in, to own them, to stop fighting hard against what they can do to you, means they can move in your body, and move you into a different place, the opposite of stuck. If therapy, or life, is beginning to make you enjoy being a girl, instead of a man, or an invalid, or a ghost, where's the illusion? Why do you turn against your dreams, your fantasies? Are dreams illusions? Even nightmares are so real you can wake from them in a cold sweat;

they have roots in your body. You unfix from the nightmare by going into the fear, letting it work out. Fantasy is part of the life-stream, turn it off and you are back with your mother. If being in love is an addiction, how is that different from saying: I have these good feelings, they won't go away, I can't control them, I can't turn them off.

So many things have loosened in you, Jenny: anger, crying, opening of old hurts. What is hardest of all for you to feel? Heart feelings, your broken heart, the grim determination never to have it broken again, the hard fight to keep a heart no-one can touch. And if no-one can touch your heart, who are you?

Since you find it so hard to love yourself, you make it hard for other people to love you. They get attracted certainly, they run to you for comfort, or excitement, or energy, but to love you is not easy. I've written enough, Jenny, and it can never be enough. I'm not going to marry you, but I'm not going to die either, because I love living, and I love you very much.

David

Encounter group, 24th July, 1972

When Martin said, 'I pass', a great surge of hot fury rose in me, I had to hold myself back from screaming and scratching his eyes out. Energy was rushing all over me. I kept breathing deeply to stay with the feeling until the circle was completed and my turn came.

I hated Martin for his total self-absorption, for all the hours I've spent working on him and the shrug of dismissal which is his only response. I shouted, 'You've got no *right* to 'pass', you've got no right not to care!'

I went deeper, I thought my guts would crack with crying. It was my father, distant, preoccupied, totally unaware of my caring. My whole childhood wasted caring for him and nothing coming back to me, worse than nothing, a gesture of dismissal and contempt.

The seeing was too big, I began to choke, I couldn't bear to face it. I said, 'I'm not going to care any more, I'm not going to spend my life caring for my uncaring father.'

The group asked me questions and I saw how the cold fathers when they crack become the hot mothers demanding I live my life for them. The excitement of the love of finding a melting father turns to hatred when they are so warmed up they are demanding to suck off me. So I go on to the next helpless cold alone father. I got the image of a long queue of dead, cold people stretching round the equator, and me at one end with a hot-water-bottle ready to warm them up. At this point, I began to laugh and laugh, it was a good feeling that took over my body as totally as sobbing. Jerry was furious at me for laughing, but I could feel it was right for me. I just laughed and laughed and remembered how both my parents had a great sense of humour.

In the Tuesday group, a few days later, I was offering Martin space for his feelings towards me, and he was refusing it. I felt more and more enraged. I went into how my Dad was deaf, he couldn't hear me. He's just standing there, preoccupied, sipping his tea and staring out of the window. I'm pawing at him, but I can't call out to him, I don't dare to.

There was a noise in the group, and this sent me deeper, into Mum and Dad rowing. They don't notice me, there's so much noise and violence in the house; they just occasionally refer to me to see who's winning. I'm their referee. I cried and cried in anger and sorrow: I see myself standing back, keeping quiet, listening to Jerry's tirades of jealousy and sorrow, listening for endless hours to Martin's problems, both of them clawing at me, wanting me, yet not noticing I exist. Mum and Dad, both so unhappy and preoccupied, killing each other across my dead body, occasionally turning to me to make a point, to win against each other; Mum saying to Dad: 'Look, now you've made the kids cry'; Dad saying, 'No, *you* made the kids cry'; and us just crying.

The rage grew inside me: I'm not going to listen any more, no more hours after midnight listening to people's problems scared that if I don't listen, they'll go away and won't care for me. I'm not going to do it any more. I'm going to sleep when I need to, I'm going to live for me.

There was a flash of white-light insight when I hit the centre and it was shattering. I felt my whole life explained, it was the cleanest, purest, clearest feeling, as if I'd found a key piece to the jig-saw puzzle of my life.

I ended up very tired and relaxed and didn't give a damn about the rest of the group; I told them they could get on with their own things, I was going to sleep. I lay there curled up, barechested, hot, sweaty and smiling.

Letter to David, 29th July, 1972

David,

There is nothing to say. I can only breathe smoothly and thank you with my whole being for your clarity and warmth.

I am having warm days full of fun and play and people and movement within myself. The only cloud to mar my expansion is the hugeness of Jerry's pain. I do not like having to grow at his expense. Guilt about him can mar the simplicity of what I am enjoying.

I am writing to you from a *pop concert*, David, can you imagine it, the first in my life. I have taken my clothes off because I am hot; no-one else has but there is an atmosphere of absolute tolerance. My dog is with me and the children here are so beautiful it makes me want a baby, and I have just received a lovely letter from Pepe who says, 'Jenny, we have the most beautiful girl in the world.' It took my thirty-nine-year-old husband an acid trip finally to see our daughter in her full beauty, but now he has and I feel my life is complete. One day he will live under the same roof as us, it is what we all want.

Thank you, David, for giving me back my dreams and showing me life can be just as beautiful as my 'illusions'. I don't know how you escaped the twisting everyone else seems to have gone through — or whether you manage to hide your twists from the therapy. All I know is I feel more whole every time I hear from you or see you.

I feel full of love for everything around me that is not made of metal.

Dream, 30th July, 1972
For years, I've had 'exam dreams' where I have to sit an exam and am not prepared for it.

   Last night, I had my first 'not taking an exam' dream. *I dreamt I am staying at home while my college is sitting their exams. I feel some sense of loss associated with not taking exams which I know I can pass with a little effort. But on the other hand, I have a sense of relief that I am no longer engaging all my energies in such an artificial task. I think of all the wonderful things I can read and know about and do which never get on to an exam. syllabus.*

   The dream has the same feel about it as when I got in from the pop concert and found Jerry wasn't in. It was a mixed feeling — loss of tension without him there to fight against, me free to enjoy myself without reference to him. Loss and relief at the same time.

Dream, 1st August, 1972
A woman is holding me tight to her chest in bed, so tight I can't breathe. I feel myself smothered and try to scream at her to let me go. The more I struggle, the tighter she holds me in determined, aggressive play. Jerry and other people are in the room but I can't get across to them the seriousness of what is happening to me because the woman is laughing. I am determined not to die and in one last effort to scream, I wake myself up.

This dream comes during the first night for some time that I have spent with Jerry. I don't think I have ever felt quite so clearly the transference on to Jerry as my mother.

One morning, Jerry saw my downcast expression when I found Martin had left without saying goodbye. Just previous to this, Jerry and I had been playing together with the dog. Now he got violently angry and said I'd better stay away from him or he'd punch me. Because I've felt so good in myself lately and cleared away so many cobwebs, in spite of my great fear of him, I was able to keep playful contact going and risk being hit. I was pushy in a way I have never been since I was about two years old. Jerry got angrier and angrier and it was really dangerous.

So I left the house alone to go shopping, and I noticed I had a rhythmic shooting pain behind my left ear (some therapists reckon your left side is your 'mummy side', your right side your 'daddy' side and all my experiences confirm this for me). It continued the whole day, a flash of lightning pain stabbing me every few seconds. I went home and went to bed. Jerry walked in and I woke up. I asked him to lie with me. We made love for the first time for ages. I felt very open towards him, I was able to kiss him which I usually can't, I felt gentle and without resentment.

But after making love, I felt depressed and fuzzy. I talked to Jerry about my sadness, how I lose all sense of self when I am with him, how I get to waiting for him to make me feel good and no longer look after myself when he's around. I cried a bit and said how unhappy I was; how, when he's not there, I am over eight years old and well able to enjoy myself, but as soon as I'm with him, I am back in the fog I lived in, dependent on my mother, before I was eight.

In the evening I went out with him, but the shooting pains in my neck were bad. On the way home, I felt worse and worse, brought down by the pain, and feeling old. At home, Jerry squirted some dreadful chemical on my neck, supposedly to relieve the pain. It went on my face as well and now I was doubly in pain: it was like a nettle rash, my face and neck burning and feeling swollen. I felt the helplessness of childhood illness or hospital operations. I cried miserably with the discomfort, yet felt no sense of blaming Jerry — after all, he was caring for me. I just cried miserably as if this is the way my world has to be, pain and discomfort and having to accept kindness from the mother who'd caused it anyway. I felt so dreadful in my body, I was glad to have Jerry spend the night with me, though the bed was horrid, and I was lost in fog.

I slept for twelve hours. When I sleep alone, I sleep for six and feel fresh. After twelve hours, I still felt tired and could have slept more. I woke in pain all over, like all the weeks and months when I lived with Jerry, and like in Spain when I was screwed up inside; and so unlike the last couple of weeks when my stomach has been soft and my body good all over. I woke up not only with the nerve-pain in my neck fully returned, but also with the whole side of my face neuralgic from Jerry's 'cure'. My head hurt, my bones were stiff and my stomach knotted.

I talked about all this to Jerry: how I am caught between two fears, the fear of suffocation by my mother and the fear of her going away. She often threatened to leave home if we didn't 'behave'. My sister remembers being dressed up ready to be sent off to an orphanage.

I felt my fear of being left when Jerry went to make tea. Yet I felt relief when he'd gone, my body relaxed and I stretched out in the bed; my stomach started unknotting. I could feel how I wanted to control Jerry to get me the drink, yet I dreaded him coming back and disturbing me. I moaned at the cup he'd brought it in, at the colour and the taste of the tea, a little moan only, not enough to make him angry, but enough to show nothing was good enough for me. At home, I used to throw a fit if my mother didn't have clean underclothes ready for me for school; I knew well the things I was allowed to complain about. The real things I couldn't even mention.

I am now left with a clear picture of what is going on in me with Jerry, but not knowing what on earth to do about it. What's new is even being able to talk to Jerry about it and giving myself the time and space to feel out clearly these warring parts of my life.

Letter from David

When I write to you, the words come easily, and at the time I write I feel very much that I am reaching you. But quite often, after a letter is posted, I get a sort of kick-back, as though expecting what I have written to turn into a load of words, ultimately useless, almost a fear that the strange magic of communication must break down under the cold impact of type, the dead pan of a white page. So your simple direct reply beginning 'there is nothing to say' was very good to have, and to know you are trusting your dreams again, especially when they are about wonderful things you can do and be when you don't have to pass exams.

There is a kind of therapy exam: it consists in being a very sick patient with very big hangups. The stronger the sickness and the bigger the hangups, the higher one scores in the therapy exam. That way one is special, a screaming hysteric at least gets attention. With me you seem to be learning that you get attention as much when you don't scream for it, that you are important even when you are ordinary, exciting even when quiet.

There was a time when anything I wrote about the therapy was full of pain. Every session was shrill with it, expressed and often latent. But the heaviness of pain is lifting, so even the pains start to get more ordinary. I told you some months ago how I saw your stomach. I said that when you breathed, when you filled out, when you let the inner charge begin to surface, the scars became unnoticed. I did not 'see' them. It is as though because you were cut and stitched, and all the pain that went with that time, you had written off your centre, you were a person without a centre. Becky came from that wound, your hate for her was mixed with your self hate. As your image of Becky changes, the wound heals. If Becky is beautiful, it is because your pain was not strong enough to crush her, as your mother's pain and your father's coldness have proved not strong enough to keep you permanently in their grip.

Let's think for a moment about what being twisted means. Everyone has twists, me included. But we're not all doomed. You've been living as though doomed, with desperation, with guilt, like someone trying to wring fun out of life before it blows up in your face. But fun won't be wrung. We're all crooked trees, like Reich said, me included — it's not that having had therapy means you don't have any twists, it's that the twists don't dominate so much, one can find spaces where the twists don't operate, and the spaces can be enlarged.

I cannot help you with the problem of Jerry's pain. His pain goes back to Auschwitz and lies deeper than yours. He gets extra points on the invalid scale, and this is one reason why he drags you down. Jerry is perhaps your pain that you are losing.

He is also perhaps your guilt that you have to face. He is also reacting against the twists still left in you, the twists knot together and hinder both of you from growing. Jerry is also your longing, which cried from Spain, which he cannot satisfy.

All I can suggest is you need more time on your own, to go into the relief and the loss and the having no-one there; time to find out how you want, who, and what it's like when you don't turn, or get turned to.

What is passion, Jenny? It is the tide that drives us all along when your own motors stop for a bit, which is why it's so frightening and suggests whirlpools and drowning. Passion is being breathed. Passion is when your neck has given up.

See you Saturday,

Love, David.

Session with David, 12th August, 1972

I discovered how all my juddering and shivering disappeared if David sat quietly and didn't talk. When he is quiet, I can relax. I don't have to entertain him any more, don't have to be ill or interesting for him. I felt safe, he would not go away. My stomach knots melted. I was able to be healthy without fear of loss.

Group, 17th August, 1972

I worked in the group by facing my mother, telling her how much I hated her, how I was just waiting for revenge, which would be leaving home, doing all the things she couldn't bear, swearing, wearing what I like, living how I like. Suddenly, without expecting it, I broke down and cried for a long time, realizing that now *she* is frightened of *me*, just as I was always — and still am — frightened of her. Then I thought of her dog and my sobbing deepened: dogs just don't look like hers does, and real gardens aren't like hers; in fact nothing looks like she says it does, nothing is really like she says it is, children are not how we were made to be, the world isn't at all like the picture she tried to give me.

The Men Who Came To Clean Up The Mews, 18th August, 1972

Two young men came down our Mews with a strange apparatus
on their backs, pointing a strange pipe at the ground. I asked
them what they were doing. They said, 'Believe it or not, people
have phoned up the Council to complain about the grass
growing between the paving stones and we're spraying the Mews
with weedkiller.' I couldn't believe it. I asked them if they
couldn't fill their machines with water and water the grass. They
didn't take me seriously. I got the children to fetch water to try
and wash the poison chemicals away. I myself had to rush
upstairs, I was cracking open. I flung myself on my bed and
sobbed my heart out: 'They're out to kill us, it's really
happening, they can't bear anything living. They're actually
paying someone to come and kill blades of grass pushing up
through the oily cobblestones.' I cried and cried, feeling
connected to all that is green and grows. I saw too the concrete,
pushing against life, often winning.

Dream, 19th August, 1972
I dream I am in hospital where we are all supposed to have
abortions. But my baby gets born. I had been pregnant without
knowing it. I like having a baby but am in conflict because of
the rational arguments about bringing more babies into the
world.
I put my baby to my breasts which, although they are thin,
seem to have milk in them.
I wonder who could be a father to my baby. I wonder about
Jerry, but notice with a jolt that the baby's eyes are pale blue
which will freak Jerry out and make him reject the baby. I
wonder if it is really Martin's baby. But it doesn't seem
important, the main thing is, it's mine.
Then I am at home. People have heard now that I have a
baby. Jack Lewis says to me in a stiff voice, 'Well, it's all very
well, Jenny, you wanting the baby, but does the baby want
you?'
I have seen my baby smile happily at me, so I say to Jack,
'Yes, look.' I open my blouse (I keep the baby inside my clothes

*next to my breast) so that he can see the baby smile. But my
own unsureness is reflected in the baby's face, and it doesn't
have the same happy expression as before.*

26th August, 1972

Jerry phoned me up from his primal therapy and said he was
allowed home for the weekend. I had mixed feelings, I was
interested to see him, but also felt my space had been taken
away.

At night, when he came to sleep with me, I felt myself
closing off, then tears came, feeling I am always nurse and can
never be the patient. I woke up in the morning sobbing. It just
went on and on, I couldn't pull myself out of the dream. Even
when I got up and washed my face, I was still in it. When I
tried to tell Jerry my dream, I just kept crying and saying, 'I
don't want you here, I want you to go away.' I realized that
because Jerry is softer now, he has become my sister and out of
the blue I am faced with the enormity of a life-time of jealousy
against her. My dream was:

*Jerry has been away doing 'something special' and has become
the centre of care and attention.*

*My mother loves him dearly. I get him alone, he is weaker
than me. I punch his head in and tell him to get out, I don't
want him around. I am in a great rage. I go back to my mother
and tell her what I have done. I am grown-up size. I block her
pathway so that she can't get to him to comfort him. She is
crying and loving him even more now. I go for her, shouting at
her that it is her fault that I am like I am. I get the dog's lead
and whip her, shouting at her each time I strike: 'Now you're
going to pay for it. You hit me when I was little and now I'm
bigger than you and you're going to feel what it's like.' She
says, 'I never hit you'. I scream, 'You did, you did, round the
head, like this,' and I keep whipping her round the head and
neck, telling her it's her fault I'm hard and twisted. I get my
hands around her neck and half-strangle her, feeling this is
what she did to me.*

Sunday group, 4th September, 1972

I took myself into my feelings without help, crying about how confused and undermined and unsure of myself I had become because of the new primal 'thing' to be always in pain, as if it's neurotic to be happy, as if I must think of myself as sick because sometimes my body feels so good. I yelled about people discarding our groups and this took me to my Mum running my Dad down. I cried about how much I love him. I felt the confusion of the rational arguments of my mother, 'We'll be so much better off without him', then screamed suddenly as I saw the trick: It was *her*, not me, that was unhappy with him. *I* wasn't; I loved Dad even if she didn't.

Our 'old' groups are my father, giving me security and continuity. But now there is something 'new', the primal groups, Mum's shiny new husband.

I wrote to David:

I'm so looking forward to seeing you, even though I know I won't be able to show you all the warmth I feel. I have been in a sad confusion, feeling so left out with Jerry, the new primal baby, getting so much help, and me struggling on still, building my own help. But now after the group last night, I feel good about myself, some of my confidence has come back. I felt undermined when I heard that a primal therapist works 'without transference' which I don't believe. I felt all the work and love and learning over these past two years in groups and with individuals and in the kitchen was being pooh-poohed and discarded. I even gave in to Jerry and wrote off for an interview with his primal therapist in case it's true that I'm 'avoiding my feelings'.

I want the kind of clarification and support you give when these doubts come up. A big part of me is bouncy and warm and confident and I know what I feel; but I do feel sad and left now some of my friends are leaving the groups.

So see you. I believe in me and you and my Dad.

With love, Jen.

Dear Jenny,

Images come to me out of your last letter and your group which was your father; the image of his arms which closed and you weren't in them. Your mother's arms inside you which hold him off and hold you split. How could you belong to him when he did not belong in the house? How could you belong to him when you were not allowed to long for him? So who rejected whom? Did he reject you, were you his unloved daughter, or did you switch him off with your mother's eyes, close your arms against him? Then that other woman, his second wife, more arms to keep you away from him.

Did you kill him then, did he die of your neglect, because you were kept away? A man is dying in a chair and you cannot reach him to bring comfort.

To love him in spite of all hurts and in the teeth of your mother is to come home to your body. The journey's worth while. You don't need primal therapy. Insights are cheaper than £300. To hell with transference, but I like helping you, your clean feelings are worth waiting for. Your own body taste of what's right for you is the only thing worth trusting.

Neurotic to be happy? No, neurotic to be where you're not, to use one feeling against another, to override, to put faces over faces, masks on masks. To be happy to be sad is to be inside you and feel you belong because you know you are you and your Dad is himself and not the run-down reject your mother saw in him. If you can love him, he is no longer dead inside you, but you can start fulfilling yourself instead of carrying him like a deformed foetus for ever. You are the one part of him that still lives, and he has a right to be proud of you.

See you Saturday,

Love, David.

It was around this time that I started reading back over my enormous collection of letters to and from David. I wrote to him:

David, we have created a beautiful poem together. 'Poetry' to me as a schoolgirl meant nonsense, pretence, snobbery. Now I see that it means perfect intellectual clarity plus warm blood flowing. I am so proud of what we have done and what we have written. I feel so good reading back now. The brilliance of your letters is all the more apparent to me now that the initial impact of them is in the past. I am still learning from them. And also at times I feel excited at my own writing, at how it has filled out and grown with me.

What a beautiful thing we have done together.

Jen.

Dear Jen,

Your filled-out feelings last longer these days — it's like a slow tide turning; I suddenly become aware that your sessions and your letters don't twist me up like they used to when the pain predominated. Happiness is breaking out in you so much more often, your letter was so much a dance of joy it took my breath away.

Therapy is a blind ship. We launch it together and no-one can say where it will travel. To know in advance where it all leads is to block it forever. There was once a Jenny who could not remember from one session to the other; you would not connect. Your writing, and perhaps mine, has played a bigger part than expected in the whole healing struggle. It's also a big thing for you to begin to *enjoy* your own writing. Enjoyment in words was so nearly spoilt for you by the intellectual language-games you took on to escape from your mother and please your father, the clever act. But amazing words have flowed out of you to chart the currents of feelings, and it is like warm blood on the paper, sometimes tortured blood, but the pulse kept moving and in the end even your head had to join in and welcome the magic that was working.

It *is* a poem that we have created, but that poem is first and foremost your life which every day is less trapped and has more space to be itself in. I want you to know that your last letter was a joy to get — one of the nicest things that ever came through a letter box. It's like one big chunk of ice melting in your hand to let all that pride and happiness through.

Love, David.

My mother's dream

At my mother's yesterday, she told me and my sister of a dream she'd had. She dreamt she had to go to a graveyard and dig up the dead bodies and rearrange them.

On digging them up, they became babies in cots, and her job was to bury them again, and smother them with earth.

Session with David, 9th September, 1972

I pissed around for an hour moaning, not facing anything, least of all David. Then I got bored with myself and wanted to play. David packed me away in cushions and held me there, strong, while I fought him. I wanted to bite him. We fought, and I felt his trembling energy, strange to perceive such energy in a man and not be frightened of it because it was pulsating within his walls, and was not trying to drown me or find an outlet in me.

I felt too, the deathliness within me, how quickly exhausted I became, feeling faint and sickly, collapsing. But here I was with David again, after an hour of withholding myself, I had him and myself back and now there was no other world. I cried with the pain and pride of being first, first-born and first in therapy. I cried because of knowing that the world I was born into was wrong and I had to find another world when I was a child; I had to cut cold paths alone while my sister settled for the suffocating warmth of my mother. I yelled, 'I don't like my sister, I like me, I don't want to be like her, I want to be me.'

Then David and I started to talk and suddenly there was no barrier. I just went into his arms and took what I wanted which was his enormous strength as big as the world, his hard hot body, strong good tension holding me firm as long as I wanted, the air passing easily through me, clearing away last fortresses. And I experienced my first totally fearless moment. I imagined my mother coming in at the door, and I just smiled at her. I asked David if he would protect me, and he said he would, she could come in. I felt my mother would not even dare to look him in the eyes, there was no way now she could put him down. He was on my side, bigger than anyone who has ever tried to kill me, firmer than her hands that tried to gag me, warmer than

all the furies that frightened me, safer than all the people who
have never left me alone. I felt we were ageless and imageless,
no-one could label us; David was loving, and I was receiving,
and the session was over, a session where nothing happened
because when I finally be how I am, it is not a happening.

Dear Jen,

I have run out of words for your last session, but you have
found them.

All your life has been a pouring out of energy to prove you
existed when you feared you didn't. So Jenny came and went
in a great rush of fierce or fizzing energy; you once said there
was so much you tripped over it. Totally different from the
glowing filled-out kind of high you are capable of now when
pleasure starts to bubble in you.

The biggest danger was other people's strong energy, if it
came to invade you. So you acted out the danger you were
afraid of, safely: you opened your body to all men, but made
sure you closed your self from them. All the while your body
gave in and 'accepted', you held fast to one momentous
instinctive decision: no-one will ever have me, they will never
catch me, never hold me down. So you resisted with your stiff
independent neck, your hungry stomach clamped on its 'no',
your eyes that avoided.

It saved you. Without it, you would have been schizoid, lost
in a maze without paths or direction. Your clear sight at
twelve of what you rejected was the only way, then, to hope to
escape from drowning. You clung to your way as the only self
you thought you had, and it led you eventually to Reichian
therapy — the therapy of storms, and of the deep|places beyond
all storms.

What I have found is that when you|become stilled, you
become filled, when you are able to wholly take, you start to
give, and anyone that could possibly confuse you with your
sister doesn't know the first thing about you. Your false pride
that saved you but blocked you from reaching is on its last legs.
Your real pride — at the wonder of yourself, and of a world
which in spite of all the horrors can lead you away from pain —
is just beginning.

You can't compete with your sister or Jerry; they tread their own roads seeking exits from their own nightmares. They can't compete with you either; your road is far on now, utterly unlike theirs. You are taking your life back into your own hands.

Love, David.

16th September, 1972

I went for my interview with the primal therapist. Although I'd decided against doing the therapy, I wanted to meet her. I went there nervous, a stranger, to a cold, strange place with a locked door. No room at the inn, money and class separating us. It was a small nightmare before I even got in the door. It was like an exam and I didn't even believe in the subject I was sitting for. 'Are *you* Jenny?' I was asked abruptly. Nothing came out of her face; I felt all wrong. 'Why do you want primal therapy?' I was thrown by the question, because I'd already answered it in a letter. I stammered and stumbled and told her I'd changed my mind and asked about joining her groups. She just shook her head, and the 'interview' was over.

It took me three quarters of an hour to drive to the East London Encounter Centre and I had to wait for over an hour to go into the therapy room. I needed to go into my feelings our way: to be asked how I felt. But in Yann's group, there is no contact, we had to lie down and were ordered to 'get into our feelings'. I cried silently for a long while, giving myself a headache. Eventually Yann came over and said, 'Say it.' I said it. I said I didn't want any more hard people, I'd had enough, I couldn't bear it, I didn't want any more hardness, that wasn't right for me. I didn't need any more hate put in me.

The next day, I had a session with David. I went into miserable feelings, of being cut up by my mother, who is an ocean drowning me, by my father who is a desert making me die of thirst, by Jerry cutting me out of his new life, by the primal therapist with her cold hard face and her arrogance, by the female magistrate in the court handing me out impossible fines and no appeal.

Then, suddenly, I got bored with all this. I looked up and

started to smile. I saw the faces of people I love. I saw myself surrounded by good friends and a tiny opening appeared in me to feel the joy of it. I lay and did nothing but chat with David for an hour. I felt how difficult it is to stay with good feelings. I remembered Alex' words: 'being neurotic is not being able to appreciate what you've got.' I gave David some oranges. I stopped trying to be a patient.

After that session, I handed David my thick thick file full of years of correspondence. I got this letter back:

Dear Jen,

I sat down to relax on the train and there was, so I thought, no end-of-the-day pain in me to dissolve after such a quiet orange-eating session. And I sat with your file, Jenny, I thought I knew it all, most of it has been in my house since three years. But suddenly it was altogether in front of me, three hours ahead to read it in, not even a meal to dilute it with.

It's too big, Jenny, it's bursting with riches and torments, some of them five years old and new as a day-old session. It is big with life and frightening with death, and it has all our pain in it, yours and Jerry's and all those other lives that weave in and out with yours. And the pain and the clarity and the innocence started to surface in me while the taste of that day's sessions was still uppermost in me. In the car, driving from the station, nearly midnight, more than a hundred miles away, I had to stop, can you imagine it, I was racked with sobs and didn't even know what was hurting so much.

It began with the thirty-year pain I and your group have been nursing you out of, and the happy pain in the side, like a stitch, from running so much to catch up with where the therapy's taken you to. And it overflowed, like your file, so much of it, and so many faces swam, N. on the stairs, a stone man looking for a kiss, D. who beat you bloody round the head, and D's new girl who has just started seeing me: she's lost, lost on the edge of suicide, her last boyfriend died at the foot of the cliffs a week or two back. People hurt so much, they can't help each other, unless. And I cried for the pride and joy of your good groups, and the sad-proud little letter from Martin, the last thing in the file, and all the failures when people drive each other into nightmare. There was NC in your file, he was grey today, there is a strong death in him I am trying to fight. And Peter, who opened so easily today when his pride fell.

And you had said, did I think the file should stay private? When already all our lives are in it, or hidden behind it, and echoes of lives back to our births and our parents before us? So I cried for the once lost people who were born out of war, whose fathers grew pregnant with cancer, or came ruined out of Auschwitz to beat them. And for those I got close to who saw some father in me, and also a tear long overdue for my own dad, a ramrod of a man, slow as a stone, and no hugs inside him. And something else I knew: the sad joy of fostering, you take someone on, you help create their life out of trust, as you said. It was good to let go and be weak for once, no longer a cheerful therapist who couldn't be unhappy, but a tired man, feeling his glad grief because you will soon outgrow him perhaps, a huge chapter of need is closing.

So I cried also for my sickness which makes me a therapist who needs to be needed, though I hide it well, and for all the long road of your therapy, the book is so heavy now, and for the giving you have done when you thought you were taking, and the taking I have done when all that mattered was giving, and for words that came when bodies couldn't.

So that is my pain that is too big for a poem and too small to belong in your book, but which is also part of it, and helped to create it. That is the song I could not sing for sobs as I sat in the car before midnight on the hill getting in touch with my truth about the happiness of sad feelings and the triumph of people who come through, and the shattered bodies on beaches of those who don't and the murdering man you tried to save in your dream, and for Vicky dead from the shock of too much light, and for that deformed baby with your face and a hole in its back whose name I never knew.

And finally I let the pleasure in, which you kept out for so long, that we did it, we did it Jenny, we were stronger than them, stronger than the huge sea of the mother you were born out of who nearly washed you away, or the cold sand of your Dad, only dreams could cling to.

Then I was ready for the last three miles home, back to my own family and able to lay down my load which I am so proud of, for another week.

And perhaps now you have reached the baby girl child woman who was buried so deep down, starved, that it was my kind of miracle to find her and loose her back to herself, you won't mind me sending you what is perhaps the first and last unsolicited letter, it is a reply to nothing, with some feelings to share about me and the people I love. And to say thank you for helping me to grow alongside you and for making the therapy in spite of this distance such heartwork.

Love, David.

Sunday group, 17th September, 1972. Letter to David

Jerry and Guy suddenly walked in, four hours after the group had started. I was shocked and thrown. I breathed, floundered, put my head down and breathed deeper and deeper, my whole body moving with my breathing, my feet starting to tingle. I started to cry, 'there are too many people, I want a small family. I never want to go outside, I don't like the world outside, I want to stay indoors forever.' I am eight years old, in the warm kitchen; I haven't broken away from my mother yet. There is a heady feeling of gas around me, no clarity, just fog; my life is all comfort and no understanding. I feel as if I am contacting a whole new chapter, as if I am at the beginning of my therapy again: the first eight years of my life, eight years of being gassed, my forehead stroked, kind words, and that abortionist and my mother, waving a gas mask in front of my face, sickly, sweet gas, confusing, seducing, taking me over, nothing solid to fight against, my head whirling, a swirl of impressions, a million nightmares explained. Me, a laughing child with bewildered eyes, Mum each night tucking me up warmly, fucking me uptightly, honey voice, 'be a better girl tomorrow dear', pethidin in my veins, sleep oozing over me, hot water bottles at my feet, a soothed forehead.

I stopped my crying suddenly to stop the heat, the terrible heat in my head, the feeling of that kitchen and the gas cooker, me stamping and bursting out with, 'I HATE YOU!' she saying, 'Of course you don't dear, all children say that at some time or other'. How can you hate someone so obviously reasonable and superior, so obviously warm and loving?

The only thing I have to hang on to, the only thing I can be sure of is MY BODY DOESN'T FEEL RIGHT. I can't be tricked out of feeling that.

I woke at three in the morning after this group, my stomach tight as a drumskin, painful as a vivisected animal. Now I feel Jerry and the primal therapists pointing at me and saying: 'Ha! You may have had all those good times, all those good feelings with David, but you'll have to come back to me in the end, the hag at the cave door. I was the only One who loved you, He gave you nothing; your father was too cold to care, you'll need me in the end, you'll see.' I feel as if I have cheated by taking some warmth, cheated myself of clarity by accepting the drunken illusion. I still have to go home to a witch under the bed.

I still need therapy, David, but I almost need someone hateful: your goodness washes all my bad feelings away.

A little faery called Rebecca came in to my room at that point and gave me a session. She be-ed my mother; she knew so well the exact the tone, the word twists, the don'ts, the uptightness, just the right voice, the escalating threats, the precise intonation of 'Jennifer'. A brilliant, shining little girl, a perfect therapist with a perfectly simple question, 'Did you feel loved when you were a baby?'

A couple of days later, I went to a 'primal' group feeling bad and hoping to get out some of the feelings that were troubling me.

There were horrible noises all around me; the group is insane, the only people who really get anywhere are those who've had sensitive body training previously. I made nice noises of my own: I just lay there humming and breathing. I was getting hot and took my clothes off and made a tent of my own out of blankets. I went to get into bad feelings, and ended up getting into good ones.

At one point, I looked up and saw Jenny P., who lives with me, and she saw me giggling at the hysteria around us and that set her off and I covered myself and laughed and laughed, and the more ridiculously false the noises off became, the more I laughed. And a connection came: *I* don't feel bad. I don't care about the misery around me, I still just don't feel bad. And I felt how often I'd had to put on a long face because my mother was sad.

But getting into good feelings didn't change the next morning awakening to a terrible tight stomach, anxiety still about how my therapy's not taking me down deep enough, how Jerry's doing it 'right' and I'm not; he's got all the help, and my working with myself is a patchwork quilt. I tried to help myself for a bit but got to feeling shittier and shittier and couldn't imagine things ever being right, and then I had to go out with Becky and my bad vibes were making her be a drag and things were just foggy nastiness. So I waited till Jenny P. came home and asked her for a session.

I got into how both my parents are the baby of their families, they don't know what it's like to be first-born. Even in the faery-stories, it's the eldest sister that is ugly, unloved, the youngest is good and beautiful and *blonde*. I was yelling 'Of course the oldest kid is ugly, no bloody wonder.' I am like Joey, our dog, standing aside while the younger pup gobbles up *his* dinner, my face getting long and thin and my cheeks hollow and my lips tight with bitterness.

I was yelling at you too, David, yelling at you for your constant canvassing of Jerry, ramming him down my throat. I hate Jerry, I don't want to hear another word about him. You're like my mother, David, saying how much happier you'd be if only your two beloved babies would love one another. *I* am the first baby, I always have been first, first and clearing the way for others. Now I see why I identified so strongly with Reich, the cold and lonely pioneer, an Aries too, going crazy with his own strength and no friends big enough to hold him down warmly and get him to yell out his pain.

First-born

When a child walks alone
it may not be only, but older.
Whoever was first-born, was only, once,
no matter how many come after,
and sometimes colder,
due to exposure perhaps
pushed out in front, sometimes severe
as a pioneer.

Why do we treat our first-born so,
wearers and bearers of all our errors,
of all we did not know?
So perhaps they are right, these older children,
thrust
first
solemn as outcasts
into the tangled world where dreams cannot comfort
and cuddly bears are clung to,
to scorn their poor their apprentice mothers.

The late-born are rosier,
their months at the breast were less experimental.
Something resembling home had begun to grow
out of earlier failures, when they were still toddlers.
The cuddly bears were more dispensable,
so they remained young even in old age,
and kept hopping from day to day as a child will
crossing a river on bright stones.
They are not in our debt still.

Pity our grown-up babies who were never quite young,
those we carried too long, or too wrong,
whose tears are stuck,
who are married to a kind of hard luck
where even success may not be a blessing;
who took the first breath but are nearer to death.

> They may live to be blazers of trails,
> seared perhaps with the mind's flame,
> or pale with fierce desire,
> but it will not come easy
> nor ever so cosy
> for them
> round the fire.
>
>   David

Letter from David, 22nd September, 1972

On all sides you sense threats: in therapy where you were first, you sold your secret down the river; so generous on top of your jealousy, you invited the whole clan to descend on me; you are the sulky pup in the litter, a bundle of hot fury. In therapy, you come to a session closed because I gave time to one of the others, and usually you can leave it open again. In life it is less easy. Who are your friends? Who will stand by you if you should ever become no longer the fire in the house, if your words should dry up, if you should start to stammer and die down into your cave of confusion Vicky escaped from the only way she knew? The tension is between the excitement and warmth of your tribe, and the confusion of the cave. To enter the cave means to face the mother you never came out of, the horror of not being born so how can you be here? It means to face your own death, or the death of that hope that life will come from *outside*, and to find there are other ways than Vicky's: to face your panic and frenzy at being nothing and no-one is the only way to find you really are someone.

There is this sad child in the photograph you sent, with no sureness of who she is: for her there are no groups, no fun and games, no possibility of travel away from it all. Flight has not begun, or the hope of it. She is numb with a longing not felt. She is there with her all-seeing eyes and she is dumb.

Your new ache does not erase the last year of growth. What you have needed, you have taken. What ground you have won, you have won. You have been nourished enough to be able to feel the terror of starving. Though you may not believe it just now, the last year is a record of your skin filling out, your eyes clearing, your breathing unlocking.

When you leave home, when you go away, it is frightening, but over the last year some of your best growth has come out of trips, a change of time scale or space scale, a chance to be alone without your tribe. The times you grow most are when you give *yourself* attention. Satisfaction comes from inside, but you fear your body is a cave and in the cave there are no people to love, only your Mum to cower into or squirm away from, rivals to stamp on, your Dad who abandoned you, a child clutching a rabbit.

You are also very beautiful. Do you believe me when I say that even when you go ugly and freezing into your private dark, or hot and desperate into your lonely rage, it will take you to find a fire burning you never knew before and to bring it back your very own which no one gave you and no wind will ever blow out.

Love, David.

Session with David, 23rd September, 1972

I went into the session not able to look at David. I hated him. I wanted him to shut up and he didn't. I started shaking my head to intensify the confusion I felt, the feeling of faintness. 'This is what it was like' I said, 'just like this.' The whirling hot bad feeling was what my childhood had been like. Jenny P. had given me confidence by saying, 'You must go into the hysteria more, Jen, if that's what you need to do.' So I said, 'Everything's so fucking reasonable' and broke right into my feelings. I screamed at David telling him I hated him. I screamed I hated the therapy, I wanted to tear my file up into little pieces, I felt I had been tricked into being a reasonable patient, every session so damn clear and writeupable; you can't write up a noise, or my body threshing around. My Mum always said, whilst screwing me up, 'I never make you do anything without giving you a good reason for it.' 'I never stopped you doing anything without a good reason.' FUCK YOUR GOOD REASONS.

I hated the heat of the room, I took my clothes off. I wanted to smash my fists through the cold cool glass, let in the cold air from the street, feel the cuts and the blood, tear up my bloody file to show how little all the words mattered, all that sense, all those beautiful puns and me still confused. I kept screaming, 'I'm going to die, I'm going mad, I'll kill you.' I couldn't bear to think of David and Mum living off me, and me being so damn reasonable about it.

Dear Jen,

I felt we had almost reached a kind of saturation point with long-distance communication; there was almost an over-charge in the air. Your storm removed any need for a while to react, to comment, to do anything else than accept it for what it was.

If I ask myself why I write what I do, it is because these yellow pages keep coming at me, your dreams fall through my letter-box, the insights and breakthroughs and blocks of your groups arrive here and reach me, so I reply. But the idea that I sit miles away keeping my cool, 'making' something out of your feelings tears me up. I don't write for a bloody public, I don't write for your group to cheer or boo, or feel their jealousies. I write to you because you are there, and because your letters cry out for the answers I cannot give.

So it doesn't matter whether I am wrong or right, whether the insights are there or not there, beautiful or ugly — a letter is like a session, something pulls inside, energy flows, there is movement, interaction, and when, occasionally, even a letter can crack you open, or bring a rush of feeling out of a bad block, that's the best 'meaning' anyone could wish for.

A little session with Jenny P., 25th September, 1972.

I talked of my Dad, how he'd come visiting when I was a kid, but would spend ages with my stepfather chatting before even announcing to me he'd arrived. This used to hurt me so badly, I cried more over my father than over all my boyfriends put together.

I spoke of Martin, how difficult it is for me to stay with him for very long, even when I feel soft towards him. I have an incapacity to absorb good contact. I told Jenny how much I'd

loved Martin last night, but how I couldn't tell him that. I
curled up and started to cry, saying 'I can't, I can't tell him.'
I cried more and more, but I wouldn't let my insides crack
open, I wouldn't go further than just feeling how I couldn't tell
my Dad how much I loved him. Jen said, 'Just breathe' and I
lay and breathed deep for several minutes and almost straight
away the block I'd caused in my head through not giving in
moved away, and I could feel the tightness in my stomach
muscles. Very soon, I was tingling all over, the prickling was
strongest in my hands and stomach, gurglings started, and the
sensations went into my feet too. I could feel a strange tightness just above my wrists; flashes like a filmstrip of my mother
holding me there too tightly, bands like bracelets where my life
energy couldn't flow properly.

The room was bluish now and when I stood up, I had an
acidy sensation of being about eight feet tall and staring down
at the room.

Group at Alex', 27th September, 1972

I was tense. Alex had become my mother for me, because he
hates Martin. No-one offered me help. I was left in silence and
I felt how I was not connected to my family. I was a monster
baby with them just staring at me, doing nothing.

As the silence dragged on, my resentment focussed on
Martin: all the times I've helped him and loved him, and now
he just sits and looks at me. I started to talk, very quietly, to
my Dad. I said, 'I'm not going to care for you any more'. I said
it over and over again and my voice got slower and slower and
deader and quieter. I stopped. I felt the deadness of my Dad in
my stomach, the cancer that was him. I saw his pale blue eyes
staring into space, not seeing me. I realized the high, energetic
love we shared was only after I was seventeen, when I satisfied
certain needs in him. I felt how when I'm down, neither my
father nor Martin would lift a finger to stop me drowning.

I started to cry, but my voice came out like my mother's, too
grown-up. I said, 'I want to cry like a little girl, I want my own
voice.' I couldn't go on. It had always been Mum crying, I had

been silent and hadn't found my voice. She was always crying about her unhappiness with Dad; there was no space for me to.

The breaking of the illusion about my Dad left me feeling very quiet and in myself; heavy, and a bit sullen, but at least a load had slipped off my shoulders: I didn't have to look after anyone any more. I didn't have to worry about making Martin feel comfortable. It didn't matter. There was nothing to be gained: I didn't have love, OK, but now at least I didn't have to give it either. I didn't have to drain myself still drier.

The next day, John gave me a session.

I got very anxious, as soon as I was quiet myself, about the noises in the house, kids yelling, dogs barking. Every noise was calling me to sort something out. I stayed, breathed, felt really awful. I felt I had swallowed it all, all the fights and tensions and bad happenings of my home when I was little. All the bad things had gone in and nothing had ever been allowed to come out. I felt sick, I'd swallowed rubber and bile and poison.

I became my mother, telling me it's all right, everything'll be alright. Go to sleep, shh! stroking my forehead. I was sitting up in the session, and yet I began to fall asleep. I could feel heavy anaesthetic pouring over me, my eyes were heavy, I couldn't open them, couldn't look up. I started to cry listlessly: 'I'm being gassed, put to sleep, I can't feel.'

Nightmare that night.
I dream I am looking for the therapy room. I go up some very narrow open stairs which lead on to a roof. A big posh in-a-hurry fellow comes up behind me (my mother!) and starts pushing me and puffing. I say, 'I'm sorry, I can't go faster, I'm afraid of heights.' I lie down so he can pass over me, which he does in a bustle, not hesitating to help me or say a word to me.

I am petrified. The stairs peter out at the top of the sloping roof and I see water down below. Then I think to myself, 'I've had enough of this dream, I'm going to wake up now, I'm just not going along with it any more, I'm not going to struggle upward when all I've got to do is wake up.'

As soon as I give up, I find I can walk quite easily up the

*sloping roof and into the building. I start looking for the
therapy room again to shiver all the nervousness out of my
body.*

Session with John M., 3rd October, 1972

I mentioned my stepfather, and John said, 'Speak to him.'

'SPEAK TO HIM? You're crazy, he doesn't exist, I NEVER
SPEAK TO HIM.' When I was about six and saw him beat up a
boy, I said I'd never speak to him again, and I never did.

I broke down and cried, 'I hate you for bringing him up,
John, he's not on my list of people I have to go through, he
doesn't exist, I made him not exist, I've got enough to cope
with with Dad and Mum and my Dad's wife and my sister. I
can't take any more, I don't have to go into him, I don't like
him, I HATE HIM.'

I was crying and squirming. I couldn't stand my stepfather's
violence, his hands covered in blood, always cutting himself,
punching his fists through plate glass windows, big muscles, a
little violent man with big shoulders and strong arms and huge
hands, all muscle and brawn, a fascist little man. I yelled at my
Mum, 'What a fucking hypocrite, saying you never hit me, you
didn't need to with a wild alsation on a lead, all you had to do
was threaten to unloose the leash and I knew he would kill me.
You used to wind him up, let him loose just a little, then call
him back just as he was about to go for me.' All through my
teenage, there he was, just waiting, panting at the leash for a
chance to get at me, a yappy little dog, ill-treated and chained
up, snarling at anything that moved and was free. Hate-filled
little man, and Mum hating him and using him, using him to
hate me with so she could have the good role of stepping in to
save me at the last minute.

After the session, I had a new feeling. I wanted to punch and
smash things, use my strength. Something had been making my
arms weak and weedy, but now my strength had come back. I
felt loads of energy and a kind of dazed amazement that I could
have tricked myself so long, kept my stepfather out of the
picture, really believe I'd wiped him out.

Now I don't have to be a floaty child, now I have got something to get my teeth into: hate and violence I can really feel. There's no confusion where my stepfather is concerned: he was just a policeman and no pretence.

Thursday Group, 5th October, 1972

Just Babs and Martin and me. I talked for a long time, about how I long to tell others my excited feelings, like how I keep falling in love lately.

I got very suddenly in touch with what it was like when I was a child coming home from school overloaded with impressions and feelings and having to keep everything secret, my head a box full of unshareable thoughts, my Mum the centre of the universe, and me just a little moon to orbit round her. The momentous feelings of my life would be just a funny anecdote for her to tell the neighbours.

And that's how I am to Becky, she's even pointed it out when I'm doing it, but I can't feel it.

Now I see my energy, my rushing around the house being the centre, as covering up a huge sadness that no-one really wants to know; my little things will be boring unless I can wrap them up in forceful energy to shove under people's noses; I am a manic who has lost touch with depression.

I started to cry when I felt my eight-year-old self, and my Mum sitting there, a smile on her face, young and energetic, the centre. And me, a wizened old child already with no-one to talk to, growing hard and black round the eyes and sore in the head, and not knowing what's wrong, but knowing I am a Nasty Child who will soon feel Ugly.

Session with David, 7th October, 1972

I felt terrible all day. I couldn't face going to David, I just didn't want to see him. It drove me crazy to think of him having seen Jerry first. I felt, David is just not worth it any more, he is of no value now that he has Jerry as well. David is not mine, he is contaminated, and I don't want him any more.

Just before the session, I was a lump of jelly. But the minute I walked in the door, I closed off and couldn't feel. I talked about about all that had been happening, and at least I didn't have the problem of trying to be nice about it, or nice to David. I told him I was fed up with coming to therapy for him, keeping him nourished; it was me coming in to the world to be my mother's audience: I felt David was feeding off me, he has a vested interest in seeing me turn out right, in seeing me grow up the way he wants. The past and present are inextricably tangled for me at the moment.

I just have feelings and don't want to be bothered with sorting them out, I just want them to flow in confusion if that's how it is, I've been reasonable too long.

I was thoroughly bad-tempered and moany, not bothering a shit about how I was coming across to David, it just didn't matter any more. I got in touch with what it was like before my sister was born, everything so sunny and exciting, and everyone's eyes on me, no competition, and how everything lost its taste and colour when she came along and nothing was ever the same again, as if I'd died. My Mum had conned me, pretended it was me having the baby, made me pregnant with expectations about her, and it was all lies to hide the horror of having to share the little I had. And then my husband made me pregnant and left me, and ever since I have lain myself open to being made pregnant with people, with having people laid on me, I am always being told I am responsible for people and hated when I am too small to look after them.

A messy session; I am stuck at not being able to express need to someone I resent: a hard little girl locked in hating and out of touch with my hunger.

Letter to David, 9th October, 1972

I read your book of poems, David, when I got home from the session. I was lonely when I read them, cut off from Jerry and sitting by the fire to find out about you.

A new David was there, how little I know you. It was disturbing to see your suit fall off and underneath was a man who knew about birth and death and loving women and about a world I don't know of corn and manure and an open skyline. I felt humbled, because I see the city David and with him I feel confident, the country girl in me will not be born for some time yet.

I cried, David, letting myself feel how much I want to be near you, to feel your warmth; and how it will cut me up to live north with you south. I did not understand many of your poems, and it did not matter. You come across so simple and so embarrassingly in touch with flesh and bleeding and women. It was difficult to separate you as I had to in that moment from my father. I feel humbled now by my projection, it does not do you credit, and I hope soon it may fall from me.

Dear Jen,

I'm so glad those earlier poems had something to say to you. If there is any kind of fresh source in me which helps to keep the therapy alive, it is in there. But I didn't guess you'd feel that so readily, and thought you might be bored by their optimism and resent it.

I don't quite know who I am with you just now since the father projection started making room for mother projections as well so none of my suits quite fits. And then times when you deal directly with a man you only know bits of. The sessions at the moment are like rounding a headland and getting into new currents. The hard little girl coming out so strong in you may be tough for those around you to take, but there's a lot of movement going on under the messy confusion. I sense something in me content to let you find your own level more and not drawing on your energy to pull things clear so much. Hope so. It does me good sometimes to step aside a little from the mainstream of your therapy and share a few small ordinary things with you, like oranges and women in poems.

Tuesday Group, 10th October, 1972

In the group, I got to talking about my embarrassment about sex. I moved on to Dad and his blasted puritanism. Red-hot anger towards him came out of me. I found I had a magnificent vocabulary of swear-words and thoroughly enjoyed shrieking at him for his narrow-mindedness. Anger came out of me too at him for dying, anger at the waste; I said, 'If you'd allowed a bit more shit to come out of you on to your superhygienic floors, maybe then the shit wouldn't have piled up in your bones and you wouldn't have died of cancer.' I hated him for dying, because he was a good friend of mine. I want him with me.

Thursday Group, 12th October, 1972

Jenny P. was yelling blue murder at me in the group. I started to shiver all over and was offered help. Hate. Hate was pouring into my body. I felt hated by so many people in that group. I felt the boisterous child in me being hated, my energy and movement being hated. I felt how I never do what I want for fear of upsetting someone and how even when I do what I like, I don't feel good because of my tension. I swore I'd never do anything ever again to please anybody. Everything I ever did was wrong anyhow. I said, 'Damn you all, you can leave me, I'm going to do what I like.' I hated everyone. I felt that everyone had left the room except the dogs. I was completely alone. Then I got to feeling that I really liked myself, there wasn't anything wrong with me. I kept saying, 'I'm nice, I'm nice, I'm good.'

Friday, 13th October

I gave Julie the final session of her intensive. It was very good and brought up loads of feelings in me. I needed desperately to cry and go into things myself. I felt how fucked-up the therapist role is. Feelings were flowing all over me. The wrong time, the wrong space. In the evening, a lot of hatred was building up in me, because a lot of hatred was being poured into me. The pot is boiling.

Session with David, next day

I was talking quite a bit when suddenly, I got into my Dad,

yelling 'He *did* love me.' I felt out why it was I felt so loved by my Dad: it was that he and I could argue, he wouldn't agree with anything I said, he hated how I thought, but he didn't hate me. As David said, he just had trouble expressing his love. I was laughing and crying at the same time with love and amusement at my Dad and his funny ways; how 'you little bugger' was about the extent of his terms of endearment, and how much more it meant to me than all Mum's smiles. The other day, I was talking to Julie about Dad and had felt him clearly in the room. She pointed out ways in which I was like him: sauntering into the room and flopping comfortably wherever I was. I started to feel how much of my Dad I have in me; up until now my great fear had been that I was totally, inseparably my mother. Suddenly I made a very basic connection, and my crying deepened: Mum had always said, 'You're just like your father', and I'd fought that desperately, because what she meant was, 'You're a cold, hard, nasty little girl.' Now, being like my father suddenly meant something good, wholesome, earthy, relaxed and at-home, as well as being a bit clumsy, noisy and rough, because that's me too, and I like that part f me.

Sunday group, 15th October, 1972

I had spent the day at my mother's house. In the group, I felt myself back to where she had charged across the lawn to Becky who was returning red-nosed and happy from picking black-berries. She pounced on Beck and said, 'Oh! You're cold, you're freezing, come in doors quickly, you've got nothing on!' Fuss, fuss, grab. I tried to slow her down, 'Mum, you haven't asked her yet whether she's cold or not.' 'But I can *see* she is,' said Mum.

I went into very deep crying about this in the group, saying, 'How long would it take before Becky didn't know whether she was cold or not?' I felt I was splitting apart inside, just a few simple words, 'you're cold' instead of 'are you cold?' the difference between allowing me to be alive, and killing me.

I cried for the four years it had taken me to get to this point, for the enormity of what I'd had to go through and wha still lay before me. I cried because I didn't really believe anyone could come right through the therapy and for so many of my friends that I felt would give up. I was exhausted at the end of my crying; I felt clear and confident, but once again very alone.

The next week, I put myself in a tiny windowless room at the East London Encounter Centre, with just a sleeping-bag on the floor, and no heating. I stayed there day and night except for twice-daily sessions with Peter Judge, who was a complete stranger to me. I wrote about this week:

Horrible projections on to Peter. I felt he hated me. He never lets anything of himself into the sessions. No-one could be more unlike David. I never know what he is thinking or feeling. This is a very uncomfortable way to do therapy. I feel fucked by formulae, my whole body hurts with them. I went into hatred of Janov's book, of therapy itself; more and more rules, things I can do wrong. I never feel right, never feel I'm right. I screamed at my mother for expecting me to turn out exactly like her and hating me as soon as I was different.

Peter kept dragging me away from present-day feelings, making me work directly with the past. After a day spent being thrown by this, I decided to use anything he said to get myself into my feelings and not let him take me out of strong feelings with any blasted techniques.

The next day he came in saying, 'What's all this about wanting to do things your way?' I said I'd worked so long just to be able to feel that I was terrified of this being taken away from me. I couldn't bear the feeling he was trying to stop me or to make me feel the way he thought I ought to. I started crying and felt soft about myself and no longer feared his criticizing me or interfering. From then on I worked as I knew best: bringing up hugely strong feelings through working on things going on now.

I was strongly affected by a girl at the centre. I let out a hell of a yell and dived into deep anger and crying, screaming at her for her dead eyes that don't see me and her dead voice that lectures me without knowing who I am. 'STOP IT!' I yelled. 'Who the hell do you think you're talking to?' I yelled and

yelled at her, but kept saying, 'I don't know who you are'.
Then suddenly I did know. Dad. I went into fury at him for me
wasting my life to get his approval, taking year after year of
crappy exams, getting good marks just so I'd have something
to talk to him about, so that he'd love me. I went on and on in
a fury I didn't know I had inside me about him: fury at him
hating women, at making me feel inferior for being a woman:
I'd tried to turn myself into a boy to suit him. I felt how he
despised his sisters, yet they were much kinder and warmer
than him. I hated him for his complete intolerance of emotion,
for wanting to turn me into an intellect machine and nearly
managing it. I felt it was his fault I had brought Becky up in
the dead, mechanical way I did, telling myself she wouldn't be
'interesting' until she could talk, and never bothering to talk to
her so that she'd learn. I felt I would break in half with all the
hate and fury, and I didn't even know these feelings were there,
I had always thought Mum did all the bad things to me. I told
Dad, 'at least Mum was better than you, at least she was
inconsistent, and that means human.' I felt sorry about Mum,
I felt she'd been right in some ways, that I had been unfair to
love Dad so much when he gave me nothing, and hate her, when
she did give me warmth.

At the end of my session, I felt Peter had warmed to me and
this cut me up: I realized how to be loved was as dangerous as
being hated. I saw myself as a child at home, cut off from all the
the others. Peter asked, 'When did you split off?' I said I didn't
know. He said, out of the blue, and hitting a nail right on the
head, 'What about being laughed at?' I'd never felt this out
before and it shocked me because it was such a huge chunk of
my childhood I'd chosen not to think of. I saw Mum and her
brothers, felt the horror of meal-times, me a foil for their jokes;
saw Mum and my sister, her ever-ready audience, laughing at
my expense. I saw Alex' sneer, Jack patronising me, the other
Peter, so many faces putting me down, using me to feel big. I
went into the biggest yelling tantrum I've ever experienced in
therapy, just noise and more noise pouring out of my gut, it
felt so good to let it come, on and on, rageful sounds, not
crying. I felt proud and strong, the more noise the better; I'd

show them how serious it is not to be taken seriously. It was the rage of a small proud girl being laughed at. I realized why I had found it so difficult to take my own pain seriously; I'd always been told, 'Come now, we're only joking, no need to take it so seriously.' Or if I didn't laugh at their jokes, I was mocked for having a 'stiff lip'. At the end of this session, I was so emptied out, there was nothing left in me except warmth and tiredness.

In the afternoon session, Peter asked me why I kept putting my arms over my face. I felt it was me given up, with nothing left outside, unable to bear looking any more. All there was outside was Mum and Dad rowing, screaming each other to pieces, killing each other with jagged hate energy. Peter said, 'Tell them to stop'. I couldn't, they couldn't hear me, I was cowering in a corner. 'Tell them!' Peter shouted. I tried, it was so hard, I can never yell when other people are making a noise. When my yell came, it came really loud, I screeched 'MUM! DAD! STOP IT!' I yelled again and again, until there was Mum, saying again, 'Now look what you've done, you've made the children cry,' and Dad was answering again, 'No, *you* made the children cry.' I screamed, 'You BOTH made me cry! Stop using me to hit each other with, I'm not a pawn, I'm not your referee.' I went wild, hitting down, 'It's not YOU, or YOU, it's BOTH OF YOU!'

After my rage was spent, I felt the sorrow at having parents that hated one another. I sobbed, 'I want you to love each other. I can't live with you hating each other.' There was my mother sighing, 'If only you two children would love one another, I'd be so happy.' I yelled 'WHAT ABOUT YOU TWO?' I cried that Dad wasn't the baddy; he was unhappy. Neither my sister nor I were the baddies either; we were all unhappy, tearing each other to pieces. Dad lost; he lost Mum and he lost us; he was alone and was sent away. And I lost him; and went away with him, in my head.

On the last day of my intensive, I had the deepest and most important session of the week. I went into the hardness I had encased myself in when Snowy was born. I turned over on my side and said, 'I don't want you any more. I don't want to live.

I want to die. I don't want anybody.' I cried and yelled, 'I don't want anyone near me. Nothing can ever be right again. I am never coming back. Nothing can ever make it better. It's too late.' There was so much of this in me, so young, I was amazed.

I reached a new pitch when suddenly I got the connection of things being done behind my back: Mum having my sister behind my back. It wouldn't have been so bad if I could have seen, if I could have been part of what was going on. I felt how important it is to let first children see the others being born. As it was, I always thought it could happen again. I shrieked at Mum to stop telling me she loved me, it didn't help. I screamed at my sister for the way she'd stormed in one night when I was looking after her baby who was crying. I yelled at her to go away and take her horrid baby with her, it wasn't my responsibility anyway. I cried about the photos of me before my sister's birth, and after: how I looked defiant and cheeky before I was two, a confused, little old woman by the time I was three. I just couldn't stop crying; I could hardly believe so much was coming out of me, that such a 'simple' thing as a new baby could cause such a big split. I felt my life really had ended when I was two, and I couldn't stop crying.

Letter from David, October 20th, 1972
Dear Jen,

The feeling of the last few weeks, as I read over your groups and sessions is that you're at another crucial turning point. It's like when after months in the accumulator, when the body has charged up enough, the tumour starts to disintegrate and comes away in big black pieces, the whole system is working overtime to excrete all the stuff away fast, and there's blood and mucus and black bile to come up from the next layer. It's as though the pride has come alive in you, it's fierce and hot, and so much ice is melting — great slabs of it, there's this huge thaw going on, so much slush, and deep waters running underneath, and a black tide, but beneath it bubbling springs, and those sudden rushes of happiness that take you over, a whole ice-age is cracking up.

The way your therapy has developed has been increasingly that you want to have your own baby: hence all the business with Peter about your right to run the thing your way. Hence the times you had to knock me back into my corner, some fussy midwife telling you to breathe at the wrong time, you know your own body better than anyone, you want help, but you want the right help. The huge drive in you that used to go into politics, the drive to survive that never let you commit suicide, has become focussed on what you need instead of into nourishing the world's babies. Suddenly all those energies are collecting and cohering and sustaining you. Perls said, 'Don't push the river'; and when the river really gets moving, it can sweep into being a whole new landscape.

There was a time, not so far ago, I wrote these letters to some girl in a distant country I had never met but dreamed existed. I didn't know quite who she was, but I wrote to tell her she was real. You wrote back full of doubts and yesnoyesnos, there were these kinks and twists and ravelled up feelings we were trying to tease simple with often fumbling fingers. But I hear such confidence and certainty coming out of what you write now. Lowen says in his new book that being in touch includes the ability to know, 'I can't love today, because there's too much hate in me.'

If feedback is a hindrance, be strongminded and throw this letter on the fire. But you managed to work with me in spite of flaws: we could have got caught up in the melt, but somehow it didn't happen that way — your horrid feelings came when they were ready to come, and woe betide anyone then who stood in their way. It's an open question if contact with me helped block them, or if it was that contact that helped you to the point you dared risk them. Either way — there was no choice, therapists are human beings, when you work with them, you meet their strengths and their weaknesses. I know that when you were 'just' a patient, in the early part of the therapy, everything went so much slower. When you started to react to me as a person, and I to you, that's when suddenly your real feelings started to get tapped, and the whole process really got under way. It's not either or. You need closeness AND you need distance. Your Mum got too close and you needed her distant. Your Dad got too distant and you needed him close.

When you told me, last session, to keep back, to keep my charge out of your way, to hold my own excitement, that's a tremendously important thing: to be separate without being cut off. To keep what space you need without going back on ice is the essence of becoming yourself; and the converse is the ability to be close without being swallowed up.

All that anger towards your Dad; I'd like to say a bit about how that seems to me. It's as though the split between your parents split your love and your hate apart. There was so much hate for each other between them that you couldn't keep in touch with the real love both still felt for you. It's like your life has been a long struggle to marry your Dad because he's all love and no hate, and to get divorced from your Mum because she's all hate and no love. The real work of therapy is to win back your own feelings, not to get close to or away from your image of theirs. Your Dad was a hung-up man, not the romantic lover you dreamed of, he had real love in him but couldn't show it easily except in the silly-bugger games. Your Mum was a hung-up woman with a lot of life in her, it's not all black and white: she both nearly suffocated you *and* yet you are a person with a lot of life in you which survived suffocation.

Sunday group, 22nd October, 1972

I'd spent the day at my mother's house with Martin's Mum.

On a day like this, there can be none of the new-found warmth in me for my mother. She is a killer, an uptight, monstrous, neighbour-conscious, diseased old woman. As soon as young life is near her — we took three-year-old Paul with us — her sickness looms high and heavy and there is no room to breathe. With someone of her own age and sex there to impress, she becomes her most cut-off and spiky. In the first ten minutes of the visit, in the kitchen, I said, laughing at someone she was telling me about, 'Silly cow'. 'NOT IN MY HOUSE PLEASE: WHEN IN ROME DO AS THE ROMANS' came the fierce command, the energy of her whole being poured into controlling me. She said the neighbours could hear me. Through god-knows-how-many-feet-thick walls her neighbours were supposed to hear and be so offended by my words that I had to shut up.

I did. I went to the wet healing autumn woods with Becky and Paul and my Mum's tortured dog. I was filled with a sadness that wouldn't climax in tears but which swelled in every part of my body.

At the dinner table, when my mother was sending out spiky vibes at something my stepfather said, he came out in mild rebellion, 'I'm sorry, but I can't help thinking what I think.'

I was too badly affected by my mother's neurosis on that day to have any room in me for sympathy for her terror, for the tension of her downsliding aristocratic background of hysteria and pretense. I was too preoccupied with being sentenced to death by the ruling slogan: KEEP UP APPEAR-ANCES AT ALL COSTS.

On the way home, I visited the other side of my family. They can't control anyone, these working-class people who don't know what to pretend so it doesn't occur to them to try. So they are dying off the alternative way, killing themselves internally; two more relatives of my father are dying of cancer; his youngest brother already went a year after him. Yet what shows through in my 'neurotic' cousin and in her kids, is the life force, bursting, bubbling, gushing out of her laughter in the middle of telling her kids off; she laughs at their cheek, admires their defiance. Her inconsistency is saving them, just as her tension and misery and fussing is killing them. She loves those kids with a fierce pride and passion, as fierce as the beatings I've seen her give them; she knows they are individuals, not just shadows of her.

So I was overfull when I got home to the group. I was soon crying bitterly. I remember little except the sudden giving in, and the way I crept further and further into the corner, trying to muzzle into the wall, trying to disappear, to get away and sobbing, 'I don't want you all here, I want to die, I want you all to go away, I'm frightened, I don't want to live'. I didn't want to feel, and I was feeling; I wanted to be dead, and my whole body was alive. I wanted to be loved, and I felt hated, watched. I wanted to love my mother, and there was no-one there but a shopkeeper, a district nurse, a headmistress.

Thursday group, 26th October, 1972

The group seemed to consist mainly of corpses. I got furious at how I spend my whole time trying to warm them up. I saw how I am still living by pleasing, by doing and helping. I saw how the only time Mum gave me her approval was when I helped her or my sister. Nothing that ever burst from me naturally was loved, only this false little self, the goody-goody girl who became a pretend rebel to hide my need for approval. I felt ill. I left the group. I cried silently in the bathroom, knowing that now I have to be truly alone.

I know now I have to stop. I feel bad because everyone may go away now there is no-one to feed them. In fact, this evening the group *did* fall to pieces almost as soon as I left. If I do not hold the world up, it will fall down. On top of me.

Session with David, 28th October, 1972

I feel thirty; not dead, but very grown-up. There is no hope any more of bouncing, of being the boisterous youngster I wasn't allowed to be. Until now, I have always thought that therapy would bring about this miracle, that I could be reincarnated in myself, become my own child again, and do it all again the happy way. Now it is suddenly before me that all is lost, and not to be regained.

My energy was very calm. David turned out the light and we lay in the room in silence for a long time.

I don't know how much I trust these quiet sessions. I suppose they are important.

Silence

When you came through the door
I looked to see it if would be peace or war;
once the blood starts its fire-dance
of fury, there isn't much chance
to be still
and see why you really want to kill.

There is a time
for the dying of a child's rage
when the black fires can burn out
in your murderous heart;
there is a time
beyond the crying of a child's tears
for your own age,
loosening your grip
on the lost years,
letting them slip
between the last light and the first dark.

There is an hour
when even you run out of power,
when there is nothing more to do at all
but stop
at the brickwall
and let your childhood fall,
the last hope drop.

There is a space
larger than any shout
for the laying of your body out,
not sprawled, as children practise dying,
but lying,
dressed
for a grown up's deeper rest.

There is a space
small as the hollow of a hand
for each slow breath;
there is a space
you understand
to put your head
and not be empty on an empty bed;
there is a way for even your pale face
to look at death
and not be dead.

> When the only sound in the room
> is the tick of a heart;
> when the only move in the house
> is the pulse of the womb,
> put out the light
> and listen to the beating of the dark.

David
October 29, 1972

The night after my session I slept with Jerry. I felt bad in the night, sick. I woke up in a terrible state. I went into the bathroom and had a dreadful feeling about David: I felt like at the end of a relationship. I felt somehow I had quarrelled with him, that everything was bad, ruined, between us, it was all over. I crawled back into bed. I started to shake my head. My father was all around me. I started to talk to Jerry about him. I wanted my Dad to come back, to come home, to walk in the door; I don't really believe he is dead, I still think he'll come swinging, whistling down the Mews one day and breeze in, turning his nose up at the dogs and the nude pictures and the smell of the house; but his belly-laugh will fill the place and he'll say what a 'nice lass' Julie is, meaning he fancies her like mad, and how he 'never could stand Yanks' when he meets Jerry. Dad is all around me, he has not gone; he is not dead, no part of me believes it. I cried, 'We weren't finished yet, it's not fair, we were only just beginning.' I realized I had always thought of myself as his wife, he was just living with another woman for the time being, but one day he would come home.

I went into my own room and fell into a thick, bad sleep for most of the day, my whole body aching as if with Asian flu. In the afternoon, Martin walked in. I felt the terrible conflict of losing Jerry by having him there. I asked him to leave and started crying very deeply. I cried on my own for about an hour with the door locked. I pictured what I wanted most in the world, and it was Jerry and Martin to hug one another and to talk about me, how they could best help me. I wanted them both to love me and love each other because they loved me.

I was crying, 'Please stop quarrelling and love one another.'
Then I reached a very bad point, it felt a bit like on an acid trip:
I suddenly felt I had invented my whole life and all the people
in it. The only thing that felt real was that brown house I lived
in until I was four. All the light, bright colours and the happy,
loving people I know now seemed like an invention. My life
stretched behind me like a Hollywood film script of chewing
gum, with Woolworths Christmas decorations. I felt I would
never be able to be with people again, now that I knew I used
them to make my life seem bright.

I spent the rest of the day in a collapsed state in bed, until
the group arrived.

In the group, Julie worked with me; she was very good.

Being ill made me feel messy; I was a mess. I wanted lots of
space around me and couldn't bear the heat of the room. I felt
I had measles or chicken-pox and was too hot; the room was
too hot and Mum was fussing around me. I wanted her to leave
me alone and let me be messy and ill and stop trying to tidy me
up. As soon as I gave in to the feeling of being messy and
stopped apologizing for it, my body pains went, all except for
the pain in my head, and a new, sharp pain in my bladder. But
at least the flu-aches in my limbs went and that was a blessed
relief. I lay quietly breathing. I told my mother how bad I was
feeling and how nothing could make me better, she was making
me worse by trying to make me better, by not letting me feel
bad. What I wanted more than anything else was to be set
down outside, on the doorstep, in the cool night air, in the rain
or deep snow. I wanted fresh air, I wanted to be free and to be
left in peace.

The pain in my bladder turned out to be tension and fear at
telling her I wanted to be alone, I wanted her to go. I faced
Martin and immediately burst into tears and told him: 'You
give me so much support, I do not want to lose you, but I
cannot be with you.' Back to my mother, I felt how I wanted
her there for me, but I wanted space between us so that *I* could
go to her. She was always coming to me when I didn't want her;
she was always on top of me. Julie suggested I talk from my
bladder. I said, 'I hurt all over, I am in pain, but you are not

going to know it. Even if you notice what I need, I am not going to admit it, I am not going to give you any satisfaction. I would rather die, rather burst, than suffer the humiliation of telling you my need. I am bursting, I am dying, I am trapped.' I felt dreadful, I felt at a dead end, a brick wall. Feeling how my mother would somehow use it if I went to her in need, I suddenly screamed in her face: 'YOU'D EAT ME!' I could feel her glee and triumph when I went to her. She was not concerned with what I felt, but with her winning. I got very angry. I screamed, 'WHAT DID YOU DO? I'M GOING TO FIND OUT WHAT YOU DID TO ME!' Over and over again I asked her, yelling and feeling very excited. I felt I was on the verge of really seeing, really knowing what she'd done to me, how she'd made it impossible for me to live, impossible for me to go out for what I wanted. Someone stirred in the room. I screamed and buried myself under the cushions. A thrill of terror ran through my legs. I was very very little, at an age when I was still separate, she was not yet inside me. My throat hurt with the joy of screaming her out of me. I felt intense excite- ment at the fear in me. It would be a total, horrible terror, but it was not locked; I knew I was on the brink, that if something really scared me, I would be able to react immediately, that the scream was loose inside me, ready to come. I was so near to seeing; I knew that intense pleasure and absolute horror were about to unite.

The next day I wrote to David:

I haven't often felt as bad as these past few days. But it is a new kind of bad. It is on top of me and I am not struggling. I am not trying to keep my head above water, not trying not to die. I *am* dying. Confusion and nightmare have brimmed over into the day; there is no longer any separation between waking and sleeping.

Thursday group, 2nd November, 1972

My stomach was knotted and hard. I knew my father was in there, hurting me. I was crying, but stuck, because I didn't want to give Dad up, the little bit of him I have. I cried bitterly, wishing my stepfather or my Dad's wife had died, not the only one I did have. The feeling was too unbearable and I cut myself short, ending up with a knotted diaphragm and a drowning feeling in my nose. My feeling is oozing out in small pieces, I can't bear to know that Dad is dead. I went down to the toilet: at every bend in the staircase I thought he would be standing there in his big overcoat with his arms outstretched. My body is his, I can feel how much I am his daughter; I am Daddy's girl, eternally stuck at flirtation-level, at about ten years old. I see how, when my boyfriend develops, grows up into a man, I start to avoid physical contact, I move away. I cannot be a grown woman when I am still married to my Daddy.

One weekend, I stayed at my sister's house and gave her several sessions. It is difficult for me to hear her speak of Dad and to know I really did have to share him, he wasn't mine alone. I helped my sister to get into her fear of Mum. Her face was the most terrifying thing I've seen, fear of death transfixing her as she screamed again and again and again. Even then, she was still locked in fear, and I was too caught up with feelings to throw her further into it, to freak her out. Tears were streaming down my face, I was cracking up with hatred and sorrow to see what Mum had made of us, tense bundles of terror. My sister's insights meant a lot to me: she saw Mum and Dad as having a passionate relationship, plenty of blood and thunder, but amazing energy between them. Then they split up and went to live with death: Dad married his cancer and Mum married a lapdog so that she wouldn't have to face so many strong feelings.

My sister has a far stronger sense of home than I have: she sees lightness and brightness and warmth, times when Dad and Mum were in harmony. I have kept no such memories.

After three days at my sister's house, I could take no more. The energy of our family is bad and I felt re-infected with tension.

Returning to my group, I felt shaky and weak after hitching home. I felt fresh and new; I've been so quiet inside myself

during these days in the north of England, everything has
slowed down inside me.

It came to my turn in the group and I had to face the most
difficult feeling of all: melting with goodness, with the love I
feel for these people who have travelled with me, this little
group of four or five friends who have stuck together because
they want to live. I went over to Alex who has been softening
consistently lately. I took his hands and broke down and gave
in to my feelings. I travelled deep into my guts, hot tingling
spreading throughout the deepest parts of me. I poured with
hot sweat and gave in for a while to the joy and the terror of
coming alive, of knowing I could never undo all this therapy
now, I could no longer go back to covering over, to going dead.
I sobbed how I understood what Alex had said once about
wanting to turn back, how there is never a guarantee of any
'happy ending' in therapy, how I understood him trying to
kill himself and didn't blame anyone for switching off or
staying dead, because it is hard, it is terrible to start to live
again, and know your own death.

Friday group with David, 10th November, 1972

It was a beautiful group, people's emotions flowing so smoothly.
I went back, the last thing I expected, to facing terrible fear. I
recalled Snowy's face when I gave her that session, saw again
the terror in her eyes. I yelled for her to come and look after
me now. I felt a great black chasm between us. We had both
lived alone, each in our fear and hatred as kids. Neither of us
had had a sister. I called and called for her, my body gave in to
need, my legs felt joined on for a change. I took a step I'd
somewhere inside me decided never to take: back to humiliation. I let out my biggest secret: that I had capitulated to my
mother in fear. When she came charging up the stairs, threatening me to stop me crying, I had called out, 'Alright, Mummy,
I'll stop, I'll stop, don't hit me, I'll be good.' I had betrayed
myself and was filled with a deep sense of shame for ever after.
I did not want to go back there, I did not want to feel such
shame. I yelled that I wanted to die, anything, anything, rather

than feel myself back in that darkened room with my monster mother coming in at the door and me going to jelly, collapsing with fear and capitulating. I'd kept this secret in particular from David: I was Dad's brave little girl, I did not want him to know how I had given in. Bringing the feeling back to adult years, I screamed with fury at Derek and Nigel and Jerry and everyone I have ever let frighten me into obedience.

David wrote this about our group, the first he ever attended:

I've had a prejudice against groups for a long time, mainly because of the gimmicks so often associated with them, partly because of the power-drive visible in many who become leaders, partly because many therapeutic groups become random or occasional events, with no continuity, and no depth relation-ships possible. Also I had grown increasingly critical of the type of bio-energetic workshop led by followers of Lowen, where everyone banged out their anger at the same time, on cue, a kind of emotional circus act.

Quite different, but I wasn't sure how, were the groups Jenny had started. I'd had regular accounts from her about these, but naturally they focussed on what she had got out of them: there was no attempt at a balanced account of the whole group, a very hard thing to do anyway. And I had very little conception of Jenny's role in that group, as leader, or initiator, or whatever she was doing when she wasn't going into things herself. But I had this suspicion, lurking at the back of me somewhere: partly a suspicion to do with the whole PNP idea, non-professionalism, no doctors, or psychiatrists, or therapists, or trained people there, just a gang of amateurs doing their thing.

Jenny's groups had been running for at least two years, but even if I'd been around on an evening when a group was held, I'd have been diffident about coming: I didn't want the build-up as 'Jenny's therapist', the curious eyes, and would have felt a gate-crasher. So I kept myself away from the idea of partici-pating.

What I finally experienced was a remarkably sensitive group where people went into their feelings easily, without any trickery, without any pressure, without any tactics, everyone following their own pace, no-one dominating or twisting, all the emotional lines clear. I had expected the particular qualities of trust and empathy and that magical something that individual therapy can reach at its best, to be difficult to reach in a group of its size; but it was like coming home, it was a river flowing with no-one pushing it, it was a group where people, like Alex, who had 'nowhere to go', could come to and be recognized as fully human, contained and held, but not pumped up to a false energy-level by any mock-therapists.

This group was 'too good to be true'. People just aren't like that. That kind of self-help is revolutionary in the deepest sense. I could not believe the seed I had planted could have grown so much or so well.

It certainly wasn't a primal group. It had no resemblance to anything Lowen ever worked out. And Reich? Reich never ran groups, he was afraid of groups, he was a lonely man with very few friends, his family joined his work or they were nothing. Reich saw the sickness of the political group but he never found the security of the therapy group. He never had that kind of family; he got on best with his caretaker. But it was Reich who wrote:

'How do you like this kind of work? It's different than what you thought, isn't it? People come and are thrown by the way we work here. They think there is some genius here who sits around, sucks his thumb, and has ideas. There is no such genius. We don't have ideas here; we work, just plain work . . . The toughest part of this work is that you can't direct it: you have to let it lead you . . . This is very deep stuff. Once you get into it, you can't get out very easily unless you turn against it and start throwing mud at me. If ever you start running from this thing, please just leave. Don't throw stones at me.'

Dear David,

It's nice of you to write up your thoughts about the group. I want to say a few things though.

First, we didn't just all walk into a room, lie down, and be able to relate in that way. It took months of (good) game-playing encounter. I don't join you in putting down other groups just because of the ceiling rocking. Our groups used to freak out the whole street; they sounded dreadful from outside. Inside, they were warm and meaningful and energy and feelings were being aroused: this is how we used to work, by playing a noise-and-movement game, and dealing with things aroused from it afterwards. People who walk in like ghosts or statues cannot be worked with on an emotion level until a spark of life has been rekindled. You saw the gentle fruit of two years (more now) of labour pains and birth cries. I mistrust any group being put down unless you have sat through it, week after week after week after week. I feel like crying when I write this: I have had enough of people judging something by a brief encounter with it. Even the messy groups and ghostly scenes at the East London Encounter Centre I visited again and again, and though I hated them for myself, there were *still people helped.* I don't want you to use our group, David, to hit others with. It *is* beautiful, and I want it recognized *by the people in it*; what the outside world says doesn't really matter.

The day after the group, I had a session with David. I went feeling already clean from the evening group, but quickly got into things. I started with the pain of containing joy: the pang of knowing I am alive and finding it hard to bear.

Then as my feelings moved into more angry ones, David intervened, suggesting to me that anger is easy, and joy isn't. For a moment, I was confused; then I knew myself, and knew I was angry. I cried and cried in anger feeling that David and my Mum wanted to stop me crying, wanted to steer me away from 'bad' feelings, which feel so good, into 'nice' feelings. I got more and more hostile towards David, feeling the therapy as oppressive. I was too hot, I wanted fresh air; I felt David was too nice, I was being conned out of my real feelings, which were noisy and fuss-making, into being a gentle, nice little girl.

I moved naturally from this back into crying about the goodness of what I have now, the groups, the tolerance between people. I have all I ever wanted, to be able to express myself without being shut up.

At the end of the session, David told me how beautiful he thought the group was last night. I burst into tears, telling David how the things I loved most — the home I have in the groups, the love I see between the people in them, and the love I have for David — are often called sick and wrong, they are being destroyed by other people's words. I cried with relief, being able at last to say the thing I most wanted to say: 'I want you to come into the family.' David said, 'I am glad to be in the family, it isn't wrong to want that'.

I felt now I could live, for this had been my biggest pain in the present, to have to feel apologetic about the things I get most pleasure out of.

Sunday group, 12th November, 1972

After two hours of exasperation with Dan, I let rip. My guts ran hot, out gushed my insults and yellings. I expected some archaic connection to emerge. The swirl of energy spent itself and settled, and it was over.

I had just experienced a strong feeling in the present, in proportion to what was happening. I sat back, a little dazed.

Thursday group, 16th November, 1972

Martin got me to face my mother and almost immediately I was back at the same place as that Friday with David: not being able to bear going back, to really be little again in that hateful house, because going back really means just that, it means feeling what it was like, with no groups and no help, absolutely alone and trapped and frantic and dying. I cried and cried for ages, stopping now and again with hopelessness or exhaustion. I was deeply in it, yet stuck too, because I didn't want to give in completely to my misery, I was scared people in the group would close in and come at me, that they couldn't stand me crying, couldn't bear the fuss I was making. I kept sobbing 'I want to die, I want to die, I can't live, my mother's tension and bad energy is all I'm made of, it's no good, I can't go on, I can't live.' I was crying that I wished I'd never started therapy, that

I'd killed myself and Becky, it was too difficult and dreadful to go on, and there was no going back.

The next morning, I woke up and cried a bit in the knowledge that I must abandon the colours and warmth which surround me and return to that brown room and those brown feelings; that I cannot reach out to the beauty around me unless I go back and grovel in the horror which was all I had.

I stayed feeling woolly, blocked and locked at the point of 'no return' and was still stuck at the Sunday group. I worked with myself for just a short time, messily, finding out at last in full clarity what my fear is: that as a child, I closed off at the point of imminent death; Mum was about to kill me, so I thought, so I died inside. If now I come alive, that moment of terror will return, and I will be screaming at my own death.

Tuesday group, 21st November, 1972

I went into the irritation I feel at corpse-like beings surrounding me. I was back with Dad standing there, sipping tea, staring blankly out at the garden, dead blue eyes, an aura of death; me, a few feet high, gazing anxiously up at him, unable to say or do anything, unable to contact him, my life a tension of watching to see how he is, waiting, hoping that one day he will notice me there, caring.

I yelled at Martin for the obscenity of his cleanliness-complex about my dogs, at my father for the same, for not wanting life or movement around him, wanting everything cleared up, especially anything that moves or makes a mess. I too am a mess to be cleared up, he cannot bear my messy emotions. I screamed at him, I hated him, I was glad he was dead, a real mess cleared up, and I was glad too that Mum is dying, another mess about to be cleared up.

When I yelled out my fury at my Dad, my whole body reacted, my legs kicked of their own accord spasmodically, I felt so good, a great weight lifted. I lay breathing for a while and then broke out in completely uncontrollable laughter which went on and on. I wasn't sure what it was about, but it was something to do with virgins and gypsies, with having thought that it was Mum's ghost in bed with me keeping me scared of sex when all along it had been Dad, a clean ghost, keeping me dead. I felt earthy now; I felt a joy of sweat and nakedness and chaotic hair, a joy in the face of Martin's frown; I felt I could roll on the floor with my dogs and he could beat his chest in frenzy and I would still laugh freely. I felt my body was my own again and I was in love with it.

Downstairs, in the kitchen, I felt a clear image of my father all around me. But now it was no longer of the romantic hero who would carry me off on his white steed and make love to me, but a bald-headed man with a pale, dead, sunken face, bitter and twisted and dying of cancer.

23rd November, 1972

The group was at Babs'. It was warm and cosy in my room and I didn't want to go. I just wanted to stay and do my crocheting. I decided not to go, and felt frightened. I sat with my fear of missing things, of losing touch and continuity. I felt dead, I was warm and closeted and mechanically making things. I caught a glimpse of the coloured wools on my bed. The red stood out. I thought with a jolt how fine it would be to kill myself now, to stop, to rest, to put an end to effort. I tried to think of my daughter, but I was not moved. It just seemed a good thing to do, a magnificent thing, something perfect and with no loose ends. The thought brought excitement to me.

I finished what I was doing, looked at the clock, and got up and went to the group. It was nice being there, being with the changing of people, feeling myself again. I had no strong emotions, but I had quiet thoughts and it was enough. I told them of my doubts about therapy, which are really realizations that there will be times when I am dead or quiet, when nothing moves within me, when the sea is calm with no big waves. I am in a period of self-containment, of not needing people. I have given up Martin and my car; I have no money. I am content with Becky and my room and the things I do. I have gone into hibernation for the winter; maybe I'll flower again in the spring, my birth-time.

Dream, 24th November, 1972
I am at my Dad's house. He has recovered from his cancer. He
and his wife and my half-brother are all there, sunburned and
friendly. It is sunny and I am starting to marvel at how good
everything is. Then I stop short and ask myself, 'Hang on, what
is wrong then?' In a flash, I realize I have created the whole
scene, and Dad really is dead.
  I wake up sobbing.

The same day, I wrote to David:

Maybe it's because the central heating is on, or the evenings are
closing in, or because I'm knitting, but I have sunken deep into
the earth, slumbering slowly, waiting for spring. My body aches,
I am seized with panic in the mornings, and yet I do not feel
bad. The newest thing of all is my separation from other people.
I feel no yearning; I am thirty and cannot be bothered to seek
out contact. Strong passions do not move me, sex is an
irrelevance. I seek nothing but Becky and colours. The nicest
things that have happened this week were sitting for an hour
having tea with a dog-crazy forty-year-old woman I met in the
park, and spending two hours with Becky while she cried out
her agonies about school.
  My childhood is remote; it has slipped away. I am not in a
hurry; the parts of it that must come back will.

Group, 28th November, 1972

I'd decided not to go, but again got a dreadful sinking feeling
that if I didn't go, I'd lose warmth and continuity. So I did go.
  I cried suddenly and quickly because I felt a dreadful schizo-
phrenia coming over me: I was cut off and confused. I was
scared to look round the group and suddenly not know who
anyone was, and to wake up one morning and not have any
memory, to find myself walking down the street muttering
unconnected words to myself. I felt I wanted the whole group
to hold hands and 'forgive one another', but I didn't know what
for. I wanted us to be faceless, with no previous memories or
images. I cried from fear, but couldn't go on.

Thursday group, 30th November, 1972

I am very blocked, I was hiding from Alex, hiding the good feelings I have about him. I felt how difficult it is to be directly loving, to say what I need.

Finally, briefly, I broke and said, 'Alex, I want you to know I am twelve years old. Please do not idolize me, please know that I am not strong, I need you to support me.' I was crying, speaking to him and Babs together then; I asked them to be with me, to see me without images, to know that I cannot hold everything up alone. I need them to see me as I am, because everyone else I know is so blinded by their projections.

They were both very soft with me.

A few nights later, I woke up with a vague feeling of my mother's chest around me. I was saying in my head: 'You know, I did love my mother once, we were so close; I don't know what happened, but I wiped it all away and have tried to forget it. And yet we were so close.'

That day, my mother and my stepfather turned up. We were having an all-day group, but hadn't started and were just sitting around. There was a lovely warm atmosphere amongst us in the room, very relaxed. A few days before this, I'd had the first letter of my life from my stepfather. It was a gentle letter and I had been cut to a dozen pieces, feeling how I had to rewrite twenty-five years of my life, realizing how I'd been artificially hard on this person I hardly knew because my parents made me angry and I couldn't show it.

So when he and my mother turned up, I just walked up to him and hugged him, not stopping to think. I sat with my arms round my Mum too, because she was crying about her illness, and I'm sure she knows she is dying. I felt easy and open with them, and they spent the afternoon in my territory.

When they had gone, I cried in the group for all the years I had hated my stepfather. He was an easy victim, not just Mum's but mine too. I was already a hardened, hungry child when he arrived, and I shut him out. Now I no longer feel safely encased in my hatred; now I may have to let everyone in, even police and traffic wardens.

This softening in me coincided with a new loving friendship I developed with Alex, someone I had seen for years as spiky, hard, cruel and cut-off. One evening when he was away, I was thinking of him warmly, wanting him, and I wrote this:

Two proud trees
growing bent but tall
backs to each other
faces to the wall
standing alone
side by side
gnarled with tension
rigid with pride

> Ugliness had clouded our young eyes
> kept us poles apart
> biting back bitter fire
> crushed under frozen earth
> a wall of snow between us
>
> Hate we had in common
> and a certain strength
> heels dug in
> straining
> not to let the hard lines blur
> or the hard times ease.

How did we thaw the icebergs of a lifetime?

Choking in a sea of bile
we surfaced, slowly,
weary smiles
opening new eyes

I felt your stiff arms
reach out in terror
hold on tightly

You saw me
writhe in my need
let the hard front drop

And our roots stretched down through the ice
found the firm earth
smouldering below,
and met.

Session with David, 9th December, 1972

I found myself fantasying making love to my mother, stroking her pussy. David said, 'Stay with the image'. It became kittens and their mother, and I broke into deep crying, going hot in my centre, feeling the pain of never having been allowed to touch my mother. I hadn't been allowed to mingle in her body, to be part of her, to reach out without concern for what part I would touch. I had lost the 'oceanic wave', bodies were no longer one continuous stream, but were divided up into war zones and no-man's-lands, taboos and no-go areas. I felt the terrible loss of unthinking contact.

At the end of the session, I was about to leave, but went back over to David and hugged him, tight and long, with arms that were not held back, with my body close against him, and for once there were no zones and no embarrassment. I kissed him on the cheek and I felt clean and clear and uncomplicated and I made myself look into his eyes. It was easy looking at David.

After the session, I went to see Alex who was living nearby. When I was trying to leave, he pointed out in a calm, innocent way the glib dismissing manner in which I was treating him. I came right down off my high, sunk to the floor and struggled to get in touch with why I was speaking to him like that. I said I was very frightened of him and his demands and that I didn't know what I felt when passionate demands were being made of me. Alex then gave me a long, quiet, clear exposé of how I escape by running from one person to another, with the groups to fall back on; how I make sure I'm never left by always having an alternative security. He said I wouldn't face deep feelings until I made a commitment to someone. Every word hit me very hard. I was in a panic inside; I felt I was going to die. I crawled to the bed and went into how I felt I was being asked to stay forever alone with him in that room, not allowed to go outside and play with anyone else or love anyone else. I felt terror, I couldn't face being trapped. I was crying, lying on my back, and kicking. As soon as I kicked strongly and made noises, terror swept down on me. I was very very young. Everything in the room, the guitar behind me, the plants, things on the wall, turned into human beings, leaning over me, threatening me. A spot on the wall turned into a spider. My sounds changed from grunting anger to high-pitched alarm.

Alex had found a way to bring on my terror: by staying in a terrifying situation and not running away.

Sunday group, 10th December, 1972

My sister was at the group, holding tight on to her feelings and on to her daughter. I was swamped with energy and when I went into it, I broke out in hysterical anger at our mother, beating the bed and shrieking at her for using us kids as an excuse not to live. 'You bloody liar, saying you were living for us and couldn't live for yourself, fucking up my life because you didn't dare to live yours.' I swore at her, saying she was all tits and no hips, all chesty smothering and no guts. I kept yelling: 'Look what you've done, look what you've done to me and Snowy.' I alternated between fury and despair at the sickness in her that had wrought so much havoc.

I was so beside myself with fury that the energy pumped up into my head and chest, my voice came out screamy, and the feelings wouldn't move down into my body. I tried kicking to get my energy to travel downwards, but my body feelings just got worse and worse. I was a head and torso with no bottom, no legs, not a leg to stand on. I kept calling out, crying to Mum to give me my legs back, give me my feet back. The top half of me was boiling hot, my legs and feet freezing. I was like a thalidomide child, the feelings were there, but no limbs to express them.

Session with Jerry, 15th December, 1972

This was the most terrifying thing that ever happened to me since I got stuck in terror on acid. This time, I got stuck in terror and I wasn't on acid. After going into a backload of fury at how I close off when verbally attacked in order to avoid rows and hot feelings, noises off started terrifying me. My dogs were outside our door. I started hallucinating. I saw Joey come in grinning, standing on his hind legs. Jerry urged me to look at the the vision. I screamed; I couldn't; I used every ounce of energy in me to keep the hallucinations at bay. It didn't work. My handbag hanging on the door started coming at me. When my dog Sally moved or yawned, it freaked me out. A pillow falling on me accidently froze me with electric horror. The room was coming alive and I was going dead. I was tingling with fear all over, but I couldn't scream it out of my body. I yelled, 'Jerry, bring me down, I want to come off the trip, it's too much.' I cried for about an hour and a half.

In the morning, Jerry and I made love and I had an easy orgasm at the same moment as him. I burst into tears and cried and cried for my mother. It was if I was crying to her to protect me from my own body feelings. Something inside me has given in.

Letter to David

Today I have just about the worst body feelings imaginable, like diarrhoea and constipation all at once. But I am pleased in my tired head. I am just not the same person any more, and that is something to be pleased about. I go into my feelings when they arise, in real life, and then they are very strong, and very frightening.

I am doing nothing, but I am working hard.

I am in despair about death, the death of my family and of the Vietnamese, and the children crying next door. But if my journey comes to an end, I will have done all I can. It is difficult to concentrate on myself with these horrors around, so easy to mourn for others, so hard to feel my own death.

We had a group on Sunday where nothing really happened, but I enjoyed some moments of intense mental clarity, so surprising it was like a sensuous pleasure. I was being attacked by Babs for 'leaving her' during an acid trip, by Marie for 'being impatient' when working with people. Alex was complaining about the group being 'clinical and cold'. For a moment, I was thrown, ready to dive head first into either defending or criticising myself. But my body receiving those words was new: I heard, sorted out, felt out, analysed what was going on through thinking with my whole body. I saw we had a group crisis on our hands: that every person had a negative trans-ference on to the group at the same moment. And somehow, I found a way to tell myself and the others what was happening. I saw how the group is only us, it is not separate from us, we are it, it is what we are, we do not leave our bags of shit outside the door with our shoes. I got this across, and the group did not crumble. I looked round at this small island of people who had clung to the boat and felt the preciousness of what we are doing.

Anyone starting therapy should be handed a leaflet; not to tell them not to smoke, drink, or masturbate, but to tell them a few simple things about what happens when hate and cold start to work loose and become a separate part and be projected outwards, and how if at this uncomfortable point they decide to change therapists, they'll only be starting again.

So I'll be writing to you, David, and visiting you once a fortnight, like I did Dad, for some time to come yet.

Bless you, love, Jen.

10th December, 1972

My mother and stepfather came over briefly to visit. I got my stepfather alone and asked him straight, 'Is Mum dying?' After a moment's silence, he said, 'It looks like it.' I felt close to him. Then we went in to Mum again. I said to her, 'If you need me to, I'll come down and look after you.' She bit her lip, and turned away to go. She was battling to hold back her tears. I could see that she would break down as soon as she got into the car. She is very bad, white and finished, very frightened.

I went up to my room and cried. I was not crying so much

for her as for the sickness of our family, the fear of death in
Mum and her proud holding-on.

20th December, 1972

I collapsed into a deep sleep this afternoon with my body
aching all over. I dreamt I was crying on someone's shoulder
saying, 'Oh I do wish I'd had a childhood without fear.'

Waking up slowly from my thick sleep, I realized all my body
pain and tension had gone. My energy had returned. I went to
the park with Sally and felt warm. Marion and Becky said it was
freezing, but my whole body was warm from my healing sleep.

A very bad Christmas

My idea of Christmas was to get all our people together, each
day in a different house, have a group session if people needed
help, then let it develop into a party if that's what happened.

It was a dismal failure. On Christmas Eve, Babs and Marie and
John were angry to turn up and find 'just a group' and not an
open party. John walked out. We went to the therapy room to
sort out our tangle of feelings and crossed expectations. I was in
a fury, which later changed to sobbing, because this was the one
time in my life when I hadn't 'laid it all on', hadn't organized
music and food and candles and atmosphere, hadn't planned,
had let it all happen, had just been myself in a scruffy house.
I felt this was the end of the road for me, this was the end of
the group. I cursed them all to hell and was left after the group
with really bad feelings. I'd alienated just about everyone, by
being myself and not trying to please.

Christmas Day was thoroughly horrid; by the end of the day,
even Alex was cut off from me. I didn't understand anything
that was happening and felt thoroughly locked and miserable.
It was just like at home with Mum saying, 'Look, it's Christmas,
what's the matter with you, can't you just come down and join
the family and be happy?'

On Boxing Day, I went over to Alex' early, having felt
suicidal the night before. I got there in a totally locked, schizoic

state, needing help desperately, but cut off from being able to ask for anything. I felt how easily I could turn into a schizophrenic. Alex, instead of working with me, made himself a meal. I lay there in a black, cold fury. Then he started to talk about himself. I got into worse and worse feelings as the day wore on. The group was a pissing awful non-starter. I went home deathly angry, ready to have a row with Jerry.

In my room, I put my face in a pillow and to my amazement broke out almost immediately in tears and growls of fury and rage.

The next day, with a sensation of suppressed calamity about me, I took seven children to a party. And had a marvellous time. I drank some cider, my body relaxed completely, I danced with the kids, I loved my dog and felt good about myself. I'd broken with everyone, but I was free and enjoying my body and my ability to move and the energy in me and my different-ness from other people.

The next day, I had this dream:

I had two babies. One was about six months old and looked like Becky, healthy, happy and loved. The other was new-born. She was tiny and wizened. A lot of the dream was spent just deciding what to call her, and I didn't decide.

I was alone in the world in a strange place with my two babies. But I was quiet and content inside; there were nurses around who were being helpful without interfering. I looked at my new baby. She wasn't pretty. She had slightly ginger hair and freckles, her eyes were constantly averted, looking sideways, never at me. Her skin was dead and unloved.

I brushed my warm face lightly on her nose and cheek, trying to bring a smile to her face, to reassure her. I felt confident that I could make her happy. I knew she was Volkhard's child, I could see she had his eyebrows, but I felt I couldn't tell him because he wouldn't believe it was his.

The greatest pleasure in the dream came simply from looking after the babies, changing them and feeding them. They were my whole world, and I was not looking for anything else.

I woke up with a longing inside me to be pregnant.

On the following day, there was a group at Babs'. I'd reached rock bottom in my feeling about the group. Tired of their projections, I was planning to leave and join a group where I was not known. Everyone else had reached rock bottom too. I walked in, and there was Babs in a great fury against me. She spat bile at me for about an hour, but didn't get anywhere because she really believed what she was saying was true. I sat through it all, but when I saw she was still stuck, I decided to let my own reactions out. This set my energy moving, my jaw juddering again — I'd thought I was frozen for ever. I felt very clear about what part of what Babs said was true, what part was pure projection and which parts made me furious. I even identified with her stiff pride and it didn't turn me off her. When I got into a shouting match with her, things really warmed up and energy began to flow in our group again. It felt like a very important turning point, upwards from the morass of Christmas. Alex went into his feelings and was so clear and beautiful I was just stunned with admiration. I felt he was the cleanest person I know. His anger cuts clean and heals everyone it touches. When he did get out-of-touch, it was as obvious as someone switching off the light. I pointed this out, and the whole group laughed together.

Finally, it was eleven o'clock at night and time for me to take space. Firstly, I looked for a way to say the very positive things I was feeling about the three others who'd been through things. I am so clumsy when I have good things to say. Then I lay down and deliberately stopped my jaw from juddering. Immediately, the energy poured down into my upper chest, heating me up and making me tingle. I was back in my dream of last night. Straight away, I broke out crying, saying, 'I want my baby back'. This meant for me, I want the good feelings of the dream, I want the baby in me back. As soon as I cried, my whole body came alive, all of me except my feet which stayed cold because I was frightened of hostility from the group. I was giving in completely to my crying, with such relief, crying my eyes out and saying, 'I'm so happy, I'm so pleased.' I was so pleased because I hadn't had to work: I had thought it would be such a struggle to get back into my feelings, and here it all was, happening for me without effort. I felt proud, as if this was my prize for working so hard with myself all these years; it was a wonderful payment.

From then on everything flowed so easily. I focussed on the party I'd danced at, how spiky and cutting I'd felt the host of the party to be, as if he were saying, 'Oh well, I suppose I'll tolerate you, Jenny. You're a bit much, but you're good for a laugh, good to get things moving.' The connection I made initially stunned me to silence: it felt as if this was the story of my childhood, a butt for Mum's jokes, someone to make *her* scene swing. At last I was able to feel hotly the scene I have remembered like a film all my life: me in the kitchen, about seven years old, in a terrible tantrum, rage bursting out all over me, and her standing there smiling patronizingly. I cried an ocean of anger and hopelessness, yelling 'Is *this* it, is this simple thing what made me want to kill myself — not being taken seriously?' I cried for Vicky, saying, 'You were angry too, didn't she take you seriously either?' Then suddenly I was with my own Mum, I became her in her Victorian parlour with her terribly-nice relatives. 'Did they laugh at you, too, Mum, is that what your trouble is?' I felt as if I were part of a chain, and suddenly screamed with anger saying, 'WELL, I BROKE THE CHAIN!' And then I felt that whatever bad things Mum had done to me, something in her had also given me the character to break that chain. Then I felt very sad again for her dying and cried, 'You are the sacrifice, I don't want you to have to be a sacrifice.' But then I got angry again and said, 'I damn nearly was, and Becky nearly was.'

After I had been going into things for over an hour, I felt clean and clear and wanted so much to join up with the rest of the group, wanted to rejoice with them, share my pleasure and gratitude. I thought Babs looked hostile though, and said so, and she said she was waiting for the group to end so she could go to bed. I got up and went to the kitchen, feeling hurt and cheated. I started to talk to Alex and got gay and merry there, feeling like a child pleased with itself, or like at the end of an acid trip. Then the kitchen was full of people again, Babs and her friend. I felt angry, I went into another room. Everyone seemed to follow, so I left the house. I walked half the way home, needing urgently to talk and dreading to find Jerry asleep. He said, 'Tell me about it in the morning.' I lay in bed, trying to be a good child. I cried a few tears, and tried to enjoy what had happened to me all on my own, curled up. But suddenly I was swept with fury at what Babs had done: cheated me of my pleasure. I longed for David and the way he rejoices with me when I have had a breakthrough. I felt this was one of the most important days of my life, a kind of 'ending' within the long therapy journey.

It was two o'clock in the morning, but I got up and phoned Alex. This was a big risk, because he's often impatient on the phone. He was a bit short with me at first, but I kept talking. Suddenly, as often happens with him, he softened and got involved and interested and really listened and told me that he's often jealous of the way I go into things and he's sure the others are. He called it 'blasting off into my soliloquys' and said I have the energy of a child which is difficult to stay with sometimes. I felt relieved to hear this, to know that the prickles I felt coming at me weren't just paranoia. I was being satisfied. I had needed something badly, had taken a risk, had gone out, and got it. I slept soundly that night, but produced this nightmare:

Cannibal dream
I was being chased, for hours on end it seemed. I was to be sacrificed and eaten. The dream was a maze of me running, running, always knowing I couldn't escape. Sometimes I ran to my mother, but she turned out to be in league with the attackers. One by one, each of the people I tried to get help from turned out to be in league with the enemy, and each time this discovery was a fierce shock. After hours of life and death chase, I had just about given up, when the whole group of them just laughed and said, 'You didn't think we really meant it, did you? You didn't really think we were going to eat you?'

Letter to David, 29th December, 1972
I don't feel able to get across the enormity of the joy and pride I feel in this bad Christmas trip turning on its own natural

wave inside my body. It seems my head is far, far behind where my body's at. My head is stuck in old grooves. I expect to be stuck; I expect to feel bad. I expect to have to work hard to feel clearly. I have never felt such sharp, sudden contrast in the therapy before: the depths of sullen, schizoid depression, then *wham bham* into good body feelings, dancing like never before, feeling at one with myself, a child showing off, yes, but with pride and pleasure and confidence. And then yesterday, the most extraordinary body movements in my session, my whole body taking over in the orgasm reflex as I cried out my need and my anger and my pleasure. All my feelings were available, and no heavy digging to be done.

Maybe when the grownups get pissed off with me and want some peace, or put me down, I will be thrown again, but my bounceability is back to stay it seems and even when my head says 'oh, my god, look at the hole I'm in', my body pops up and says, 'oh? I hadn't noticed' and carries on regardless.

Well David, what an amazing thing it is we have explored.

Jen.

The same day, I wrote this letter to my mother. She never answered it:

Dear Mum,

I want to tell you that I am thirty and feel younger and happier than ever in my life before. I have been on a long and rocky journey these past four years and I am far enough up the mountain now to see back down over where I have come from, and to see it in perspective.

Last night, in one of our groups, I went through one of the most important emotional breakthroughs so far where I got beyond the anger and fury I have felt about being laughed at as a child, not taken seriously, to a feeling of being part of a chain — it was almost as if I could see you sitting as a tiny child in the Victorian atmosphere of your family and being talked out of your rage or hurt by polite voices, jollied out of the things you were feeling when you were still a warm little animal in tight dresses and a tight world. And I was calling out to you and saying, 'Is that right, is that what they did to you when you were little?' Is that why you had to laugh at me, to tell me I didn't mean it when I was angry as a child? And I felt terrible sorrow for you, that in a way you are a sacrifice — there wasn't any therapy or clarity about emotions when you were in the CP with all its great ideas about freedom. I am not putting down what was going on then, but I feel that the kind of help that is available today just wasn't around then. I nearly died before I got to it, I nearly killed myself in my twenties because of the pentup fury and chaos of feelings inside me that I didn't understand. I was nearly a sacrifice too, and Becky was nearly a sacrifice, because not understanding my own childhood, how could I understand hers?

So what is happening to me now is that I am working through the nightmare feelings inside me enough to get glimpses of the sunlight in between, of the many good things you gave me, especially the ability to stand up and fight and to feel things strongly and to question authority, and the warmth that you must have given me when I was very tiny, because I feel a tremendous capacity in me to love life and living things and that can only come through a mother's warmth.

I have had to fight you for a long time in order to survive, because you are a very strong woman on the surface, and you damn nearly crushed the life out of me. But my fight is nearing its end, and now that I am feeling the weakness and fear inside me, I can also get in touch with the weakness and fear inside you, and that makes me feel very close to you and makes me suffer when I see you holding in your softer feelings as I held mine in for so long. One day can be a lifetime and I believe you can begin to live at sixty-two or at thirty, and that for me doesn't mean 'putting a brave face on it', but letting go and sobbing if you feel frightened and reaching out for help if you feel in need. I closed off from you when I was about eight, and it has taken me four years of therapy to go through my childhood again and bring alive the deadened parts of my body so I can feel again. I have a long way to go, but I would like to share what I have gained so far with you.

My love, Jenny

Letter from David, January 1st, 1973

Dear Jen,

Your letter to your Mum was unbelievable. That you can let her see your softness now, let yourself be moved by her. You are down at the roots of healing.

As 1972 ends, I want to rejoice with you at the breaking of that chain — the chain Reich said was 6,000 years long. And to send my love to you for the New Year, and to Becky and your Mum; and to all those working with you, and sometimes against you, to break chains or make joins.

David.

The tide turns

I paid my maiden aunts a New Year visit, reluctantly.

I held my feelings all day with those sad aunties and their fourteen-year-old she-dog, perturbed at her own unheld-peeing. My Mum's elder sister, proud, with all her insides taken out so she can no longer hold her shit; my Mum's aunt, still beautiful through her death-white skin and black-ringed eyes; my Mum's cousin, driving her car with the murderous insensitivity with which she must once have driven the girlchildren of her school. And then in the afternoon, my swollen mother with her pasty face, a spark of the old life coming out of her now and again, a few words of unconscious put-down to her older sister for cruelties long buried, then the overwhelming sadness and fear, the everheld tears behind glazed eyes. My family is so female, but where are the mothers?

My stepfather still lives. From a different generation, he patiently tries to live for the old; son of country-people, he knows the aged cannot be left to die alone without incurring the sky's wrath. But his push is still there, the male push he was never allowed to express with my mother. And it is urging him back to work, to give up being nursemaid to his ailing wife; back to work where he can be a man, where people know his worth, where he is not just a worm that may some day turn. But her need is great now, even she cannot hide her dependency. An intimacy he is allowed at last that no other may share, in the middle of her frightened nights, the intimacy of her terror, of her bursting lungs and pounding heart and tear-filled legs.

He could talk with me now, talk out his worries. Such contact had always been within reach, but I said, 'NO, if I cannot have my Dad, I will not have you.' So the hug I gave him at the end of the day was the only real life of that day, except for the shells I found on the beach, homes of animals that had given up their lives naturally, quickly, in the fullness of time.

On 3rd January, I had a session with Jenny P. who lives in our house. I worked on painful feelings about some of my closest friends leaving the therapy groups we had developed and going into primal therapy. Thinking of one girl I was particularly fond of, I was crying, 'You have given up warmth and darkness for the bright lights; you have exchanged a difficult and growing relationship for the con of the quick cure, the big names, the new labels. You have thrown me and our friendship away.' I cried for the trust we had lost, for the sister I could have had, for the quarrels we were on the verge of having that would have healed and sealed our love for good.

I saw my friend as my sister, coming into a ready-made world, the path through the jungle already cut; not scared to yell out loud for what she needs, like I am. I cried once more with the pain of being first, of being the first to push my head out, to cut that path. I hated the precious babies who come second. I remembered the struggle of the years when there was no other therapy, just David and me and a lot of people to fight against.

After my session, I lay with warmth all around me; I lay and looked at the bright warm colours in a child's room that was no longer hostile or frightening. I was going to get up and hug Jen for her help, the kitchen-help, bathroom-help, stairway-help, the help that is so here-and-now that I too had almost passed it by, almost missed this warm help lying in the dark corners of a place called home, almost fallen into the trap and gone out into the cold city to seek the bright lights and the big names and the latest brand of Omo. But then I woke up, and found I had slept half way through the night, the sleep of a child fed.

Letter to David, 4th January, 1973
My very dear David,

Can it be that these things can come together, the releasing flow of my period coinciding with the wave opening within me?

David, you know what I was going to do yesterday, before the session with Jen? I was planning to put myself away for another week, find myself somewhere cold and hard where I don't want to be, and have intensive therapy. Sure, I need a lot of therapy at the moment, but the putting away, I see that now as a mixture of fear of being left behind, fear of not 'doing it properly', of the pointing finger which says, 'You are no good, you are a fraud because you have not done it The Only Way', and also this anxiety I have about pleasure, that I am not supposed to feel the joy and contact I do in my life as I have made it: that somehow to find the joys I have struggled four years in therapy for means that I am neurotic; if I were becoming 'really healthy', I would be eternally sad and soulful and would go around with a halo of Primal Pain shining above my head, so that everyone would see and know immediately, 'Ah, she has crucified herself in the befitting manner.'

But I let in Jenny P., the little sparrow of sunlight that sings me songs in the kitchen, and I let myself know that to stay at home is the most difficult thing in the world, to stay with the worries and dirt and ecstasy of the dogs, to stay with Becky's need for me, and with mine to be accepted and recognized and loved for what is big inside me as well as what is little.

David, I love you so much because you have helped me to love myself and my stepfather and my mother and to break a chain so terrifying that no brute force could move it; you helped with the persuasion and respect that comes from having also been a link in a terrible chain and escaped.

5th January, 1973

Exhausted after a day of intense interaction, I collapsed into m room late at night and cried because of all the demands on me.

There is no space for me. I realized how I am a controlled claustrophobic, the walls were coming in on me now, the street and the neighbours so close, people above me in the attic and below me in the kitchen, my ever-opening door and my room getting as narrow as a crack between moving rocks. Terror was moving up; lying clothes gathered themselves together to become pouncing animals, my dog Sally became an unpredictable monster when I turned my back, and if I didn't look, I could feel Alex rear up and grin and stretch his claws. But I could feel, too, a warm kernel in the very middle of me, and I knew I was ready to scream at the terror.

But then, Jerry began to sob enormously in the next room: my crying had started him off. I stopped, I shut down. I was in a cold fury of hatred. My beautiful feeling had been taken away. I went almost psychotic: I truly believed it was Impossible to cry when someone else was crying. He was the baby, I had to be grown up. I could not compete: the other couple in the house could not cope with us both crying at the same time, that's what I imagined. I had to stop.

It wasn't until Jerry actually stopped crying that I slowly wakened to the fact that it wasn't a cosmic law that I couldn't compete. This horrid experience was worthwhile just to realize the total lack of insight I have into myself when I am locked in something deep.

Session with Jerry, 6th January, 1973

Jerry is leaving the house for an experimental two weeks tomorrow. He sat in the kitchen with me and delivered what I call one of his 'tragedy' speeches. I went numb. I listened, there was a silence like death inside me. I kind of side-stepped out of my body and said to myself: 'Is this happening to me? Does he mean me?' Tears came, and I asked Jerry for help.

He was a bit rough working with me, but I got through to some vital realizations. I started by asking my mother what she'd done to me. I felt the dumbness of my early childhood return; I was silent for a long while. Then I told my Mum very quietly, 'Mum, — I can go inside other people.' Then, 'I will be a very good therapist when I grow up.' At that, I burst into agonized sobbing, feeling how good I was at being for other people. I continued, 'It's good you taught me to be generous, that's a good thing to be. You taught me not to tread on ants because...' and then I screamed and went into very deep, horrified crying. The rest of her teaching was, 'BECAUSE THE ANT MIGHT BE OUT SHOPPING FOR ITS MOTHER AND SHE WOULD WORRY WHERE IT HAD GOT TO.' I nearly went crazy, seeing for the first time the monstrosity of this simple, twisted sentence. I screamed, 'Mum, you should never have said that. Do you see what you did? You should have said, 'because it hurts to have a great big foot come down on you and crush you to death.' I felt I was struggling for my life, I was drowning, and yelling to Jerry to bring me out of the flood of feeling. I held Jerry's hand to gain the strength to go further. I saw the word SCHIZOPHRENIC written in the air, and could hear it. I cried that I was all present, with no past, no legs or roots. I hadn't existed as a child. I cried that I was a victim out of Laing's books, not Janov's. Always inside other people, great lover, friend, therapist: a ghost can get under anyone's skin. I understood now the awkward, slipping feeling I get when people pay me compliments. I feel it has nothing to do with me, I had no choice other than to be 'kind and giving'. It means nothing to me to be told I am those things. I want to be told I am cheeky and boisterous and impossible.

I felt I had come from outer space and landed in my Mum's house and there she was telling me she is my mother, and that is my sister, and this is my aunt — and I am listening and looking and trying to understand, but I am frowning, none of it means anything to me, I feel no connection with these strange people.

As my session ended, I understood my envy of the people who have been hit, like Julie and Jerry, because they have stories to tell, they can tell dreadful tales of being beaten and locked in cupboards, but I have nothing to tell, just a perfect mother saying, 'Don't tread on ants because their mother might worry where they've got to.'

Just then, Becky came to my room. I asked her what she

thought about ants. She said, 'Ugh! They're horrid squiggly creatures that sting me.' I said, 'What! You mean to say you can't make yourself into an ant and feel what it's like to be one? ' She said, 'No. I'm my very own me.'

Letter to David, 7th January, 1973
Dear David,

I feel that this is the climax of the joining of life and therapy, that the two can never again be separate for me. Long ago, the groups were a first step. Working with Jenny P. many months ago was a further step: to ask a friend to help me live. But it was the day Alex got me to stay with my feelings and with him and not run home to 'session my feelings away' that I learnt my biggest lesson in therapy. And now being with Alex is just one long encounter group, which means simply that my life is no longer lived in a fog between sessions. Living becomes a full-time occupation instead of something I do two or three times a week when the 'space' is available.

This is a period of intense learning for me. I am feeling scared of dying again, which means I am savouring life so fully that the loss of my past is bitter to me and I do not want to lose my future. I am greedy for each moment. The groups, which so recently were oxygen and water to me, have once again become occasions when I enjoy my skill as a therapist and often also become very weary of it. The times I go best into my own feelings are when the tiredness of the night or the tightbellied anxiety of the morning is upon me. Or suddenly, alone, my hands on a typewriter, no separation between the words I am writing and the feelings behind them.

I am smaller than ever before. I am that ant, not so much concerned, however, with the foot that threatens to crush me, as with the amazing natural organization of life around me. Now I have allowed myself to sink into chaos, perfect order emerges. I understand now why men out-of-touch with their feelings have not been able to perceive such order without inventing some string-pulling god to explain it.

I started my relationship with Jerry in a tradition, on both our parts, of hiding need. I am relating to Alex in a tradition of public feelings, public anger, yelled-out need, open sadness.

I am having what was Jerry's room soundproofed in order to start giving therapy again. I do not enjoy being an ant who is more concerned about my waiting mother than about my own fear, but as the lunatic reasonableness of my background has given me a certain ability, I will enjoy using it.

Sunday group, same day

As always, noises 'off' were alarming me. I lay down and got into terror. A paper flower above me became a threatening face, every movement in the room freaked me. Trying to tell my mother about my fear, I realized I was telling her about herself, her other self, the snarling monster. If I let myself see that this gentle woman standing over me was the same person as that monster, then she would be the monster all the time and I would be stuck in total terror forever.

I started trying to control the people in the room not to frighten me, like my Mum, who had been freaked by any sudden move on my part. I was furious when I saw this and screamed at her, 'If you're frightened, find a fucking grown-up to look after you and don't feed me with your fear.' I play-acted Mum's hysterical 'heart-attack' fit. Immediately, I felt an ice-cold hostility coming into me. I looked up at Alex and asked, 'Did you say, *that's enough of that*, when I screamed? ' He has said no such thing. I felt out the words I had projected and a calamitous realization hit me: I was getting in touch with my father, with how *he* had treated me in my early years. I saw how I was stuck between Scylla and Charybdis: Mum pumping me full of hysterical fears, and when I tried to spew it out of my body, there was dad's icy contempt, shutting me up, 'silly hysterical little bitch'. I swore and raged at him, hating him hotly, feeling glad he was dead; I yelled at both of them for the bloody marvellous team they made. And I felt my own despair.

I came out of this session shattered. I knew I'd only let a tiny bit of this 'new' side of Dad come into me. I feel I cannot be the same person again now that I have seen him. I was subdued, broken. I saw how many of the things I have blamed Mum for were his fault too. In the toilet, I looked at my face in the mirror. My eyes were big, big with fear. I felt I could never go on gaiety trips again.

Alex and me

I can feel all over my body a hunger I used to confuse with sexual frustration. I want unending contact with Alex, and yet I hate it too, because I can feel my chains, feel I am not free; my hunger is so great that there is anger just below the surface because I cannot feel fulfilment even when he gives his body to me.

Somewhere in the timeless hours of the night, we wake up and talk. I am able to tell Alex of the times I have taken sex without any warm feeling for the guy I am with, just to keep the cold away. I told him how to be offered a hot penis that says 'I want you' is like offering a full breast to a starving baby; to say 'no' is unthinkable. Alex is full of tolerance for the things I tell him; I don't ever remember experiencing such acceptance since the first session with David. A friendship like this is as precious as a good mother.

One afternoon, I fell deeply asleep on my bed alone in the late afternoon. I woke up anxious. I was scared to be found sleeping there, wrapped in the sensuousness of giving in to a pressing need. Alex came in and lay too close. I moved him away and talked about the hazy feeling I have already after only a couple of days of him being here; how I have lost my outline, I am not born. I want to be attached to his skin the whole time; the more contact I have, the more I want, on and on forever. If he moves away to prepare food or have a bath, I am desolated; rage and fury follow quickly. I have to hold myself back from rushing after him. I am a very unseparate toddler and something about my mother is preventing me from growing up.

Working on this feeling, the smoothly rebounding yo-yo of time took me on a much more recent journey. I let myself imagine Mum coming in at the door, finding me lying on the bed in the afternoon, sleeping not to schedule. She is heavy; she keeps bringing me cups of tea every morning of my life. It seems to be a nice thing to do, but it is veiled control. I am being woken up. Even when I am married, she does the same thing, a sexual intrusion. She has her claws into my waking and my sleeping, my breathing and my shitting.

I get the shudders to think I am anything like her. Alex asks me: 'How would you like to be?' I say I want to be someone who glides around. I want to have an air of serenity about me, I want to spread peace and calm wherever I go. I want never to frighten anybody, never to be the sort of person people can have witch-mother transferences on to. I want to relax people just by being with them. I want to be my age.

My voice is calm and quiet when I say these things; Alex is very much with me; his face is soft and alive. He tells me, 'Jen, you are already so much like this; you have a very rigid image of yourself.' I feel sadness and pleasure at his words; I cannot feel this is me, I have been so differently defined.

Then I imagine Mum coming to visit me. I say to her, 'Sit down, Mum. I'll get the chair you like. Don't worry about anything, you don't have to do anything, I'll fetch you anything you want. Just sit and breathe. I want you to cry, you can cry, it's all right. I haven't got to go anywhere, I haven't got to do anything, I'll stay with you, I've got all the time in the world, I am absolutely with you.'

That's what I wanted her to give me when I was a baby. I was sad thinking, 'I don't give Becky that.'

I moved on then to feelings aroused in me by my sister's therapy writings, which I had seen last night. She talked of Mum's violence to me when I was a teenager. Somehow, there was something sensuous about feeling Mum beating my head on the floor: for if Mum was beating me up, it meant I *was* different from her, separate from her; I *had* got away, and become a person of my own. It meant I was becoming sexual. I was following my body and going on my own way, and she couldn't stand it. As I cried with the humiliation of letting her beat me up without resistance, my body felt long and I had long, thin legs; I was thirteen.

I had a bath after the session and could think and feel clearly for the first time for days. The house feels marvellous, light and bright and warm, with winter grey and dirt outside. It feels like a good Christmas. There is no structuring of time. I lie awake with Alex for hours in the middle of the night. I sleep any time, morning, afternoon or evening. Sometimes at nine o'clock at night, the day is just beginning. My mother really is losing control of me. I feel relaxed with Becky. She comes to me and the way we hold each other is sometimes loose and complete. She said once, with more naturalness and passion than any lover: 'Oh, I do love you.' I only went a tiny bit tight.

Letter from David, 9th January, 1973
Dear Jen,

Yes, waves are opening in you, everything you write now has a different quality, such an unstuckness, whatever dark days come there is a centre of sun in you now no bitterness will put out. There are so many new currents and inflexions in what you write, I can't find words for the quality, it's a sound in your words which reminds me of your head no longer cold to hold; your writing flows amazingly little ant, it will be a marvellous life you are shaping as you cut loose the strings of hysteria. Ants are survivors, they come through fire and flood. You are turning your nightmares inside out so that the fears can be faced in the daylight.

You seem so much more able to give to and take from where your true need steers you; no-one has the power to rob you of what you have won. For so long, the people in your life existed in what you wrote only like shadows, all the colour was in your feelings, people were the ghosts you had to control, while you felt you had no existence outside them. If you were two-dimensional once, on your long journey to breathe, they seemed paper-thin. Now as you write, they take a life of their own.

To be able to love not only your Dad you never had, but your Mum who never let you have yourself would be to become three-dimensional, but there are four dimensions in you now: neurosis is stuck time, and you have set yours free, so there are these ongoing rhythms of the waves that come to me from your letter. So you will never wear that halo of primal pain; neurosis is the crucifixion, not therapy. Therapy means getting down off the cross and being able to walk and see the sun again; not the passion of wounds forever. It means living and one day dying in your own time and space, from which you can reach those still trapped out of their bodies perhaps, and those waking with you from sleep.

Love, David.

11th January, 1973

Alex moved into the house a few days ago.

The house is zinging. I have discovered I do not mind carting cups of tea up and down stairs when men are making me a home; I do not mind doing other people's washing up when the other people are my people. I sit in the kitchen. I tell Jenny P. gently about what I get from Alex. She bursts into tears. Something is happening in this house. The hammers are banging upstairs, soundproofing the therapy room. The cooking is steaming in the kitchen. Becky is crying a lot lately. She is crying for her Daddy. She is telling me she hates me. And she is telling me she loves me. Her friend has fallen in love with Alex. I have fallen in love with life.

Four years after the beginning of my therapy, I, who was cold and ugly, have come together with someone else I thought was cold and ugly. We relate not as two halves to make ourselves feel whole, but as two amazingly different individuals whose heads met first, and whose bodies followed.

Session with David, first for five weeks, 13th January, 1973

I was talking about pleasure and the primal pain thing when I burst into tears, saying, 'I have been in primal isolation all my life.' I cried, 'David, it's not right for me, it's not right for me, it really isn't. I go cold and dead when I'm alone. I feel, I open, when I am close to someone. David, I do not have to be alone any more.' I felt the crushing weight of what I'd nearly done to myself these last six months with the whole 'primal trip': I'd humbled myself inside, been unconfident of where I was at,

thought I was 'doing it wrong'. I'd almost automatically
assumed Jerry was somehow 'ahead' of me and that the others
were right, whilst all the time my body and my feelings were
screaming out that they were not. I said, 'David, I nearly fell
in the trap', and then I started crying much deeper, calling
out to David; and I held him like I've never held anyone before
in my life, and sobbed my guts out, held tight on to him and
knew what he meant that time he said his problem with my
sister was to get her to stop clinging and his problem with me
was to get me to cling. I felt now just how right he was,
clinging opened me to my roots, I felt David's body crying with
me. I cried on and on, saying how primal isolation might be
right for people who had pampered themselves, rich people
from the Jewish culture, but it certainly wasn't right for
Scottish Presbyterians like Alex or communist atheists, people
from the puritanical cultures. I had never given myself anything,
I'd lived as a stoic, constantly depriving myself, and *that* was
my defence. To sleep when I want, eat only food I like and not
'what is good for me', to love a person and really let him in, to
let myself rejoice in the comfort and safety of a total relationship, these things are what soften me up, what 'get me into my
feelings'. I sobbed to think of what I'd nearly done to myself,
how I'd nearly fallen into the trap of further deprivation, and
how wrong it would have been for someone as cold and lonely
as Alex has been to have that kind of therapy. I realized how
Jerry had nearly convinced me to give up David, give up the
comfort, the love, the healing, because I was *enjoying* it, give up
my groups because I revelled in them, give up Martin because I
got so much fun out of our relationship.

   When I had stopped crying, I just lay and looked at David.
We were both a bit shy. David said, 'You have been a very loyal
patient.'

That same day, I cut my hair. I was cleaning the kitchen floor.
My hair was a nuisance. I suddenly saw that I had not changed
it for twenty-two years: I had clung to the protection of my
long hair, hair to make me feel female, to make me attractive,
sexy, loved. I have hidden the boy in me, the long-limbed free-

moving pube, the aggressive, sure-minded, growing child.

I went upstairs and closeted myself with a good mirror, a pair of scissors, behind a locked door. I took my time. I do not have rose-bud lips, a button nose, skin like peaches and cream. I am angular, I am strong. I started cutting, I cut away the dead ends I had clung on to, I cut away the white hairs I had sighingly let grow. I cut away the annoying fuzz that flaps in my face when I bend down. I cut slowly, non-aggressively. I thought and felt all the time I cut. I was prepared to cut all my hair off and have a woolly crew-cut if that's where the trip took me. My new shoulder-length hair bounced; it was pleased with itself, and with getting rid of the dead weight. My pale forehead breathed easier without the mat of undergrowth suffocating it. My ears called out to be free, and I responded. My cheeks complained at the itching ends. I freed them. I shook my head and cut away any hair that got in the way of feeling free.

I am left with long bushy hair that feels good. I have let the boy in me surface, and consequently feel fully female, fully sexual. I am loved so I have no need to try and feel pretty. The kids responded joyfully as they burst in the door.

Sunday, 14th January, 1973

After my session yesterday, I had gone to bed feeling healthy and open and cleared out. Then up came the next set of traumas to be faced, a whole nightful of nightmares, each one ending with a strong emotion and the frustration of not being able to express it.

But something else has been happening in the middle of my nights this past week: Alex listens. I can't believe it's happening: this isn't a therapy session, in the middle of the night. Alex is not duty-bound to lie and take my feelings. Yet not only is he not cutting off when I tell him about my sexual frustrations, he is holding me, holding me while I rant and rave. He does not let go. I cry in anger at being a little girl. Alex breathes, he is moved inside. Not only does he listen, stay with me, hold me, he is moved. This can't be happening: my man says he can feel what it must be like to be a girl.

I was able to tell him: Boys can do what they like. Sex is easy for them. Girls have to wait, they cannot take what they want. Girls have to pretend not to want. Girls have to be eternally grown-up. They have constantly to stroke the male ego to keep it erect. I may not hint at dissatisfaction, at despair, because that would reflect on my man, he would deflate, he would not be able to stand up, he would not be able to hold me up. He would hate me; he might kill me. He would leave me in the cold until I reassured him once more that he was perfect. Men are always my mother. She is an over-inflated balloon. Even the sight of a pin that might prick her sends her into a violent fury of fear and she bursts all over me.

The next day, I phoned Jerry. I could hardly believe it was him speaking to me. He said all the things I thought could never come from him: that he trusts the way I am doing things, that he was moved to insight about himself by watching Alex and me at the Friday group. A helpful friendship is growing under the debris of our broken dreams. His openness made me cry.

He came to the Sunday group, it was good to have him there. He helped to work on me. I felt how I hold back from 'going mad'. This for me means letting my greatest schizoid terror come up: that I have invented or dreamed my life, that everything is really happening within the confines of a padded cell at Bexley Mental Hospital, that this house, the people around me, the therapy, are all hallucinations and I will wake up to find ECT electrodes round my head and nurses bending over me smiling and saying, 'You'll be alright, just keep still, everything will be alright, you've been very ill, dear.'

After the group, I went to bed and Jerry came to say goodbye. He sat on the bed, and I burst into tears. I cried bitterly about the last six months. I felt how I'd lost my partner to another woman; how it was really Jerry that had left me, not the other way round, when he went off to that therapy; how I'd closed down for ever on him when I heard with shock that he was going to pay someone all that money for doing what we do anyway, when we could put our money together and get a green place in the clean air. I couldn't stop crying with relief and with the backlog of stored-up pain, and the sadness of not being able to turn the clock back. Alex came in, and he and Jerry held hands for a moment. After Jerry left, I carried on crying. I cried because therapy had been a world I had created to counteract the world of horror I was used to, and now suddenly the plague had contaminated this world too: an authoritarian therapy had appeared, like the authoritarian left-wing parties that mushroom on the soil of people's desire for freedom.

23rd January, 1973

In the night, with Alex, I got so high that the whole of my body came alive. I was very near to orgasm when I suddenly burst into tears. This is something that has happened many times: I call for my mother, as if I am calling to her to protect me from my feelings, as if I'm saying, 'I'll be good, I'm on your side, I won't feel this.' The difference this time was that I saw something that made me cry more and more: I saw a two-inch gap in my body at my waist-line. Below the line, I belonged to my father. Above it, I was my mother's. No energy could transfer across that line; I could not join chest and genital emotions. My lower half was secret, passionate, desperate, very much alive, but with no acknowledged identity. My upper half I accept, though I swallow my anger at having to give up my lower half. If I start to give in to Dad, to orgasm, to earth-feelings, terror seizes me: I will lose Mum, I will be hit.

During a very short session the next day, I remembered how my sister and I were always pretty united when we went to Dad's cold house. We cuddled together against the deadness of the atmosphere. Only when Mum was around did we fight to kill.

I was struck, between tears and laughter, by a sudden overwhelming feeling of the *fourness* of us: feeling the presence of my sister. I started to talk to her: did we play together, Snowy? I started to feel that I *had* loved her as a child, that when we'd quarrelled and weren't speaking, life got boring and dull, so that slowly in our children's way, we'd made approaches to one

another to have someone to play with. I have been very moved
by Leila Berg's book, 'Look at Kids', and saw how if only Snow
and me had been left alone to fight it out, we'd have sorted
things out in our own passionate and yet matter-of-fact way. I
was crying and I asked Snowy: 'Did you love me too, Snow? '
This thought was completely new to me; I had done so much to
deserve her hate, pouring mine into her.

I felt sunny and relieved at the end of this. A thirty-year
imbalance had been redressed: I'd had to fight so hard against
my Mum's sugar-pills in order to stay alive, that I'd made
everything black. Now that I doubt myself less and am not
afraid of losing touch with the hurt, I have room for the good
things. I feel as if I can allow my scowl to drop and my smile to
break out without losing myself.

2nd February, 1973

In a very bad state indeed, I got Alex to try and help me. I
couldn't find my way into anything. Then, when he went away
to the toilet, something loosened in me and I was able to kick.
I kicked vigorously and straight away got a very strong sensation
of my father just about two inches above my face. He was
menacing, his face and teeth and chest were huge. I was very
young, and very frightened. Things were coming at me, and
this time it wasn't Mum. I cried out, 'No! not you! I've got
enough to deal with already, without you as well.' My feeling
felt a life-time old, too big to bear, like a white flashing light
inside my head. So Dad had threatened me too. I felt crushed in
my head like when it all gets too much when you are very small.

Afterwards, I went into a schizoid state. I couldn't look at
Alex. I felt I was going to have a breakdown. I could hardly
move. I was relieved when he went to sleep somewhere else. I
imagined killing myself and how the whole house would fall
apart and the whole therapy scene too and how everyone would
have to give up therapy and my book would be no good and
Jerry would go mad and I don't know what David would do,
write a poem maybe.

And then I fell asleep. Alex came to me in the middle of the

night. I'd forgotten my hostility. I felt he was my good father.
I reached out my arms to him gladly and let contact seep back
into my body. My whole body was open and pouring with
energy. I thought, 'Well, however unhealthy I try to be, the four
years do tell.'

At this stage, David was somewhat alarmed at my wild mood
swings. So he did write a poem, the story of my therapy:

There was this hand
that was no good at holding;
it could not clutch
because there was no wrist;
it could not cling
for that would have been death
because it had no arm.
It was a man's hand
joined some way
to the body of a girl.

This hand was a claw
afraid to scratch
a hook that was flinched from.
Sometimes the hand hurt terribly.
Once it locked itself up with a razor
sometimes it wanted to turn into a fist
to break windows and let air in,
but somehow even when it wanted to die
it never slashed itself off.

The hand was good at stopping holes,
it could strangle unwanted sounds
tidy rooms, block up the mouth cries
of madness. It could carry
people. Once or twice
when there was nothing to hold on to,
and even stronghands can go weak as water,
it nearly drowned.
Once or twice, life nearly slipped through its fingers.

The hand did not want to know it belonged to a girl
afraid to be a woman;
it did not want to know it was joined to a wrist
that was joined to an arm
that belonged to a shoulder
that flowed into the neck
and above that the face it was used to hiding.
For a long time it did not want to let eyes peep through
its fingers.
It was a very shy hand.

But the hand wanted to say hello.
Sometimes it dared to reach out and give things,
oranges, or something to hold on to,
but still it was afraid to take,
it did not want to turn into a cup;
playing was not its function.

But the hand worked:
it squeezed some of its hate into a ball
and threw it across the room;
it opened so grief could run out of it;
when it was terrified it shook like a leaf
and learned to stop torturing itself.
The hand helped the head
to shape words;
it began to write about
its own pain.
It was a big hand with strong bones,
and when it sat up typing half the night
its fingers were wet with tears.
Although it was dumb, it learned to speak.

Big little hand hard to hold
that came so alone out of dark
little blue little cold hand
that can lie
in the grip of the warm
in the hollow of a neck of a man
and not break
out of touch
when you cry,
let the ache,
as you curl and uncurl
slip out of you.
Old little young little hand of a girl
hold tight.

David

5th February, 1973
Dear David,

I'm back! I've been gone for about five days, but I'm in my skin again, and I don't really know how the going happened, or the coming back. The tide just turns, and here I am.

Yesterday, we had a big twelve-hour group. All our new patients had joined in. Good work, chaos, fun, deadness, happenings; people came, people left; people slept, I slept. Outrageous goings-on no therapy book has catalogued. Sometimes the way to love someone is to laugh at their pathetic defences, rape them into fighting back when once they were raped out of it. And the three 'therapists', Peter, Alex and me, all jumping over one another while our 'patients' looked on, stunned, or amused, or indifferent.

And this morning, I gave a session to Jeff. I lay there, quieter than you. I watched my anxiousness to intervene, accepted his reprimands, and it just happened, a five-minute-long two hours of peace and learning for me, no words, while Jeff went into his body, left behind his Ph.D and his head that drives him crazy. He is outrageous, he makes sounds and movements that I don't dare to, this person coming to me for therapy and teaching me so much. This guy, who had been so hostile, curled up tired at the end, nearly crying with relief and just looked up and said,

'I'm so glad I found you and this place.' How could I tell him, David, there was no way to tell him. I just held the hand he reached out, held it, so together in our separateness, over seas of different life-experiences. He just happened to be somewhere at the right time and knew someone who knew me, and what I know now is that if you start every day knowing nothing, life is pretty wonderful.

David, take only my happiness seriously now, and not my swings down.

5th March, 1973

At eleven o'clock at night, I went to the therapy room and started working on myself, focussing firstly on the annoyance I feel at Alex' gaiety round the house, which I feel as a cover-up for other feelings. He is like my Mum, singing always, no matter what is going on inside her, or inside me. I moved on to David: I felt he was overgay at where I am at. I started crying and went on a big trip about me being his potted plant and he is gloating over me, and really things aren't OK at all. I feel he is sitting back and saying, 'the job's done' and here I am still fighting to keep alive. My trip deepened and got very bad: I felt David was insane, a maniac, and I am his monster and he needs me to keep his own madness going, and he has to praise me no matter what is going on. I got to feeling I had dragged a whole band of disciples after me, getting them all to believe in therapy but god is mad and I am on the cross and suddenly I see it is all credo and doesn't work and we've created this massive superstructure and really there's nothing I can do even to help myself. And my father has forsaken me.

I am swimming, I am really alone. Therapy has fallen away; David has fallen. The house is madness, nothing is left.

After a lot of crying, I surfaced for a while, looked up and felt how organizing my relationship with Alex in the fitting manner is still following Mum's way; following my 'mad' feelings about Mark, having a session at midnight, not writing up my therapy-sessions, filling the house with people, this is letting go of Mum, letting my legs judder was to be not-her, was to be in a way that would horrify her. I let go of her in that moment, and she faded into the distance. Straight away, my crying softened and deepened, the sounds came from the middlest part of me and I cried and cried for my Daddy, just saying his name, each sound travelling right through my body with no blocking, long and clear and soft till I had finished. My body was very young and I was very separate from the other people who had come in. It was one o'clock and I went to bed.

10th March, 1973

What has been happening?

I haven't been doing anything. Structures have dropped away. I often don't do the shopping or cleaning 'at the right time'. I never read. I haven't been writing. I haven't been high or terribly low. Sometimes I think I'm pretty dead. Yesterday I went out, weak, after a few days with a dreadful sore throat after that session about my Dad. I thought I'd find myself dead, but a bird singing on a dirt-stained 'green' at Shepherds Bush made me cry and telling an old woman it wasn't safe to cross the road brought contact back to the steel and poison madness of our highly-organized roads. I felt weak, but alive, and even laughed a little to see only one person sitting in each of those poison-spewing metal monsters, knowing it all has to come to an end, even without me trying to do anything about it.

I feel ready to leave the city now. Even the word therapy gives me claustrophobia. I have given up all idea of system or working through steadily to my core. Maybe the primal people are right and you can programme and structure growth, but I have started on a muddy path through an overgrown wood and keep getting lost just standing looking at the trees. I guess I will wander on my way as best I can, I cannot start a streamlined campaign to eradicate my mother and father from my veins at this stage. I feel ready to open to the sorrow when it hits me and will hope to open to pleasure also. I am tired, and the problems of the people around me who hope for my help appal me. My credo is no longer clear-cut; all I see is muddling through as best we can. I cannot be a primal therapist without becoming a machine, and I have worked long enough to do away with that. My throat hurts and I seek comfort cuddled up in the nearest arms available; I know no other way. I leave people to die when I have no strength to move, and open my face to them when the mood takes me. I have failed in all my images, but I feel closer to Becky and the dog and the grass than ever before.

On my birthday, 11th April, my mother phoned me. Her voice was broken, young, helpless, frightened, her pretences fallen away. She is admitting in her own way that the end has come for her. When I told my sister that she will die soon, Snowy scoffed and said, 'She's not dying! She'll live for another twenty years.' I felt then that Mum had lost Snowy and that it was like back at the beginning, just me and her.

In my next session with David, I felt as if going back to the beginning, back to my Mum, meant laying myself open to anyone who wants to harm me. I broke down, feeling suddenly what it was like to be little with my parents: both of them immersed in a hermetically-sealed system of ideas, both strong and determined. They had to be strong to be commies in the Cold War. They were people staunchly standing alone, broken out of their background moulds; they'd struggled hard for identity. I cried, 'It's no fun, no bloody fun being born to strong parents.' There was no room to breathe, no room for my individuality. I remembered how often I'd longed for a little brown Mum, a weak one, a nobody, someone I could look after.

A day in my life at PNP house, 30th April 1973

On the way home, there was my next-door neighbour and her two kids walking along in front of me, the kids crying as usual, she dragging them and nagging them, me tensing to hold back the freak I feel at the way they are being killed. Then she smacked her boy for crying. I went berserk. I yelled down the street, out of control, 'Carol, leave your kids alone!'. She turned back on me, all held-fury and drawn-up dignity, and said, 'I beg your pardon!' I thought she was going to hit me. She is big, and crazy. She told me I need a psychiatrist, that everyone in our house is insane, that she will call the police if there's any more banging, and that I am a drug addict. She also informed me her kids need disciplining. I told her she is a fucking cow.

My knees had turned to jelly by the time I got home. I felt near to tears. With my anger released, I felt soft towards my neighbour, wanting to tell her I understand, I know what tension can do. I felt so bad, I decided to write to her and went upstairs to do so. I was only half way up when there was a knock at the front door. Carol, plus two kids. She said, 'I want to tell you I don't like being shouted at in the street.' I was ready for battle. But she was crying already, collapsing on my shoulder, smelling of perfume and booze, sobbing, 'I've got enough to put up with in that house, I'm at my wits' end.' I was crying too, holding her. I kept saying, 'I know Carol, I know'. I took her to the kitchen and she stayed and talked and talked and talked. I showed her round the house so that it wouldn't be so mysterious to her; and I tried to tell her about the therapy.

I was bowled over by this experience, so beautiful, emotions flowing free and this brave, alive, hysterical woman daring to come to me — I dared not go to her — because she has nowhere to turn to, and something warms her to me in spite of her image of drugged-up hippies.

Meanwhile, some straight guy had arrived to find out about PNP. He sat in the kitchen with all this going on round him. I don't know if he ever got anything out of the experience, but he never came back. Then a woman from across the road came in crying; her husband hadn't come home in time to look after the kid, and she had to get to work. The kitchen was already full of little kids, one more made no difference. Then Helge arrived for his session, he was annoyed at being kept waiting. What was happening in the kitchen seemed more immediate to me and he had to wait. Finally though, I tore myself away and went to see him, forgetting Mark had told me to watch the cooking that he'd started while he had his bath. The cooking burnt. In the middle of the session I was giving, Mark pushed in to the therapy room, furious about half a dozen things at once.

I tried to cool him and continued giving the session. Then there was Becky hovering at the door. I said, 'It better be important.' She said, 'It is. Mark is tearing up your books.'

My nerve endings screeched. Panic for my file. I rushed into my room, which was covered with the snowflakes of tense anger, layered thick with book pages. I couldn't cope, and left, crying. Becky got Alex to deal with Mark.

Then I heard Becky crying, and Mark shouting. That was it, I had to give up the session. Mark was still tearing up books and I was furious. I yelled at him to stop, he went for me and threw me across the floor and Alex leapt, and I screamed at Alex not to hit him, and we dragged him instead to the therapy room, him fighting like five furies, and held him down so that he could yell and storm. I yelled at him in his face and he yelled back his hatred and I felt warm and safe and was glad at what we were doing. Tearing up books is better than leaving forever or taking cold pills. I felt in that moment that Mark was winning his battle. When he was quiet, I left him for a while. I went back later, and he was lying grinning to himself, an aura of peace surrounding him.

The next day, as I had planned, I took acid. My new friend Steve was in the kitchen and was being his usual honest self about not wanting Mark there. I felt threatened by this conflict and went upstairs on my own and cried, thinking of Mark and saying, 'I am so frightened to lose you, but I must be myself.' Then Mark came up and I spent two quiet hours with him. I was so peaceful, my body fullblooded lying there and looking at this beautiful boy who was soon to leave, and I was calm about it.

As soon as he left the room, and it had been so good with him, I burst into tears, saying to myself, 'I am so good at covering up how much I want you'. For over an hour, I worked with myself alone in that room, and this was the best part of the trip. I cried and cried for my Dad, for Mark, and when I abandoned myself to wanting him, the threat of Mum at the door came, and I was so proud of myself, because I was finally able to work with that fear, alone in the therapy room. I faced each wave of it set off by my dog stirring or the ghosts creaking in the walls or a sound outside. I yelled, 'get out of here, get out of me, leave me alone, let me be by myself, let me cry for my Dad.' I was sitting up, facing the room and my fear, giving in to it, riding my calm storm. I felt how desperate is my need to be alone, away from my mother, and how everyone that intrudes becomes her: the neighbours, the police, the shopkeepers. I had to find a way to be alone, but she was in the walls. I cried and screamed myself to a standstill and lay ready to open my stomach to breathing as never before.

But then Steve came in. I didn't want him there, I hadn't finished with myself. I said I wanted more time, I would come out and play later. But he said, 'I'm afraid this is reality, I'm here and you'll have to deal with it.'

Looking back, I know that I copped out. I should have risked losing him and got rid of him, energetically, not by politely asking him to go.

But I accepted his presence, his pleasance, I did not fight, I resigned myself to sharing my space once more. I still felt very good in my body after what I'd been through, hot with pulsating energy. I was very alive and very high and very sensitive. This was my downfall. Helge came in for a session, having refused to work with Alex, and I agreed to help him with Steve. I could see every shadow that passed across his mind, I was an angel of perception. BUT I FUCKED MYSELF UP. I left myself behind. All seemed well at first, but then I caught a shadow crossing Steve's face which I took as fedupness at me working with Helge. That did it. I was split. I needed Steve; my security was threatened. Something seized up inside me, I knew I had strangled a big feeling, my energy turned, I went cold. I asked Steve to take over. I lay back to be with myself and tried to get back to my good body again.

I leave the room, go downstairs. It is good again. I peep round my kitchen, feel the awkwardness of my strangely grown body with the damaged child inside, feel my un-at-homeness in my home, my checking up, sneaking, peering, to see whether everything is alright, whether everyone is there. I peer round corners, hate the hallway, the mess and dilapidation; and I feel its meaning: I am not comfortable in these walls. I feel an urge born of new health, to know this house and the people in it. I open Mike's door, without knocking, peer round, see his dying face and NEED written all over it. I shudder and shut the door before I can get caught up with that one. I climb the stairs, stop halfway, hearing Alex whistling in the bathroom. I feel at home on the stairs, my soft body sinking into the wood; I lean there, more relaxed and comfortable than on many a bed. I melt into the stairs and giggle to myself, I am enjoying being alive and loving myself.

I go into my room, my dog is there. Oh, Sally, you really are a different creature from me, I see how you are covered with fur and do not look like me. Your body quivers as I enter, your eyes turn to me, pleased recognition; you do not bother to move your lazy body; but your tail vibrates furiously to tell me I am someone you know and love. I start to talk to you. You do not answer! Oh, this is something new, a frustration, I cannot get you to answer me. You hear me, but my words mean nothing to you. I see! I have to speak your language if I want something from you. I have to growl and bite on a sheet for you to tug at, I have to lower my head and grab you with my teeth. Well, I won't! I feel how lonely I am, you are not like me, I have smooth skin. How can it be that you are alive, yet a different creature. Well, you really are a dumb creature. And your nose is a funny black spot. You are no good to me, I cannot play with you. I am alone; you are not a me.

So I curl up tense and cold in my bed. I have lost myself, tense about the arguing voices in the hallway. Where is the warm blood and the red light and my filled body? This can't go on. I must get back to myself. I go back to the therapy room; I lie down and breathe and make sounds and crying wells up. Well, that's all there is to therapy, isn't it? You cry and scream and react and it comes right. Doesn't it?

IT DOESN'T. This is bad, I am getting terrified, I am screaming at each wave of terror as it comes. I am doing all the Right Things. But my terror gets worse. Everything is changing into a very bad mother. I see Helge's face everywhere; he is my mother, and I am him. In my mind, I see Steve's and Alex' faces; they will help me. But their expressions change, they are becoming Her. Now the carrier-bag hanging on the wall is threatening. I have lost myself. It is very bad.

I run to the door and scream for Steve. He comes to help. I think it will be alright, he'll help me find myself, but no, it is still happening. I am still doing all the Right Things. I am crying softly with sadness, screaming with terror. I am saying, 'Mum, you are killing me, I am dying of fright, you have frightened me to death. I am already dead, I died then and everything since has been an invention. Mum, I cannot live when you frighten me so.'

But how is it that I am crying and yelling and feeling, and yet I do not exist? I have no centre: where is my crying coming from? This is a feeling I do not recognize: a feeling with noise, but I am in my head. My body is dead. I am all head and shoulders, and there is no me, only periphery.

I hold Steve's warm hand. I sob and cry about how my parents are quarrelling over me, I am made so important, and yet I do not exist. There is only their quarrelling; I have gone so dead and quiet I am not here, and yet I remain the All-Important subject of their quarrels. God help me, all these people quarrelling over someone who doesn't exist, in my present life as in the past. And yet I am in pain, in a terrible nightmare, a bodyless being in terror.

I say to Steve: 'I am never in one place. I cannot be with Him and Her together; they are not together. They were quarrelling before I was born. Was I conceived during a quarrel? I was born into the Split, there never was a joined-up place to get back to. My therapy cannot work, because I have no unified root, only a forked treetrunk, to work back to. So, with no beginning to get back to, the therapy becomes a nightmare. I can feel Mum; I can feel Dad; I am them, but I have no me.'

Steve says, 'Be with one of them.' I feel his warm hand and I feel how good my life is in the present. I let myself be comforted and I cry: 'Mummy, I want to be here with you. But I want you to let Daddy in too. I want you to love him. If you do not love him, you do not love me, because I am both of you.' I cry for a short while and then stay silent in a deep and terrible sadness.

The children come in, and the dog. Here is magic Kate who somehow always pings into existence when I take a trip. The kids are playing, they are alive. I am flattened and killed. I am sobbing still, feeling guilty for spoiling their world. I cry with the safety and warmth of Steve to nourish me. I am crying because I have died.

I lay after that for many hours in my room, in really bad body pain. Steve read me a beautiful poem he had written about the day we came together. I asked him to read it over and over again. Such peace, to let another person take the stage. I lay quietly, taken on a gentle trip by the rolling waves of his lines. I could not believe there could be such peace. Can I then feel music in my body, know at last a body pleasure from words used previously only to kill me?

Then Becky told her stories. This beautiful child. I lay on the floor and looked into her mouth and eyes: deep, questioning eyes, shaded somewhat with the pain of past hurts. There is no forgetting there in those eyes, she knows. She can never trust I may not strike again. There is a deep depression in my little girl. My heart aches as I see the wisdom in this little body, with baby's hands yet and fresh skin that can wince with the pain of a too-loud word, whose fibres cannot be fooled by any double-talk, by a reasonable word covering a tense muscle.

I stroked her to sleep and felt the death in my own body. I felt the peace and sadness, the dreaminess of this amazing boy from the railways who tells me in an accent that would make my mother's hair fall out, 'I'm the most uneducated person you'll ever meet', and who cannot open his mouth without wisdom and humour gushing from it; who writes poetry that lands me face to face with my own prejudices about such things not belonging to the working classes, and who after just a few weeks of knowing us gives therapy with the ease with which he pressed tube train buttons for eighteen months. The walls of my walled-in world are crumbling and their dust is soft to lie in.

So this is living, to lie with the knots of confusion in my stomach, the pain of brain battery in my head, and the scarlet peace of three beautiful beings surrounding me. My own mind too, is at peace, accepting that I cannot understand what happened to me today, that I can never be the same again, that from now on I must look open-eyed at the people I feud with and say, 'You know, I am very frightened.'

Earlier on, in the therapy room, I had worked with a mirror. I looked at my face. 'Look at it kindly, Jen, do not hate the mean chin and puckered mouth, the hungry teeth and that nose: am I really so ugly? Look rather at the eyes, crisscrossed with a century of knife-cuts. Don't look unkindly as They did: heal yourself with kind looks. Look, there is Mum's sister in your face; she always said you were like her sister, mean and cruel. And look! There is Dad in me, so clear. And Mum of course. So I really am all of them; what a strange creature.' Then I become scared staring in the silence. 'Who are you in there?' I have to stop, mirrors are bad, it makes me Two.

Later, in the kitchen, I let myself feel beautiful again. I am swathed in warm summer colours, the same orange as on the beach in Spain that time. It is difficult to sit here with these people when the giggling stops. I lie on the kitchen floor (is it alright to do that?). Jerry pops into my mind. The many faces of Jerry: strained and pale, ugly; then full and shiny-black, warm and strong; so funny you are, Jerry, what good times we had! His jokes, his strength comes through to me, then his hurt, and the sending away. I must tell you I am with you now. It is one o'clock, but I must speak to you. You can be angry if you like, I am going to phone you.

He is not angry. My 2p runs out, spent on giggles and teeth-chattering. He phones back and I put on an irate voice: 'How dare you phone this house at this time of night! Don't you know it's a hospital? ' He asks for the psychiatric unit. 'Can I speak to one of the patients? ' I hand the phone to Mike and he puts on one of his voices. He becomes the middle-aged German Jewish psychiatrist, high-pitched and hysterical. 'Vat iz deez, vy do you phone like deez, vat do you vant? ' Jerry can't make out who he is; I am in pain with laughing so much.

Then I talk to you Jerry lying on the bathroom floor for an hour. I tell you of my bodyless feelings today, but it does not come any clearer.

When we have separated, I lie still on the bathroom floor. It is so good to be alone. The gurglings of the water-cistern work on my stomach, popping the bubbles inside me, one by one, bubbles of tension bursting, to let my juices flow. I am coming back into myself. I will stay up all night.

In the morning, I wake tense and frightened after only two hours sleep. Calamity is all around me. This is the end, I am going to have to kill myself. Someone is coming for a session in one hour and I am dead tired. I cannot cope. And how am I going to explain to Mark the warmth I have with Steve; it will threaten him so. The pressure and conflict is too great; I am overladen with burdens once more. Hadn't I put them down? How is it that when I pick up warmth, I find myself with a stone round my neck? I must go away, I must die. And I have promised to go swimming with Becky. Swimming! And I can hardly stand, let alone walk. I cannot be a mother.

At the sink, trying to wash up, I desperately need help. Alex is there but I cannot say anything; I feel he is hostile. I cannot collapse because too many people are leaning on me, and I will be crushed under their weight when they fall down on top of me.

Suddenly, the dirty fork I am washing has no meaning. I stop, sit down. Alex asks me at last, 'How was your trip?' Tears come, and I say, very very frightening. I want to talk about it.

I recount what happened, and this time it makes sense. I see where I took wrong turnings. I see my need to be alone, and how scared I am of taking space, aggressively. An hour later, I am cleared out and in myself once more.

The last day of April, 1973
Dear David,

How to describe these days I am living through? I want to relish them forever. It is hard to remember not to try to hang on to happiness but to let it wane when it must.

I am frightened, nervous, neurotic, yes, spots and tightness and terrors in the waking night. But David, I am so full of joy I want to cry. My neurosis and my health are no longer things apart from my daily life. I live in a world that makes me cry to write about.

Yesterday Lazĺo complained 'so much hate and aggression in the group tonight.' YES, BEAUTIFUL WONDERFUL YES! I revel in the joy of the heat of that aggression, those people who in wanting to kill each other come so close together, closer than they've ever been to anyone before. I am proud of the fury that fell from me that set everyone going in our group, that electrified the energyless air of our stuffy room. I am amazed and amazed at the courage of these people, some of whom have been with us only a few days, who face the snake pit that can turn into a rose garden, these people who are so hungry to live they will risk the terror of an acidpill rather than live in the twilight forever.

I want to write another book, more like the one you wanted from me, that has People in it; the people who are my world, who are really here, whom I have not invented. I want to write of the love I see between people, twenty-year-old Steve who sits and works with the tenderness of a good mother on forty-five-year-old Ted, whose face alone can dissolve me to tears; Dan who reaches out again and again and again, desperately, to Martin; and Martin who kicks him back every time because of a fossilized fear of male contact and then one day gives in and lies sobbing in his arms for hours on end; Pete, who with his cheek turns up here without asking, takes acid, and then turns the whole house on with his vibes, awakening warmth and love in Steve and Helge that magic, because not their cold fathers, must have put there; Alex, swinging dangerously between ugly schizo-phrenia and the full-blooded fury that makes his face round and his eyes look straight in heat and self-assertion when the pride he picked up somewhere on the streets of Scotland is goaded to flame; Mark, who stays away because it aches so much to have to feel again, but whose honesty in the quiet hours keeps the contact going and whose aliveness to other people makes him forget his own game sometimes, of staying closed in pride; Mike who having retreated into largactyl to 'gain strength' as he says, returns, effectively having gained strength; his pain is white and terrible, I hardly dare reach out to him, it would be like touching someone burnt all over; and Helge, new to all this, brave and desperate, moving nervously, never still, trying to keep off the nightmare of his pale mother jumping from his tense bedroom to her death when he was three.

And what of my Becky who lives through this stormy sea, riding the waves with perfect serenity, falling into her own pits and fighting out her needs? My child, baby born of my brittleness and her father's plastered-over rage, grown up too soon like all the first-borns and only-borns before you, I am trying to give you back what I have stolen from you. I am paying you back slowly, the hugs you get are still asked-for, I still do not think to come to you. But your rocking-days will come; I will carry you through the babyhood I stole from you.

Letter to Mark, 4th May, 1973

Many good things are happening between me and you, slowly, quietly. But one thing I don't like is I feel I am colluding with you in keeping you safe by silently pretending you are the only soul in my universe. I can't live in this trap, it hurts my stomach; so I am going to try and tell you what you mean to me, and what other people are for me. For whatever reasons, I find it very exciting that you are a big hard man with a hot stormy sea just under the surface. I feel a deep pleasure when I watch you swim in that sea for a while; and I feel a deep pleasure when I allow myself to swim in my own sea in front of you. Swimming in my sea means being honest with you. Even when it means risking losing you; *especially* when it means risking losing you.

I wonder what you think I do when you're not here? Whatever you think I do, I must tell you; I carry on living, and that means relating; relating closely, on the level we have built in our groups. I am not a stranger to the people around me, and I do not lie to them about my feelings.

So I want to tell you about my relationship with Steve, because he is the person who is giving me most when you are not here. I do not want to pretend to you that he is 'nobody' or 'anybody' or of no significance to me. Steve is amazing. He is a very alive twenty-year-old whose freshness and no-bullshit honesty heal me; I cannot play games or pretend or hide in front of him. I feel accepted by him in a way I don't feel it from anyone else except perhaps Babs and Peter. There are things in

him that drive me crazy of course, things that awaken old
insecurities in me, like the way I feel him drifting off when I am
talking to him or reading to him. His independence and in-his-
self-ness throw me constantly back on my own internal
resources, and this makes me feel hurt and humbled and very
vulnerable. But I can listen to him endlessly, it fascinates me to
watch him, hear him read his things or talk. I know this may
puzzle, anger, hurt you, but that's how it is.

Steve cannot replace you, and because of this I have kept my
friendship with him quite hidden from you. But I cannot live
with myself if I have to pretend; I feel it has come down to you
dying or me killing myself. I am killing myself if I pretend to be
the sort of woman you need to fit in with your pain-cushioning;
I feel I am killing you if how I am forces you to leave this house
in pain and pride forever.

Letter from David, 7th May, 1973

Some feedback on last session, as you asked.

I see three strands in what is going on at present. They are all
related to identity.

To have an identity, you need a past. When you started
therapy, you were burning your bridges behind you, so there
was no continuity. Therapy became a process of opening up to
that past, of allowing all the projections to be felt, of thawing
out your cold shield so that feelings could run (instead of you
running to avoid them). Your book is the record of that process:
it is filled with immense energy, the energy it takes to explore
so much so intensely: it is a very strong sea you swim in.

So the first strand, the building of an identity through
owning back your past, assimilating it, going into your feelings,
swimming in that sea, is the most obvious strand.

The second strand is the fear that you have no identity, the
schizophrenic terror of being swallowed, of being taken over, of
being two-dimensional, of waking up to find nothing has
changed, of not being believed. The fear under acid was linked
to what you felt when you saw your Mum and Dad looking
back at you out of your face. So who is Jenny? All the energy
you pour out in your groups, where you are threatened by low-

energy situations, where you are threatened by the waiting atmosphere, which leads you time and again to jump in and activate, all this energy rides above your death-layer which you got in touch with again under acid, though you don't need acid to reach it.

It's as though at one level, the despair is a fear to be left alone, the need to hang on to the parent-figure, to prevent any more divorces, to stop outside splits. But the only way to stop outside splits is to keep yourself split. If, to keep Mark, you suppress the truth about Steve, you split yourself. If you heal yourself through honesty, you risk the outside split: that Mark will go cold on you, deny you, cut you up with words. It is what he could do to your sense of identity that you are afraid of, not his physical strength or his power to harm himself which your letter does so much to forestall.

At another level, the despair is a fear at not being left alone, at being smothered by people. You seem to structure your life so that you get smothered by people, who you then need your explosive energy to burst a clean therapeutic path out of. Acid asks questions: what if you cry and it does not lead you out, what if you rage and it does not lead you to a new identity? To be left alone is perhaps the most important freedom you have had to fight for: you won it, I think, from me in the therapy — you had to fight me for it because I saw more readily the other fear, the fear to be left, the need to cling. When you found I wasn't going to go away, it became important I didn't get too close, didn't try to steer the therapy, allowed you to flounder, withstood the voices that whispered that I aided and abetted you in your neurosis.

The third strand of identity is the new thing emerging, since Christmas, or more recently than that, alongside all that you have been working out with Mark, but perhaps not part of that: the ability to live in the present. The wheel starts to come full circle. Once before, you were in the present, but trapped in it then without a past. Steve is your present because, so you say, you see him without projections, and he sees you without projections. To be alone means you have also the freedom and the right to be alone with someone else. You have never surrendered to one person because you have always divided yourself between two. Before Christmas, you thought you had found the answer to that — some kind of monogamous tie with Alex. Maybe you just haven't found a man yet who can relate to the whole of you, there is a lot of you to relate to.

So while acid asks three questions, it also points towards the directness of your realization that to be in the present feels good: there is joy in it, and peace, and sometimes great hurt, but it is not split. Your relationship with Mark contains within it the three main stages I see your therapy as falling into now.

The first and longest stage was the thawing-out stage, when your hysterical character, the frozen defence pattern, slowly softened. Then came a period when instead of defending yourself against hysteria, you were prepared to let it take you over, the pain of the past instead of being dammed back by your character defences, came flooding in full strength, it could burst, more and more easily, into the present, to provide the sea you swam in.

But what if the flood runs dry? Who are you when not exploding or defended against explosions? Your old fear rears its head *precisely* when the chance to take a fundamental new step forward exists. You could move forward to the kind of immediacy — a quite new kind of immediacy concerned with new ways of moving and of being still which your body tasted last session and your head is in touch with through your amazing writing. But to move forward means so much dissolving: more slabs of neurosis have to go, more projections have to die, and the schizophrenic nightmare is that you will be dissolved as well. If the old Jenny goes, your nightmare is there will be no-one left but the ghost of your mother filling your skin and looking out of your eyes. Acid asks: who are you when you stop exploding, when you dare to let people in (and out) without control, or possession, or projection; when you trust yourself to believe what you see because your seeing is so much clearer when you let your honesty act from you, and give it space and time not to be pressurized. Health for you will be life with all your energy, but without pressure. And that is the taste that trickles through what you are writing now. Hysterics need pressure, or they are nothing. You cannot disappear into the void, you are too firmly entrenched now.

Two sessions back, you realized how you were suppressing your anger towards Mark, how you were letting him walk over you. You walked towards love and it could have become a trap again. But the projection on Mark that would, three years ago, have left you hung-up and desperate, is now something that you can work with.

In that same session, you directed your rage at Mark: you faced him, you exploded out at him. The problem of life is that people explode back, books get cut up, a lot of destructive anger flies around which is only therapeutic if it can be connected back to its infantile source. Acid asks: who am I when two people are trying to tear me in half?

To become unhysterical in the way you relate to Mark you have to get beyond both the suppressed scream and the expressed scream: you have to face him not with your infantile anger, but with your adult honesty. That brings us bang up to date. To find yourself, you have to risk losing Mark.

You have this intense need to be recognized: everyone has to meet your Mum to prove she really exists, that you didn't invent her, or she you. Having your group to share the rage and the grief with was a necessary part of growth for a person who had once been so shy. Needing a companion to witness Mark when he cuts you down with words, defends you from the threat to your identity when the person you love treats you with rationalized hate. Your joy and your peace and the way you can nourish hope out of hurt, are not your mother, or your father; they are not illusory. But they are provisional, they are tentative, they are tap roots for the identity you can move towards if relationships cease to impose strangleholds. Not everyone will recognize the path you are on, the forces to keep you neurotic are quite strong. You won't always get the affirmation so easily for the non-explosive growths as you have done for the explosive ones. I still think you need to experience quiet energy and find you don't die. I still think you can move towards being filled with high energy pouring into you out of the present, instead of exploding out of you from the past. If you rest from energizing the world, do you disappear? All the signs are that when you let yourself be energized by the truths you read in Becky's face, or by Sally, a Steve poem, music, the body of your man, you enrich your life — the opposite of disappearing. To preserve the essence of yourself and your therapeutic journey, you pruned everyone else out of your book, they became ghosts flitting through the pages of your life. If they enter your vision, these people who are not from the remote past of your childhood, but from your present, if you see them as not you, and get tangled with them less, if they begin to fill your book but leave you more space to be alone with whoever you choose in your life, then it's one hell of a change, and one hell of a risk (there are no certainties left when a neurosis gets given up). Acid tells you all your old 'solutions' may now need revaluing, there is so much for you to see when your eyes turn outwards and you are not fighting to stop the world from looking like your Mum, or keeping it behaving like your Dad.

One further thought, huge in its obviousness: has any man that you wanted ever given you up? What you risk with Mark is just that. The way to prevent it is what you have always done before, held a large part of yourself back which the man you want is always trying to reach. If your letter to Mark represents honesty, hysteria is dishonesty. Your letter to Mark takes nothing from him but risks that he takes all of himself from you. Hysteria leads sooner or later to your rejecting the man you once loved, when you are ready to.

You had a broken heart once, in the split you were born into, from which your father became the one who was thrown out. That is the grief your neurotic life-style protected you from feeling, and which your therapeutic life led you back to. What you risk now with Mark is the grief of losing him if he takes himself away because of his reaction to your letter. You can only spare yourself the risk of that grief by suppressing your letter, and with it yourself, and the gateway out of neurosis.

I would rather see you broken in grief but growing from it towards health, than trapped forever in a protection-racket. It is paradoxical that temper tantrums are safer to go into than quiet honesty. Your letter is braver than any anger outburst. You can indulge your anger but still stay protected from grief. Mark may find your rage easier to deal with than your truth; just as it will be easy for you to handle a demonic Mark tearing up your books, but difficult to exist in the face of a cold Mark freezing you out of his world.

Mark is neither your father you must cling to at any price, nor your mother you must reject at any cost. He is a hurt man who could trap you once more into being a saviour. The energies of a saviour pour into rescuing abandoned people. It is risk of abandonment you have to face if you heal your split. To be given up by the man is to be thrown back, you fear, into your mother. What you see as your death-trap is your life-gate.

Love, David.

9th May, 1973.

Dear David,

Do I detect a degree of fatherly fussing in your long letter, for which many thankyous? A touch of tension at the outcome of this tale?

Anyway, my love, what happened was: I had some very bad moments of pre-execution diarrhoea, I sunk into a kind of sleeping jelly, wondering if it would all pass off, but time was ticking by, the letter lying like a bomb in my room. I gave Mark the letter and watched his face.

The next day, in the afternoon, Mark left, perhaps for good. We had spent one more night together. He understood my position, that I could not sell myself to him by promising him security; I understood his position that he could not sell himself to me by becoming 'just one' when he needs to be the 'only one'. I let him walk out of here and he managed to walk out of here. We were not cold and we were not angry and we did not abuse one another. Neither did we cry.

I watched him walk down the Mews. He is very beautiful. I discovered there was no hole in my heart when he had gone; but I discovered there was still a warm place in my heart for him when he had gone.

That evening, I had a couple of hours of subdued elation. I

waited for the bomb to go off inside me, the catastrophes and cataclysms at being left. None such. Quiet relief; respect for Mark, and for myself. I slept well.

The next day, I was more subdued, and not at all elated. I was alone, not lonely, but not particularly alive either. In the evening, I had the choice of going over to Steve's, but I stayed with Becky and fell asleep early.

This morning, your letter comes, and I am consolidated in my position. I am feeling a few quiet things, such as that I do not want to see Jerry for some time, because that confuses me, but most of all because I do not enjoy myself with him; that I do not want to sleep with Steve, because I don't want to be a therapist in bed; and that the thing I have stuck to most of my life, that I need a man in order to live, no longer seems to be true. So be it. Steve has taught me to go back to my painting and drawing and writing, and there are good times with him. And anyway, I have a lot of quarrelling to do with Becky.

Yet a new ending, David. How many more endings and beginnings? I think now they will be gentler, uncharged by the poison of past volcanoes.

With thanks to you, my friend.

○   ○   ○

In the middle of May, Steve, Becky and I, Babs and Peter and their kids all joined the 'Greenpeace' walk from London to Paris to protest at the French hydrogen-bomb tests.

We passed through the seaside town where my mother was living and I was to take Steve to meet her. But a few days before we reached the coast, the police came to find me on the walk. My mother had died, as I had long expected, of a heart-attack.

Letter to David, 15th May, 1973
    Mum finally went, quickly, in the night.
    I'm an orphan now, David.
    I hope they'll soon both be out of me. (Not their good bits.)

Dear Jen,

At least your Mum is not suffering any more. I am glad Steve was with you when you heard the news.

Yes, Jen, they will soon both be out of you. Though you are technically an orphan, you were most without parents when they were both alive. You belong now and have your own roots, so even marching has a stability in it.

Love, David.

My sister, Becky and I went to my Mum's cremation. My step-father wouldn't let anyone see Mum; I was disappointed; I had wanted to look at her without her avoiding me. Because my stepfather was too grieved to get things together himself, he put the funeral in the hands of professionals. Consequently, I had the freaky experience of unwilling attendance at my first religious ceremony since school. We were told that 'our sister would have eternal life'. Heaven forbid.

Becky was crying. She told me the prayers made her cry. I picked her up and held her in my arms and her crying made me cry. At least then there was a bit of life in that place. My sister made her own private, secret protest. She wore a long skirt and no knickers underneath. She also pointed out how my atheist Mum would have poked fun at the proceedings. I didn't like to tell the priest my Mum thought she was descended from space-men, just like Reich.

Letter to David, 18th May, 1973

I am enjoying myself in my mother's house for the first time in my life. I can leave the door open when I take a bath. I can make a cup of tea and wash up, no-one will take it out of my hands, do it for me, tell me how to do it. I can take the dog for a walk without asking. We slept in sleeping-bags on the carpet on the dining-room floor. I can put a new toilet roll in the bathroom when the old one runs out without being accused of criticizing Mum's household management. If I wanted to, I could walk into the kitchen right now and take something to eat without having to sit at a properly laid table.

But then, terror comes in the night. Mum is standing by the

bathroom door where I last saw her alive. She is coming back to haunt me because I am enjoying her house, being friendly with her husband. None of my recent soft feelings for her can seep through now, because I am so frightened. I am not doing things as she would have wanted. Such a strange feeling, to move through this house without being watched. And can it be that I am really lying here in this hot sun on this fresh lawn, the dogs at my side, Steve by my side, my sister in the kitchen, my child in the bath washing her hair of all things — we were never allowed to wash our hair in the bath, I never discovered why.

Letter from David
Dear Jen,

It is too much, you are breaking so many taboos at once. You are not supposed to be an orphan having fun, you are not supposed to be bouncing with life in the house of the dead.

To take your therapy into the heart of her home is a kind of delicious sacrilege which will do all your cells a power of good. How do you manage to grow younger when death is at your elbow?

My elation, however, was shortlived. That same evening, I was back with my friends on the Greenpeace walk: my stepfather had taken back his request that we stay with him. He wanted to 'keep the house as she would have wanted it', that is, perfectly dead. And that means, without me in it.

I felt split to pieces, confused, ungrounded, explosive. Had I made a fool of myself, believing I could be accepted at last in that sterile house? We found a basement room at the place where the peace-walkers were staying the night, and Babs tried to help me with my feelings. I started to cry immediately. Suddenly, Babs leant forward and gently removed something from my jumper. 'What was that?' I asked. She looked at me strangely. 'Something you don't like.' I looked on the floor and saw the big black spider. That did it; I burst into tears. It was her. She was haunting me, she was on me. She'd come back as a spider. I felt she was more powerful now that she was dead; I knew she'd come back and get me for enjoying myself, for enjoying being allowed to drive my stepfather's car at her funeral, for committing the ultimate taboo: I'd cried for my *father* on the day of her funeral, moved by meeting his sister for the first time since his death.

Two days later, in Oostende, we managed to have some more sessions. I had been seized up with fear at what the other marchers would 'think' when Steve made so much noise in his session. I worked by remembering how I'd been paralytic with embarrassment and fear about the other marchers waking when Steve was talking and laughing after we made love the first night of the march. I went into the things I wanted to say, 'Please be quiet, please don't frighten me, please don't move, don't breathe, go dead like me.' Immediately I connected with my first sexual affair, when I was fourteen, making love in my mother's house, always terrified and hating my lover for breathing loud or doing anything to endanger me. I was crying, saying how ashamed I was, I couldn't even tell these friends of mine of the connection I'd made. I spoke out the attitude that I was locked in: 'I have never been near a man, no man has ever touched me; I don't like men, only women; I have never been in bed with Alex, or Mark; I am yours, Mummy, you can come and take me away any time you want. I will come with you, none of these people are important to me; I'll leave them any time, I'm not really here anyway, I'm just pretending.' I cried remembering the words of Kate in 'Family Life': 'You can have me too, doctor, if you like; anyone can have me. It doesn't really matter what you do to me if I don't exist, does it?'

Then I asked my Mum, 'Well, what *would* you do if you came in at the door? You wouldn't even dare to see, to look, would you?' Babs said, 'Make her see.' and then I realized it was me who couldn't face what I was doing. That made me very angry indeed, furious at being so screwed up, at being robbed of myself. I was full of hatred for my mother; now she is dead, she is everywhere, coming between me and my friends, turning into other people at the door.

I worked now by being my mother fully, to bring her to the surface and get her out of me. I jumped, started, shrieked with

shock, freaked with her hysterical movements. I let the shock
she'd put in me come out a little; I let my body shake and
convulse and a shriek came out of me. I felt immense gratitude
to my friends, to Babs and Steve, for being allowed to go crazy,
allowed to come out with the hysteria that was in my bones. I
shook my head wildly, I went hot all over; and that was like
sex, like I am sometimes in sex. I was kneeling and sweating and
letting the sounds erupt out of me. The room was dark and in a
heap from all our sessions. My mother had left the room for a
while.

I laughed and laughed with relief. I felt like on a trip with
Jerry. Then I cried softly, wanting Jerry very much, feeling he
was the only person I'd ever let myself go with, on trips, when
I'd let flow out of me what was in me, tears and laughter and
freaked fear, and he had stayed and seen me through so much
of my story.

Then me and Babs competed doing headstands, and I lay
around the room while Steve was crying about something, and
felt hungry.

A week later, the walk was over, the French border-police
having smashed up our posters and chucked us all over the road
and stopped us entering France. I called at my mother's house
with Steve. No-one was in. I got in a window and we took over
the place and space for hours on end. When my sister and my
stepfather arrived home in the evening, Steve was wearing my
skirt and using the phone, and I'd had to phone the police
because I'd let the dog off his lead for a change, and he'd run
off.

My stepfather was furious; he stormed off in the car to look
for the dog and didn't come back until the middle of the night.

My sister, if you please, was wearing one of my mother's
dresses and had her hair scraped back off her face with a scarf
round it. She was tight and drawn, her skin white; she couldn't
look at me or speak to me; she went upstairs and lay on her bed.
The ground was trying to swallow me up, so I repacked, ready
to leave straightaway. I went in to see my sister and ended up
giving her a session that lasted several hours. She was in terror;

loads of energy was swirling all over the place, but she was too frightened to really let go. She cried about how she found it quite easy to keep the peace with our stepfather by being how he needed her to be, but recognized that if she stepped out of line, she'd be chucked out like I was. She said how all her life she'd played the 'hate Jenny' game, going over to their side, and yet now she felt she had killed herself because 'you were the only thing that was alive in that house.' I was stunned. I couldn't believe I was hearing her saying these things. Finally, she got through to the point I'd reached of feeling like a forked tree, split, being dragged apart. At the moment, she felt split between me and my stepfather. The session ended because she couldn't face the split; she was still terribly tense, terrified he would come home when she was crying.

I sat talking with her and she criticized me for facing 'non-therapy people' such as Mum and my stepfather with my feelings; this was vindictive she said. I swallowed this, and did myself a lot of damage.

I went in to Steve who was asleep in bed, and covered in anxious sweat. My stepfather had come home. I was frightened. I couldn't wait to get out of that house. I was scared to open doors, scared to move or put lights on or go into the bathroom. Home again.

In the middle of the night, the door of our bedroom opened. I woke immediately and lay there, wide-eyed and bare-chested, with Steve asleep beside me. My stepfather walked in, stared, and walked out again. What did he want? What was he going to do? I couldn't get back to sleep. I thought maybe he was going to kill us. I wanted to get out of there. Every time I dozed off, I awoke with a start, not daring to leave the door unguarded by my eyes. My Mum's coat was hanging on that door.

All that evening I had been seeing ghosts, doors opening, reflections in the windows. The whole place was haunted; this fully-lighted, perfectly solid modern little house was more scary than any creaking old mansion. Horror for me is in bright flooding light, soft carpets and perfectly painted woodwork.

Steve and I escaped at eight o'clock in the morning. On the train home, having been quiet in myself for several hours, I realized that although my head was bad and I needed a session, my body felt beautiful. I felt long and slim in my trousers and Steve's jumper. I was sexual, I felt alive and in the world. I was here, not in that glasshouse of insanity. I said, looking at Steve as we stepped off the bus in love, 'I hope it lasts.'

Back home, in the group, I yelled at my sister for killing her kids and yet being so concerned about me killing my stepfather. I screamed and screamed, but the sound was coming from my chest, not from my stomach, because of the overload I guess. I felt I would kill any grown-up to save a child. I felt impotent and furious against the adult world. It was a ghastly feeling, being too small to fight these huge big dead things twisting my life. I got a picture of my stepfather in my mind and said, 'What's the matter with you that you have swallowed Mum so', but I was crying with self-doubt, feeling there was something the matter with me because everyone was on the other side; he was trying to convince me how good my mother was. Then I was screaming, 'But I *remember* what it was like, you can't take that away.'

Jan got me to lie and just breathe. My body started to come back, I could feel exactly where I was blocked, above my genital. I breathed more and more and a four-year circuit closed: I was back on a couch with this still-unknown friend of mine, David, giving me a session in the days when I made no connections, just sank into body feelings. I was back there, blue and yellow lights flashing, my whole body suffused with amazing energy; I felt everyone in the room must be able to see the porcupine quills of electricity sticking out all over my skin. My hands and arms are throbbing, bristling with thistles, my face too, nearly my legs, yes, my legs and feet too. I am joining up. The bad trip is over, I am becoming three-dimensional. People in the room have lost me, but I cannot communicate what is going on without losing it. I am smiling, I am wet with tears, I am saying, 'Hello, body, hello me, I'm back, I've been away thirty years, I'm joining up, I'm coming, I'm coming, I'm nearly here, I'm coming back. I'm coming all the way this time, no-one is going to stop me, all the way this time.'

I didn't come back all the way, though, because Jan said,

seeing me stroke my legs, crying, 'Do you like yourself?' and that brought me back to the outside. I lay down once more and breathed.

This time I went back to that room as a child. They are all there, Dad and Mum and my stepfather and my sister. I can taste the room, the smooth whiteness of this horrible feeling; I remember my nightmare of the cat and dog chasing each other at jet speed through the room, out of the window, back in at the the door, out the window again, round and round, faster and faster, shrieking, and me lying paralyzed in my bed, watching. Yes, the room and the white feeling, that is all there. But there is someone missing. Who is it? It's me! I'm there, but I am a different colour. I am black. Suddenly, I let out a blood-curdling scream and thrash around yelling, 'You tried to make me forget, but I didn't, you tried to take away my memory, but you can't. I REMEMBER, I REMEMBER!'

29th May, 1973
Dear David,

'What are you celebrating?' Steve asked me as he walked in just now. It seems the sun is shining around my skin.

I will tell you what I am celebrating, but first I want to tell you a bit I missed out of that long session yesterday.

When I got my body back, I lay quiet and started to cry for you. I cried, 'I want David, I want him here because he has seen me through, he has seen me through the whole story and always believed me, I never had to prove anything, he never questioned me, it was true because I said so.' I was crying, 'I love you so much and I want you here now, now that I am coming back, now that my therapy is ending.' And for those minutes, there was only the present, just you and Steve and Jerry and the people in the room, and Dad and Mum didn't matter. I cried and smiled and said, 'And I've been faithful to you, I've stayed with you' and flashing through my head were all those times of doubt last summer, the leavings and changings and trips about therapy, the right way and the wrong way, which are so far from me now. I was also saying, 'I have stayed with myself, I have been faithful to myself.' I knew, too, that I would have died without you. I cried and said, 'How did it happen that I found you? How could I be so lucky?' The mystery and magic of that will never leave me I think, because it *is* a miracle, and no-one else would do. I have learnt that from you, David, in your letter that still sticks in my mind: 'you are not replaceable' you said to me. *You* are not replaceable, David. 'Therapy' wasn't what I needed, I needed *you*.

So I am celebrating! I would like to tell you about this peace walk we went on to stop their bomb tests. On the march, Babs and Peter and Steve and me and our four kids were loved by the rest of the walkers; we were alive and loved, and found place and space to give each other sessions in those weeks, we were a PNP community within a wider community, and were accepted with no games and no pretending.

At times, I ended up, quite relaxedly, organizing the march; all that means is getting people on their feet and keeping the front with the back, just like therapy really. And painting banners and placards, just for fun. Steve has taught me that drawing is for fun, and so we drew on the pavements, and on people's clothes and on each other's skin; we painted our way across Kent and Belgium, and my banners flew and were washed away by Flemish sun and broken up by French police and renewed again, because there are a thousand happy brush-strokes in my hands; and Peter read Khalil Gibran to me while I painted Dutch words and got brown in the sun.

And how to tell you about Steve? I am embarrassed to have so many good feelings, shy to know how well I can relate now; anxious about not being believed after the good times with Alex — they *were* good times. Well, it is better times still, and that's the truth, I can't hide it from you or Mark or any mourning people round corners; our faces shine with it, the mess in the room is witness to it, the days that have no names or numbers tell it, and the people who get moved towards us prove it. Becky's jealousy of Steve is perhaps the strongest, saddest witness.

This boy and I said to one another when we started our relationship: 'All I want is affection, nothing serious, no sex of course.' Well, we certainly got the affection, and nothing too serious, but our relationship is extraordinarily sexual, in a way I have never known before: blatantly, amusingly, openly sexual, 'a couple of schoolkids' as a girl we both fell in love with on the march called us.

Letter to David, 31st May, 1973

On Tuesday, in walked Jerry. Peter, Alex, Steve, Jan and me were in the kitchen in high spirits, friendly, joking, brown-skinned. What happened?

My stomach swelled up with painful tension, swelled up as if I were pregnant. I felt Jerry as a black crow, sitting, hovering, brooding, spying, peeking, watching, wanting. Unhappy: saying he was happy. Judging: saying he felt open. Demanding: saying he wanted nothing. I didn't want to be alone with him; he wanted to be alone with me. I wanted to stay gay; he wanted to be serious. When he went, he said: 'Let's keep it as I said, no contact with one another.'

I was blocked, swollen, solid. I struggled with my feelings and got through to guilt; guilt at leaving him, guilt at leaving Alex. I felt ungrounded: Jerry had said, 'Oh, well, you're always high at the beginning of a relationship.'

I couldn't look at Alex, couldn't face him. I don't think I have ever felt so blocked, so avoiding. I got depressed, wept a few tears, about my fear of my energy swinging, as it did from Alex to Mark, of my unfathomable feelings sweeping me away from Steve. I moved on to my stepfather: him telling me in his letters how friends of his and Mum's had 'confirmed' that Mum was a kind, generous, loving person; so there was no reason for me to hate her, I was wrong; there was something wrong with me.

Huge anger at my sister came up about her telling me in secret that she shared my feelings about the family, but presented a front to keep in with them. I screamed at her for thinking it was alright to encounter a little kid with her feelings, but not Mum or our stepfather.

I recalled the incident when I was about thirteen and Mum stormed into my room, threw my books round the room, got hold of my hair and beat my head on the floor, all for 'making a noise', banging a door I think, when my precious sister was in bed with a cold. I remembered my silence, how I did not fight back, didn't make a sound. I screamed and cried now at the insanity of our family which says: it's OK to be beaten to death, as long as you don't make a sound and disturb the neighbours. Our next-door neighbours of those times were at Mum's funeral. In a letter to my stepfather, this lady wrote: 'I know Jenny won't be of much use to you at this time.' She had spoken to me as polite as can be the day of the funeral, sweet smiles masking her disapproval of me. I yelled at her now in the session: you were next door, you weren't in the house, you don't know a thing. I realized how my stepfather would say I was insane to think that this incident with Mum really happened, and how Mum, if she were alive, would find a way to whitewash it, laugh it off with some clever joke. I am crying: 'You try to make me forget, you try to make me insane, but I do remember, and I will hang on to these memories.'

The session was a mess; I can't remember all I went into. I know I have not felt good since Jerry's visit and that the session didn't make me feel better.

Next morning, I felt very bad after sex with Steve. All my sex problems are coming up again, though this time I am seeing them a bit clearer. I realize how there is a deep deep fury in my limbs which will not come through into my muscles and how this fury is locked away, smoothed away by people being nice to me. 'I have nothing to be angry about.'

I had a session with Jan, a very messy one. I am struggling and it does not help to have him overdirecting me. My fury is locked. I felt how I am 'co-opted' by men: Peter and Steve saying how I am a comrade, how I'm like a man, not someone to be fought. I am being patted on the back, but I look puzzled in my eyes. Patting me on the back, that doesn't help when I am left, frustrated in sex! Then I am absolutely a woman and can no longer pretend I belong to the ruling class. Then I am inferior, my body is inferior; I am no longer on top. My anger is stolen from me: I give it up in exchange for not being left alone.

I saw the trap and know what I must do: regardless of any

good feelings about Steve, regardless of whether or not it is his 'fault', I must blast out my feelings at the time, not help my comrade and fuck myself over. I must make an issue of my feelings, not swallow them and make Jerry's mistake of saying, 'This is a feeling from the past, it has nothing to do with you, therefore I will not express it.' I can rip into fury and violence at Steve without ripping him apart as long as I am aware of what I'm doing.

At four o'clock in the middle of the next night, sleeping alone, I awoke in terror. My mother was standing, smiling over me, in my dream. I am lying, screaming at her. She is being sarcastic, clever, controlling. I say, 'You cunt'; I am screaming and shouting and telling her she is a liar.

She says I shouldn't make such a noise. I scream and shout more and more, louder and louder.

I wake up. The walls, my skin, the air, are zinging with fear. I go into the lighted hallway and the lighted bathroom. But light is no comfort, it is just as electric with fear. I lock the bathroom door; someone will come up behind me as I am washing my teeth. I have to get in to Steve before I am killed. I bundle clumsily into the dark therapy room; I don't know where he is lying. I fall over his head and he cries out in his sleep, but doesn't wake up. I lie beside him, trying to comfort myself, knowing that such fear is far too frightening to face!

I lie remembering what it is like to be five years old, to scream out in the night and have Dad pick me up and take me to bed. I savour my memories deliciously, I am so pleased and proud to have such early memories. I go back over all the ones I have, treasuring them: four at Leicester, two before my sister was born. I see Mum's pregnant stomach, I see our Dalmation dog; I remember Wally and Nan, our landlords who loved me. I see the layout of the house, remember the scene when Mum threatened to leave me, just after my sister was born. I contrast the sunny, cheeky feeling I have about myself when I was tiny with the terrorized, paralyzed little girl I became during the worst years of the breakup between Mum and Dad.

I go back to sleep and have another very long-winded nightmare about a horror film I am watching where the actors are in the cinema with me and the projector is by my side, and the horror of the plot hinges on a man who is a baby himself having a baby. I wake up with stomach pains and tension for the first time since I have known Steve.

This morning, I got a hatefilled letter from Jerry. Amongst other things, he writes: 'I see you as a controlling, frightened person with a lot of energy, just like your mother. I just won't close my eyes to your out-of-touchness,' and 'Don't call or write me. Any letters will be destroyed lying unopened in my special incinerator.'

I got an energy-rush and a fit of laughing when I read the letter, and was very angry too. But also I was sad to see how I can be unnerved and derailed in my deepest layers by such insults: how my security is so flimsy that I can be quickly brainwashed into thinking I've invented the fact that my name is Jenny, that my body flows with hot energy, that my mother was a maniac and that I wanted my father. I wished Jerry was in the room, and cursed him for chucking insults and then closing the door on any comeback. I cursed also my own real out-of-touchness which was not to allow my hostility to come out at him the day he was here with his hang-dog look.

Well, David, I suppose that's how it's going to be: every time I clear myself out, another huge thing will come up. At the moment, I am struggling again: there is a huge rage in my pelvis which is blocked by fear. My body hurts again. This will be a difficult hurdle. This is a time when I must read back over the past weeks to know that I do exist, and so does my health and my love. I am not despairing, but I am weary sometimes of the enormity of it all.

Yes, I am still full of love. I love myself so much that after an hour, Jerry's letter bores me. I love Steve so much that I feel happy and secure when he leaves the house or the room. He is a shining alive child and I feel we are made of the same material

I miss you, David. But there hasn't been a 'gap' in the therapy, as you say. How can you say such a thing, David! A gap, indeed. What do you think I am doing when I lie in the grass, sweat in my dreams, roll with my dog, feel the warm skin of my friend, open my eyes wide in the street and dare to look at the faces in passing buses?

There is a little hunger in my throat to see you. It is not neurotic to miss a good friend!

I will write soon to tell you how I cross this hurdle.

Jen.

Dear Jen,

So much to take in, from what you wrote. I can only sit back, open to what comes from you, and say a few things. You give yourself the best feedback in the world these days.

So many new things, new ways of feeling, new roads out of feelings, in what you say. You are a changing-colour-Jenny and your letters get like the sea, all moods, all colours, never still for long, and so much movement in them. No-one will ever succeed in freezing you again, because even when ice forms on the very top, it gets pushed away before it can gel. Even when crying splits you to pieces, again you reform and each time the life is clearer in you.

So your stepfather threw you out with one hand and offered you his home with the other! Is a hurtful, insensitive Jenny all that he and that neighbour and Jerry (sometimes) can see? How little they know you. You were 'sensitive' when you froze, when you were trapped in shyness, when you blocked the scream, and crying was a silence in the night. How well you used to protect people from you. Now you are so much more alive, you are 'insensitive'. You are 'insensitive' because you speak truth and not lies, because you face people instead of looking away. The only safe way to protect other people from Jenny being alive is for Jenny to die. That trip is over, and people will have to look after their own feelings.

Your letter to your stepfather is beautiful; there is nothing cruel in it. But the images, the images you have to keep shaking off: cruel-Jenny, witch-Jenny, malicious-Jenny, it is the role they cast you in. The unfeeling girl who dances on her mother's grave, the ungrateful daughter with her boisterous friends who come trampling over the carpet to harrass the grieving husband. You were soft towards your stepfather when that was appropriate, you have a great openness for him, your feelings are clear, there is no cloudiness there. As in the letter to Mark.

Honesty doesn't cut, it heals. So where are these people you keep hurting, I would like to meet them. Your Mum? Yes, honesty hurts, but there is no hate in it. Lies hurt more and there is plenty of hate in that. She could have buried you with herself in the lies, if we had let her. If she swelled up with dropsy, like you once wrote, from suppressed tears, those are the lies that kill. She was your strength and she was your terrible weakness: she was your eyes and she was your blindness; she was your protection and your prison. I never met your Mum, only once, looking down on the top of her head at the hotel, many moons ago. But I have been working with her a long time. I got to know her in your body and her tentacles in your mind. I got to know her softness and her hardness, her terror and her hysteria. But Jerry is wrong, you are not just like your mother. These life-songs of letters you write did not come out of your mother, they are a language as alien to her as the back of the moon, they are your language from your life, and nothing else anywhere is like them. Sometimes in the therapy I lose you, and sometimes we meet again. I ask you again, where are these people you are so hurtful to, whose homes are you wrecking, where is the debris of the hate and insensitivity you are supposed to nurse? Jerry? But when, in your sadness and his incredible grief he moved out last autumn, it was his first step to independence. He is fighting his own battle with *his* mother in you. Alex? But you parted in friendship. Mark? But you blessed him with truth. I have seen you blazing with fury, but fury is hot and people can learn to cope with it, like with any storm not cooped up, the sun can follow. Hate is cold and deadly. I have never known anyone with less hate than you. Hate before you came alive, yes. All the hate of a cold marriage gone dead that rooted in you before the therapy started, the hate whose cold fingers have left the touch you sometimes see on Becky's beautiful body, or in it.

There is one thing I disagree about, when you wrote to your stepfather that all that you are must have been due to him and her and your Dad and anyone else who moved and breathed around you. 'Everything I am', you wrote, 'is from the home I grew up in.' Almost, not quite. It is the 'not-quite' we have to work with; it's that bit of breathing, electrifying, being-in-the-world that you are as well, which has nothing to do with home, even if you brought it with you from the womb. It is something so deep no-one wants to be it for long, and there you are again, in that amazing session you had with Jan, which has nothing to do with houses or carpets or Mums and Dads, but with the daring to be alive everyone is so frightened of. Hello Jen, hello new body out of someone's womb that kept on growing and didn't die, it's good to hear from you. It is not you who are doing the inventing, the inventions were theirs. They invented the falsehood that you were a not-nice Jennifer who could be wicked, that your body choked with dead ice, that your mother was a model of sanity and your father a figure to hate. Speak the truth again: from the madhouse of your mother came a Jenny full of hot life and a lot of love, who learned to unstrangle and is still unstrangling all the chokeholds that were put on you. Yes, there is time for celebration.

But when it came to your not replaceable letter, I cried with the shock of your love which has so many wonders in it, and for where you have got to which is sometimes with me and sometimes without me. I cried from the pain and the healing of holding and of letting go, and for the fact that you stayed with yourself even when you believed for so long you had no self to stay with. The mystery and magic is not projection, it is nobody's fantasy: I never knew when I cast myself out towards you in your loneliness sometimes across half a continent that my words would take root in your body and be part of your growth, that you would quote them back at me years later in a way that would call me open. If I believed in you always, it cannot be explained. Some things are unexplainable. Did you come to life so hugely and delicately because I believed you would; or did I believe you would because I could see the passion dormant under your skin? I stayed with you because, in spite of your home that wasn't, you made the therapy which wasn't a therapy work; and however much it can hurt coming alive out of a death, you, who had always run away, learned to stay and face whatever self was there.

How can there be an end when there are so many beginnings?

No-one can take me away from you, because what matters
between us you have made your own. You taught me to believe
in your kind of miracle. If this kind of connection was neurotic,
you would be hung up on me; fear of getting hung-up was your
neurosis, not opening to love. Keeping me impersonal, and
therefore yourself at vanishing point was the sickness; not being
free to use the space and time and love that we set flowing to
find yourself — how could that kind of connection be bad when
it was so much of your need? I was wrong, there has been no
gap. I miss you, too. How come you chose as your therapist a
man you had never seen?

I love you Jen, David.

A writing to me from Steve

Skin and who is under mine. Things I know. Skin is very
smooth and brown. Attitude in a horizontal (friendly) position
is like a pussy-cat; also, looking up from underneath, face is
very calming and warmth vibrating out from the brown eyes,
especially in hair, nice when let down flowing; actually vibrates
when I'm tripping; also she makes pussy cat-like sounds when
being friendly.

Looking at old photos seems like a different person, much
older. I feel you are now a child like me, before going to school.

You gave me skin and heat.

Now I am not scared; but I am when you get old and coping
clinically and withdrawn, your voice then is like icy accusing
fingers I feel pointing. I'm alone and want to go quickly, be
alone and not feel threatened. This could be the voice of my
father and a thousand schoolteachers.

At twenty, I turned to mysticism, small wonder behind every
puff of marijuana is anger at the adversaries of my youth, at the
skinhead politicos coercing me through guilt feelings into Saving
the World, being true to my 'class' and selling sixty Workers'
Press a day come rain, shine or snowstorm.

Glad that you are the first friend of this new lifetime, from
the moment I walked into the house when you thought I was a
virgin/homosexual/school-inspector, and I thought you were a

man. Was too soon then for you to recognize the light behind my eyes at your surprise when I was 'so lucid' despite my accent — that light was from knowing I could transcend certain old and phoney barriers, leap over certain well-worn games and into a warm and friendly understanding which I hoped then would grow brighter, for all to see. And now something has.

Yes, I am afraid, or threatened, when you are going into feelings, especially with your family — is that past what makes you? Sometimes I feel it is a completely different person that came out of all that, you couldn't have lived through that childhood in that horrible family, you can't be the same one.

4th June, 1973

I don't like writing when all I have to say is very bad, very bad indeed. The downers are much worse when the skin is freer to feel them. This time there is no mitigation, no comfort, no hope: I am anti-therapy, I think of suicide. It is true that today there is enough enjoyment in me returned to write, thanks to Alex, he has helped me today.

Undermined, ungrounded; that's what I've been, a bad wave turned. Ever since Jerry's visit, but the insecurity was there waiting and ready to come out. I didn't believe in myself, I wanted to tear up my therapy file again. I felt David needed to believe in me to believe in therapy. I felt angry for enjoying myself, I didn't believe the good things or the good times. It seems one dose of the outside world — my Mum's funeral, because that's when things really turned — and I am poisoned.

I thought perhaps maybe I'd escaped at last from the land of two dimensions and blocked feelings and ungrounding. I thought maybe I was permanently on the other side of the rainbow, though I knew of course it would rain and storm and snow again. But I didn't think there'd be a drought, the clanking of skeletons and a parched mouth. I thought maybe I'd be safe from Jan and the poison in him and people like him, but no, I am infected, affected, bowled over, hating myself for not being able to cope with diseased insults, him telling me I am 'out-of-touch' and go into my feelings 'in a superficial way'. The result is I become just those things, and my fury is locked, buried deeper than ever, not reaching my muscles, just my voice.

And how can I deal with Steve and my feelings about him and how can he deal with me? He is only just starting his therapy, only just starting to know how his family is surrounding him always. He cannot stand being reminded of his floppy mother: and that is what I become when I cry, when I cannot cope. He cannot be big for me, and I cannot help him when I am locked in the anger of disappointment, the humiliation of feeling my own dependency and not being able to cope with the feelings when he leaves me and goes his way. When I am in myself, his going is something else to savour, to explore, a newness and exciting, enjoying the sadness of it maybe, it is a stimulation. But when I am black or blue, I lock tight into the old anger of Mum having another baby, hatred and revenge and self-destruction fill my thoughts and my body deflates suddenly to locked two-dimensionalness.

I don't want to write this nightmare of death.

On Sunday, after planning the day before happily to go to Spain for the summer with Steve and Becky, and my friends coming after, I awoke Sunday morning filled with anxiety, a deep fear surging up from long ago; I didn't know where from, I was just terrified to leave 'home'. I wanted to tell Steve, but he was asleep. I went in to my sister; she seemed asleep. All I wanted was comfort, I didn't want to feel that fear all on my own. Steve woke eventually, and I told him, but it didn't register. He was off to Peter's for the day. I was alone and lost with those bad feelings and needed him. I watched him walk away feeling I had to bear him going, I had to 'deal with it', be grown-up.

When it was time for the group, for Steve to come home, he didn't. I was sad, but with myself. Quite late, Steve and Peter and Babs arrived, Steve quite freaked having taken *two* acid tabs; he hugged me and cried a bit in the street, which was beautiful, but I was too deeply sad and depressed to open up. He had gone to other people, taken himself away from me, our contact was broken, our intimacy lost, and I couldn't cope. I was quiet and white inside, glazed. I helped others a bit in the group. Near the end, I bounced over to Steve, but he rejected me angrily.

It's no good trying to piece together the bits since that day: I know I held Steve that night while he cried and felt warm towards him in spite of my hurt. I know he was away for a lot of the next day and Alex gave me a session and crying a lot helped me a bit, even though it was about not believing in therapy and being a complete failure, depressed and blocked.

The next day, late in the afternoon, after spending the day in the sun, I got home and Steve was trying to make contact again, asking to talk to me, but I almost ignored him; I couldn't face my feelings about him. I felt the cutoffness inside me had reached crisis proportions, and the only thing I could do was take an acid trip.

I took it, and the physical effects came on immediately. I went with my body and was straightaway deep in it. My hair and the blanket felt like mucus on my face. I made sounds and they came, strange straining noises that came up from inside me, each sound very very long. Something big was happening, and I got Alex to sit with me.

My body had taken over. I was contracting and releasing; grunting sounds were pushing out of me. I thought a woman must sound like that when she has a baby naturally. I was a baby, straining to be born. The sensations and the sounds went on and on, it was the most exhilarating experience just to be in that, but what an effort to fight for my life, what exhaustion, and then periods of deep peace, deep relaxation after the straining; and then the tension and contracting and urging would come back, so naturally, of their own accord. And when a thought got in the way, it was so clear, I could see it written there in my head, popping up to interrupt my being born. Was I really allowed to do this, to be born in my own time, with no-one hurrying me, with no-one offering instructions or suggestions? Could Alex bear to sit with me while I was born? Tears came as I saw: if Jan was here, *he'd tell me how to be born.* I realized the preciousness of having someone there who was silent, but attentive. At one point, Alex went off to get his dinner and a book, and that was so beautiful, I laughed and laughed. For me, it meant he was so relaxed about being there, about seeing me through; all I needed anyway was his physical and energetic presence. I laughed also at the contrast between how amazingly important it was to me to be born, and how matter-of-fact for Alex; of course, it happens every day; people are being born all the time. More and more laughing came as I started getting comic-strip images of Alex as Bugs Bunny sitting on the beach in a deckchair, wearing a straw hat and casually watching me being born.

And then I was deeply back in my body again; the urging came back, there was a lot of work to be done. It was such a strain, as if each straining, grunting noise was my body fighting to live. My own tears and mucus round my face became part of fighting to breathe, I felt them as the blood and mucus from my mother's body. I felt what a dangerous thing the whole process is, what a fight. I felt how completely vulnerable I was, and how to relax totally would mean opening myself to being killed: anything could get at me. I saw how necessary my tensions, my defences are: how they protect me from feeling the full horror of being a helpless baby, unprotected.

Then the worst thing happened: Becky came in. I asked her to leave but she didn't. She kept coming back, sulky. That was the end of my fight to breathe.

One of those dreadful things that can only be understood after the trip is over was happening: what I needed to do was literally fight for my life, fight for the right to be born without interruption. But because it was my own child threatening me, I copped out completely, rationalized. I did not scream at my own child to leave me. I felt I would kill her by doing so. So I went quiet. She did go, but I'd lost myself. I got tied up on the head trip of 'Is it alright to face children with your feelings even when they are murderous anger?' I started asking Alex all kinds of daft therapy questions. I was losing myself rapidly. I got into joking and giggling with him, and before I knew it, I was gone completely, lost. It was terrible. I asked Alex, politely of course, to leave, so that I could find myself. He went; I was avoiding, and his parting was tense. I lay there alone

with everything stilled inside me. Jan came in for something. He
was tense and smiley and darting around and talking fast. I
couldn't hear him, so our exchange was confused and messed
up. He went. So I'd sent Becky away, Alex away; and I couldn't
relate to Jan. Bad.

I lay for what seemed like hours alone in that room. Dead.
I had no muscles, my skin was kind of melted and flabby. I was
old and dead. My head was working overtime. I wanted Becky
and Sally; but then I stopped the want, telling myself I only
wanted them because they were alive and I wanted them to
liven me up. I was punishing myself for being dead by going
deader.

I took my clothes off. I didn't even know if I was 'allowed'
to do this, I was so uncentred and cut-off. For a few moments
when I sucked my thumb, I came out of my head for a bit and
could feel and that was good. I came alive a bit also when I sat
up instead of lying collapsed. But mainly, I lay curled up,
waiting, wasting life. I felt how easy it would be to turn into
Mike, shut myself away in a room for ever, take valium and
keep everyone out.

Eventually I thought: if this is how I am, well that's that, I
may as well accept that the therapy's a failure, all my images of
myself and my hoped-for health are false, so I may as well go
out and relate to the world as I am.

I got up, wrapped myself in a blanket, and went to find
Becky. She was watching TV. I climbed up to her attic and
tried to get her attention by sitting in front of the telly, by
throwing orange peel at it, by asking her endless daft questions
about the programme. Especially, I kept asking, 'Do they mean
it? Are they serious?' The picture was really affecting me:
people with masks on who kept changing character, suddenly,
from evil to kind and back again. Then there was a comedy
piece about depression and being loved and taking pills. I
laughed at every joke.

I sat, knowing I was dead, hugging the wooden beams of the
attic, feeling humble and that I wanted to face people with
what I was. Mark had phoned during the day and so had Babs,

and I hadn't spoken to them: more people that I'd pushed away by the state I was in. I suddenly knew I wanted to face Steve, it was time to face him. I called out for him, loudly, from the attic. Alex appeared and I felt embarrassed because it was Steve I wanted. He said Steve had gone to his old home. That was difficult to swallow. The door banged, Alex was gone and I thought, right, that's it, now you're really doing it, really cutting everyone out and you're going to be alone.

I went down to get my dog, Sally. She wouldn't move and looked weird and wouldn't come upstairs. I tried to get her up and all she would do was lie on her back with all her paws in the air and look sickly, kind of leering at me, with stiff, unmoving energy. I decided she was dying. Something was really wrong, all she would do was cower and stare at me sideways. I couldn't see any energy coming out of her; usually she is flickering with it. She didn't even snarl and snap when I tried to move her like she usually does. I thought, that's it, now I've killed my own dog with my deadness. Her fur looked strange, lank and unhealthy and I recoiled from going too close to her because I thought she was diseased and dying. I went to get her some food and felt how my own split about buying meat, about killing for food, about killing when you have to live, had killed Sally: she was dying of my schizophrenia, my own blocked killing instincts.

I lay down under the stairs and cowered and tried to see the world from her point of view. It didn't help, I couldn't make out what was wrong. Jan and Becky were playing in the hall-way. I sat under the stairs, and let myself be entertained. I had time for them; I opened myself to really seeing Jan, my enemy. The way I looked at it was, I didn't have myself, I'd failed, I was dead, so there were no grounds for criticizing him for anything he did. I felt gentle towards the idea of him going out drinking every night. I saw the heartbreak behind his quick talking and sparky movements and felt how every bit of contact anyone can get, however they do it, is valid; I didn't blame the hash smokers, or Jerry for any of his things. I felt we were all in a last-ditch stand and had to get warmth as best we could. I saw a lot of love and life in Jan; he's like a kid with no exit and still desperately trying to be loved and trying to live. He went out.

Becky and I sat in the kitchen, eating and throwing food around, me that is, Becky wouldn't throw food around. The house was in the most incredible mess. It didn't matter. I let Becky lead, I revered completely her capacity to know what she wanted; I let the life in her guide me. It was good eating with her in the kitchen, bashing my food up with a knife when I thought of Steve, trying to get Becky to come out with hostility towards me, and not managing it.

We went up to bed. I lay and looked at Becky's beautiful face and started making faces at her. She opened her mouth wide and made monster faces and I screamed and energy came rushing, and she laughed her head off saying, 'I can't believe it, my own mother and *she's* scared of *me*!' I wanted to go further, but Becky was tired and wanted to sleep. I saw how wrong I had been earlier not to follow my instinct and go to her then.

I stroked her to sleep and then got up. I decided to renew contact with the people I'd cut off today, to face them as I was: depressed, amazingly so, on an acid trip, something I didn't know was possible. Alex isn't on the phone. Babs was in bed. Mark answered. It was a difficult conversation, but I kept it slow and didn't rush away on any guilt trip of being responsible for his life. I dialled Steve's number, but just then Jan came in, manic from his drinking. He sat and talked and I listened quietly, respecting him absolutely, not trying to get away, because nothing I wanted to do was as important as listening to him. He and I joked about phoning Steve to tell him to come home as it was his cleaning day. Steve was not amused. He hummed and haahed about coming back and kept asking why I wanted him there. I wanted him home, and that's all I could say.

I sat around with Jan listening to stories about the woods. I realized how unspoilt he is. His room was lit by candlelight and he gave me some body perfume to put on and I poured too much on and stunk. I was very quiet the whole time. I went into the therapy room to wait for Steve.

By one o'clock, I realized he wasn't coming. I cried a few tears and thought for a long time. I knew that if I waited till morning to see him, this time I wouldn't cut off, I wouldn't go off. I knew now it was Steve I wanted and no-one else would do. At least I knew that.

I thought, 'I'll walk to his house.' The determination cheered me somewhat, but I knew I didn't have the physical strength to walk so many miles. I phoned him anyway and said, 'I'm coming over.' I dressed for the outside world and felt quite beautiful in spite of my deadness inside. I wrapped myself in an Indian bedspread, Steve's, and hailed a taxi for the first time in my life. I was terrified of his driving; I was furious, feeling he is trying to kill me before I get there.

Steve and his room were in technicolour. Sitting there in his torn shirt on his own territory, he looked stormy amongst the clouds painted on his walls, self-contained and looking at me as if I were mad. He talked a lot about the last few days and his anger at me for cutting off and not facing him. Every word he said was right, but my mouth wouldn't open and I couldn't answer or come out with my feelings; they were too strong. I felt I would go crazy, the more he said, the more sense he made, the more the words died in my chest; every cell in my body was going out towards him, but nothing would come out of me.

In the morning, as he lay sleeping, I wrote him a letter, and left:

Steve,

The words stone cold dead stuck in my head can come out perhaps through my hand. It seems I have had a relapse into almost total emotional catatonia, I could quite well imagine myself cutting off forever like a junkie in a graveyard, waiting to die. With you, I got quickly addicted to a paradise constant good acid trip of bright orange colours and ever-ready warmth and contact and I let you get into my veins and come all over my body, and when you went, I backed up and fell into the biggest trap of all, retreating when I should have yelled, 'Please stay!' Steve, if you knew how I see you: like a magic fairy come to turn my pumpkins into coaches, my fleas into dragons. Do you know what a proud stiff woman is like? I am so stiff inside I wonder I don't snap when you hug me; I am so proud, I have

eaten the whole world with my face turned to one side
pretending not to be hungry. I have attended my own funeral
and smelt my own body rotting and watched the children
dancing on my grave without a shadow passing across my face.
But I know that if I want an after-life, I better sit back and
watch those children and learn because I am blind and cannot
lead the full-eyed.

And I WILL COME BACK, Steve, I did already come here
last night, though all I could bring you was a corpse. Steve, a
slap round the face from you is more precious than a thousand
words; I treasure your anger like I treasure my own moments of
fullbloodedness. DO NOT RESPECT MY IMAGE, Steve; but
please do not turn away, there's a person dying underneath.
How can I, Aries, first-born, open my paralysed mouth and
say, 'Steve, every clean red word that comes out of you is right.'
Never listen to me when my eyes are dead and arrogant, listen
only to the beating of your own heart and trust it.

I will come back, you know, I am going to have you because
I know what's good when I see it. The mad woman has a baby
kicking inside and I will get out and play with you again.

And then I went home, in long clothes, with a bedspread on my
shoulder, knowing that all my previous life and images had
come to an end; no more goals of perfect health, no more
clarity or perfectly logical therapy, hardly able to face myself
because myself is something so totally collapsed; I felt like a
junkie, not even with the illusion any more of being able to
keep things together. All I could do was humiliate myself and
get what warmth and contact I could. I felt completely in
Steve's power and accepting of the fact.

The strange thing was, I didn't feel bad; there was pleasure,
even a little smile, at giving in to my new capsized self. I got
home after going shopping with Becky, brown and hot on a
sunny day, high and very awake; I knew Steve would be there
and all I wanted to do was see him. He was in the bath, but
wouldn't open the door. I pretended to saw it down and set
light to it, but he wasn't joking. Suddenly, I knew I didn't know
Steve, that I couldn't handle him, and that I couldn't handle the

explosions inside me about being shut out. I found my letter amongst his things and tore it up. Me tearing things up now, that's new! Soon Steve stormed downstairs, shouting at me for tearing the letter up, and we both went up to the therapy room with Alex. He carried on shouting. This was really bad, I was sinking. At every loud word, I got stiller and stiller inside until I was completely walled-off again. In the end, I couldn't even hear his words.

Alex worked with me. And he worked a miracle. I thought I was cut-off for ever and wanted to kill myself. Alex tried to get me to say 'I exist.' I couldn't. But Alex was so patient and so insistent and gentle, that somehow he got through to me and I started crying.

I went back to when I was two years and one month old. Mum had shut me in the darkened sitting-room with the new baby there in a pram. I had punched the baby in the stomach and Mum had said, 'That's it. I'm leaving home.' I was sobbing, standing at the window watching to see her go, believing her implicitly, my world at an end. I couldn't argue, couldn't call her back, she'd shut the door and there was no comeback; she *was* going and that's all there was to it.

Then, instead of her leaving, the baker came up the path. I was howling and the baby was howling, so she let me out, I clung to her skirt. As she opened the door to the baker, she smiled gaily and said breezily, 'I don't know, once one starts, they all start, don't they!' A frivolous ending; the execution never actually came. I felt in my session how I was stuck in tragedies with frivolous endings. I remembered a dream about how I was going to be eaten and every person in my family that I turned to for help turned out to be in league with the cannibals and when it got to the moment I was to die, suddenly they all turned round and said, 'Silly girl, you didn't *really* think we'd eat you, did you?' I feel throughout my life, my tragedies have been brushed aside, 'Surely you don't take it *seriously*?'

Steve and I went for a walk in the park after our sessions. We still weren't communicating. There is no life in me when I don't feel loved. As soon as he held my hand on the grass, I fell deeply asleep; it was the only time I felt good and secure. Eventually, I managed to tell him that I have to feel loved in order to live. I needed nursing back to life, holding. Therapy isn't just 'going into' things, but also coming out of them; I needed to be nourished back to healing and wholeness. But Steve was in another universe. Back at home, he sat in himself, smoking, then left the room. I was going mad, I had never felt so bad. I lay on my bed and fought with sounds and with my body and eventually I dared let out my crying. I kept saying, 'Don't think you're going to have me when I'm sunny if you hate me when I'm down.' I cried for a long time and felt worse and worse, especially as there was loud music being played in the house. I cried that I would never go back to Steve if I had to get through this thing on my own without his help. I cried on and on and on, but there was no relief, it was not good; my chest was breaking, but there was nothing therapeutic about it, it didn't feel like a 'session', I got through to nothing. All I wanted was to be comforted by Steve and nothing else would do; I wanted him to come and let me yell at him and then be comforted by him.

Slowly, it dawned on me that he wasn't even in the house. I looked in every room; the whole house was empty except for Becky. I just couldn't believe he'd leave the house when I was crying; I was completely destroyed. I went back to the therapy room and cried myself to exhaustion. I decided then to dare to go into the pub to find Steve and ask him to come home. I went like a ghost into that crowded smoke and Jan tapped me on the shoulder, 'Steve's not here, he's gone to see some friends.' I went home, splitting still more on top of all the other cracks; I wondered how far this could go inside me; I knew I'd better phone someone quick. Peter answered and was really soft; he is so good at times like this; he listened to my slowed-down voice.

While I was talking to him, Steve walked in. Another frivolous ending. Mum opening the door to the baker, smiling gaily. Steve walking in, amazed that anything was wrong. I tried to face him, but my emotions were spent, my voice like glass, my tears exhausted, my body finished; I didn't feel real. Steve started to cry, and I left him, deliberately.

He came in soon and talked softly to me; he seemed quite
broken up. I had come down now from the cold hysteria of my
nightmare. I could look at him, even see him. My body was
tired now, in a good way. So there *was* relief from all the
terrible cutting of that crying; I was surprised. Steve talked
some more, and I went over to him and told him I wished I
wasn't, but I was in love with him.

I slept thick and well that night and woke up feeling quite
strong; aggressive too, I don't take so much humiliation easily.
We went to Richmond Park together. The journey was bad,
sitting there side by side, miles apart. I felt we were really
finished, and this was the dragged-out ending. In the park, we
agreed to separate for a few days. I went off for a walk alone,
to imagine my days and to plan for being alone in the world
again. I went on the swings and felt sick. I knew I'd be so angry
at Steve going away that I'd cut off for good. I was angry at
myself for making such a fool of myself so soon after getting to
know him, angry that there was no-one else I wanted. I went
back over to Steve and told him my thoughts. He said, 'Well,
that's it, I'm coming to the group tonight, and we'll just have to
face one another.'

I don't know how we came through. It was a miracle and I'm
not sure what happened. I don't have to be given much to get
my cheek back. I just remember looking at him and saying, 'I
hate you.' And I remember starting to tell him all the horrible
things I'd like to do to him. I remember chucking water over
him and him hitting me too hard round the head. We played,
and it was serious. We went on the swings and worked out ways
of killing one another. Our aggression turned sexual and became
soft feelings and someone had switched the lights on again.

David once told me, 'Pain is when the person you want is
irreplaceable and you can't control them not to hurt you.'

On the way home, we went into a pub. The cider Steve
bought me was strong and the air was singing round me; I had
that teenage feeling of discothèques and cigarette smoke and
being with my boy whose body I was allowed to touch, anywhere. The atmosphere was electric and sexualized and I felt
like a woman, shy and proud and knowing the other men in the

pub were looking at me. I was purringly content and didn't have many clothes on and was blissfully scruffy and brown from our hot day in the park.

My happiness is flimsy and fragile and can go away, but now I know I can go to hell and back and die and still not go away in pride and I suppose that is something to be glad about, because it certainly hasn't happened like this before.

I eventually got into the group about ten thirty, having been waylaid by Steve in the bathroom. I told Babs a bit about what had been going on and looked into her lovely eyes and tears came into mine as I felt the pain of being alive and needing love and I said, 'What's happening to me, Babs, I don't understand any more what's going on.' And she said, 'It's good not to understand, Jenny, to be without your head for a bit; you've always had your head. It's because of where you're at in your therapy that the pain of being left is so great.' So I didn't struggle to 'get into things' and when she left the group, she hugged me.

Session with Steve, 12th June, 1973

Sitting up, looking at Steve, I held his hands and broke immediately: I couldn't bear to take in his skin, his face, so soft and round. I sobbed that I didn't want to come back, how many more times must I be born, each time so painful? Then suddenly I was my elder sister, the one who took six days to come out and then died from the forceps in her head. I was her, struggling in that dead body and meeting her fate. I sobbed to think of my mother's body. 'Oh no, it can't be true, I can't believe that I came out of her.' I was suffocated before I was born.

Then suddenly I felt I'd done the same to my own first-born, Becky's twin, Nicole; she fought three days to come out of my tight body, only to be yanked out the other way under bright lights in an arena of medical students, her head full of water. I became her too and was wracked with sobs to know the pain of my baby.

I looked at Steve's face again. As I stared, I couldn't believe my horrified eyes: another face began to superimpose itself over his, a lion's face. I couldn't bear to look for long; I sobbed and cried, knowing in that moment that this horror is always there, lying just below the surface of my consciousness, knowing in this moment that that monster face is imprinted on my eyeballs forever, embedded in the cells of my brain. As I looked at Steve again, I knew my eyes were those of a baby, focussing intently, seeing with microscopic awareness, looking, searching this face in front of me which was my everything, the rest of the room blurred and unimportant now. I knew I would be able to see every change, every passage of energy, every shadow that crossed this face and I understood the wisdom and the agony of a baby whose mother is pretending.

Eyeblock

No baby
blind from the light
from a split sky
makes sense of the cracks
in the mirror.

When a world snaps
like a baby's back in the womb
when the sun becomes glass
in a cold house
it is no wonder eyes have their terrible struggle.

Seeing is easy:
there is the dead mother inside you
to ever look at,
you cannot unwrap her.
There is the dead father outside you
to ever look for
buried alive, his laugh still lingers.

Looking now,
endlessly looking,
screwing a hole in the clouds
scanning a face which could be a horizon
waiting like dying
you make me your mirror,
your dreams roll over my cheekbones.

From a foot's distance
you peer from the end of a tunnel
where birthcries are lifelong.
Your eyes squeeze the vision in, the light out.
Your hands strain the hinges of time,
wrists wrestle with history,
wrenching you back to the one space we sit in.

David

Session with Babs, 22nd June, 1973

I start feeling the split in me between arrogance and humility.
I am humble with Steve because I need the good feelings he
gives me. I talk to Mum: 'I will give myself to you, do anything
you say, let you think and feel for me, relate to the world for
me, take me to the toilet. Yes, I admit I cannot live, I cannot
speak to strangers, I will stay home forever, unmarried,
incapable, I will hide in your skirts, if you will just look after
me and come home to me each day.' And all the time I am
hating her, seeing her as sickly, inferior, not worthy of me. But
she is all I have, I have to swallow my pride, wallow in my
humility.

Then my baby sister is born and she steals the humble-pie
trip from me, she does it better; she plays the game better. So
only arrogance and cold pride are left to me.

I speak to Mum: 'I want the warm times back.'

I break immediately, the giving-in is terrible. I am whirling
down through a plug-hole, passing Jerry and the warm times
with him on the way. My swallowed pride is cutting me up as I
digest it, I am tiny again. 'I want the warm times back.' The

sounds crash out of me, long, long, longer than any breath can be, sending me back, back to my beginnings, I welcome now the retching that heralds the long dive downwards. 'I want the warm times back.' Each time I say that, another wave of feeling bursts over me. Brown, I want those brown rooms in Leicester, that brown house. That is my home, there I existed, there I could feel, I felt myself, I felt alive, before the baby came, there I was a little queen, battered and torn already, but alone and whole and at the centre, feeling and struggling and still living.

There is pleasure in the wrenching pain: so it is true, I did exist, I was there in the world all those years ago, before I died when my sister was born. I WANT TO GO BACK, I WANT TO GO BACK THERE, to be myself again. I, who always cried never to go back, am crying now to be that child again, in the days before I died.

Now Babs' youngest child is talking to her in the therapy room. A soft, white, blond, blue-eyed whimpering second-child is taking my space, taking away the attention of this dark woman who is helping me. I am taken out of where I am; I can't get the space and time I need to grow. I see my life as a cracked stream of interruptions. I had unfinished business with my mother so that now, when I am not cut off by someone else, I cut myself off, I know no other way. My relationships do not conclude, my sexual feelings do not conclude; there are no endings. I lost my endings somewhere back at my beginnings.

I feel torn apart, I am howling with the hopelessness of it all; I feel Jerry's 'I'll burn your letters'; see Jan slamming out of the door in fury, leaving me with mine; doors closing everywhere, no-one can stand my noises, no-one can take what comes out of me; Dad dies to avoid me; Mum dies to get away from me; my stepfather breaks off contact because he cannot bear his feelings about me; Alex hears me as his complaining mother, Steve as his; my one friend Babs has her own children to cope with; no-one can hear me to the end.

I am quiet. I look at Babs. She says smiling, 'I think you are going to have to kill your sister.'

A Visit to Jerry's

Steve and Becky and me went over to Jerry's. Somehow I was
open. I could see Jerry. I went for a long walk with him.
Yesterday, I had felt close to him, as I listened to John
Lennon's primal record, crying. I'd felt connected to him. It is
difficult to admit these things, very difficult to let my defensive-
ness drop, difficult to forget all the bad images I have had of
him and the bad times I've had through him, the ungroundings
I have suffered. But there he was, quite soft and ordinary, and
not on any guru trips. It was fun to let him buy me ice cream
and a jumble-sale dress and show me along the canal, and to
play in the park. We were no longer stiff or distant or defensive.
I felt the strings tugging; he is my person and I do not want him
to move away.

Back at his house, he admitted to Steve how difficult it is for
him to acknowledge anyone as being 'my boyfriend'; he still
thinks of me as 'on vacation' and that I'll come back some day.
As he said these things, I began to cry but would not give in to
the feeling, which was that I too think of myself as his errant
girlfriend, that we two really belong together, and I am just
away for the time being.

As we left, I determined to deal with what has been opened
up and to explore these feelings.

Back home, I came face to face with my old life. Trev was
there, Trev from the beginning of my therapy, with his hair cut
short like when I first knew him when he was nineteen. He is
twenty-five now, plays the sitar and has sat at home for two
years, had ECT in hospital and is going to sea, up to Newcastle
where my Dad died, and where I got the boat to go and see
Trev in a Swedish jail all those years ago, before I knew David.

So six years have passed, Trev? I just sat and stared and
stared and couldn't get enough of looking now that my eyes are
open and I don't avoid the penetrating twinkle in his and the
smile always playing round his lips, which is love and not
sarcasm as I used to see it. He is a beautiful person, so much life
twisted up in his bent body, and so much love still bursting
through; he is a genius, a Jesus, whose dim parents will never

see him. I hope his day will come. He talked of old times in an alive artistic way and struck chords in my heart and there were warm vibes between him and Steve, and Trev said how lucky Steve was to have me and that made my heart hurt. I felt so sad for him, I wanted to do anything for him, but all I could do was make him some egg sandwiches and kiss him goodbye. He said, 'So you kiss people now?' and was gone. So much love still between us in spite of those bad times when he overran my house with his illness and I couldn't see him straight because of mine.

I ached with knowing my age, to know what it is to look back on a life half-lived with so much life in it that I couldn't feel then; to know how sometimes it seems I was more important to others than to myself. How these meetings and partings hurt.

A day with Jerry, 27th June 1973

Steve was trying to help me in the therapy room when Jerry walked in. I called him over, he was sitting tense and awkward and looking angry against the wall. He came over and said he didn't want to feel like a grown-up any more, didn't want to be stiff and different. I asked him, 'How could you feel one with us, how could you join in and play?' An old grin I knew from way back broke out as he said, 'Take my clothes off.' He took his shirt off and I saw a Jerry I knew; he lay down and I held his hand and we breathed. Later, Babs came and joined us. I started to feel safe and good and ready to be with them all and explore. I played with Jerry later, he was making me laugh like so often before. Then I just lay and looked at him and told him I was sorry for the pain I'd caused him and that I loved him. I held him gently while he cried.

I knew I wanted to spend more time with him. It was pouring with rain, but with a long skirt and bare arms and feet, I went out into the streets and the parks with Jerry and my dog feeling long and slim and warm. There was hardly anyone about in the park on this hot rainy day. We went to the pond and they'd pulled mountains of green water-weed out of it; it was piled up high and steaming. The water was warm; there were no park-police around now, so I paddled and waded in and sat in it, talking and talking with Jerry. It was a relief just to say a few of the things I felt — how I wanted him to live with us when we move to the country, and not go off into a separate life; how I felt possessive towards him, and couldn't bear to think of him going off and joining some middle-class scene. He was small Jerry today, not up on his throne and he talked of the back streets of New York and he said, 'I know who my people are.'

After he left, I sat on the wet grass for a long time, and then walked home with my dog.

Thursday group, 28th June 1973

What a horrid group, crowded with unwelcome faces from the far distant past; a kind of forced energy I couldn't bear, sounds I didn't believe; I was sickened and embarrassed. I looked hungrily at Steve to suck up some of the radiant health in his face, looked frantically at Alex to reassure myself he wasn't being fooled by the games of the girl he was working with. I sat withheld and stunned while this wild group whirled round me; I wanted so much to leave, but I let the tension build up right to the end of the evening, and then Alex worked with me, magnificently. First, there were the false faces: Mum with her plastered-on smile that hid a snarl; me locked in pretending to believe in it, because if I didn't, it would change, crack, crumble, and she would become a monster of fury. I related this block immediately to how I withhold the truth of my opinions from so many people, terrified to break through their masks. I pretend I think they are real and healthy, knowing instinctively the volcano that will erupt if I confront them.

I moved then to anger at the new people; those who drop in occasionally but who give nothing. How my attitude has changed! Now I am no longer willing to help anyone I get nothing from. I got into immense anger about the house, yelling that if I were sure of the place in the Lakes we are after, I'd let the bloody house crumble. I enjoyed my beautiful anger, relishing the thought of the bailiffs coming, of the walls falling down, of people knocking at the door and no-one to answer, Mummy's gone away. I was feeling three years of anger and pressure, cleaning this house, making it good for others, no-one ever making it good for me. Hate and more hate poured out of me, I even felt hostility towards Steve for the way I look after him and make his life comfortable. I swore I'd never do another thing for any weak people: once again I felt the 'weak' people as angry, threatening me with their blue passive eyes and pale bodies, waiting to be picked up (Dad!), and felt how I relate to the dark-eyed people, the hardbodied doers (Mum!).

I felt tremendous gratitude towards Alex after my long session, and felt strong and aggressive in myself, very cocky towards Steve, quite separate from him and well able to withstand him, but friendly and open too.

Sunday group, 1st July, 1973

I was feeling almost too good to work on anything, but then I started to be aware of my impatience when working with Steve. I got help for myself and went on a long and complicated journey which wound its way back to my sister: big, blue eyes, chubby cheeks, passivity which says: 'I am so innocent, why do all these nasty people around me bug me so?' I felt my hatred of the 'goodies'. Surprisingly, I realized I identified with Jan, not Steve, in an encounter earlier that evening where Jan was so obviously the 'baddy'. Sickening feelings about the goodies: they have no guts. Back to my sister, the goody of the family, being a real child when she played with me alone, then changing miraculously into an angel when Mum was there; betraying me always, friendly with me when alone, turning against me as soon as there was a threesome; secretly criticizing Mum and my stepfather, but never facing them, and me, the baddy, losing all. I felt I was only just starting to loosen the big blocks inside me about my sister.

Then I saw Mum, how she'd always pretended she wanted my sister and me to be friends, but when we started to get close, it was obvious: YOU DON'T WANT US TO GET TOGETHER, because then your game would be up, there'd be mutiny in the ranks, we'd communicate and tell each other the truth, and your version of our lives would vanish in smoke.

Then I got a strange, new feeling. I saw Mum and her scene as a bad Hollywood movie and this was the showdown: Mum, the little gangster, and she'd run out of bullets, a Nixon without his bombs, a traffic warden without his uniform. It was a horrid feeling, seeing Mum deflated, about an inch high, a terrified bully, cornered, with nothing left but death. I cried a strange, new crying, lying limp and calm on my side, feeling more separate from my mother than ever before, knowing her emptiness: she was a puffed-up, painted figure with a six-shooter, and her day had come. I lay, feeling out her absence.

Letter to David, 3rd July, 1973

It seems we will not have the house in the Lakes, and Steve is talking about finding a space for himself to live. I am thrown back again on myself: Steve thinking of the house problem in terms of himself made me realize there is only me, Becky and Sally; that's all I am responsible for, and no-one is responsible for me. This made me very quiet and grown-up.

In the night, I awoke in a fright, calling out and screaming, so I thought, kicking and yelling for Steve. I'd had a vision, I thought I was awake, of voices and lights at my door, and some-one with crepe-soled shoes on. Fear was all over my body and it was even more frightening to hear Steve tell me I hadn't screamed at all, he'd been awake the whole time.

My whole body was paralysed, especially my arms, I was locked in fear. I associated this vision immediately with a powerful session I'd given my sister when she got in touch with the night Dad left, when she was three and I five years old. Steve making me realize I don't have a family has brought that night back to me.

So, David, technically, things are bad, and quite a lot of bad feelings are coming up, with amazing regularity, a strange logic out of strange chaos. But I do not feel bad. Jerry has got me back into physical things, bats and balls and running in the parks. Yes, technically, things are glum, setbacks every day. But emotionally, I have great support, Babs and Laszlo close to me,

Jerry close in his separateness, Steve's sense of self setting me
back on myself, new and frightening, but I will face it and not
cut off from him, our love is strong.

David wrote back:
Dear Jen,
    I have been reading Mike Barnett's version of PNP and the
Jenny-who-everyone-depends-on. It's strangely out-of-date
already, back in a time when Jerry still lived there, before he
was separate enough to be that kind of close.
    So things are bad, but you do not feel bad. Your worst times
now seem when you get stuck in pleasure anxiety. Steve is so
right for you, no wonder you get the bottom falling away if he's
physically not there. To dare to enjoy him is to invite the basic
punishment: departure.
    He is not some third party I write about who gets excluded.
He is Steve who is lucky to have you and who helps your
therapy along without getting too involved. I don't think he will
let you cast him in roles, he will be Steve, for you to take, or
leave, or have fits over. If I gave advice, it would be to let in the
pleasure-pride your body won't burst with, and to let the infant
in you rage at his absence when you have to.
    Steve is better than I imagined him — he said I had known
you 'longer than any of us', but I reckon he sees you one of the
clearest. He won't tangle in your games, he won't lie down and
die when your eyes go stony; unlike Mike Barnett who respects
the man in you but cannot love you, Steve seems to relate to
the woman in you.
    Enough of my ramblings — I hope your technical hitches get
sorted out soon, that Spain warms to you, that Becky warms to
Steve, that your kind of creative chaos has some wonders in
store for you in spite of all setbacks.
    If you don't cut off from Steve, your mother will really die,
her lease of power over you will finally run out, her wrists that
dared me to break the spell will have abandoned her struggle in
you.

                                                    Love, David

Letter to David from Spain, 11th July 1973
Dear David,

I dreamt of you last night. I dreamt that Heather was telling me she'd invited you home for the weekend and that I was trying not to be jealous about it, but I was, because I knew I would never dare to invite you home for the weekend. Strange that this should come up now, it really happened, you know, years ago: she told me she'd invited you home for supper, and I was shocked because you were my David, but I'd never dare such intimacy.

I am very burnt at the moment, and that makes it difficult to think. I have been through some more very bad times, been to the bottom of nowhere; and I have had moments — whole days even — of great joy.

The Tuesday before I left, I spent the day at Jerry's. He was saying how I should live alone, it would get me into more things in my therapy. I didn't get into a hard knot with him arguing about this, I was generally more open to him, and him to me, but I certainly felt undermined by what he was saying, frightened of bad things happening to me if I 'kept safe' with Steve.

The next day, I felt really bad. Alex helped me and I spent one and a half hours crying in resentment, a resentment that covered everyone, I couldn't even look at Alex. I didn't ever want to do anything for anyone again, not for Steve or anyone. I felt I was drowning in a never-ending sea of resentment against anyone I'd ever put first, because no-one looked after me. I stayed on my own with a headache afterwards and felt very in myself and on my own.

On Thursday morning, Steve and I had sex and it really hurt me, I guess I was tight inside with all the anger which hasn't come out at being the one doing all the looking after and sorting out. I started crying and needed him to encourage me to open to my feelings, but he didn't and I went into a very schizzy state where huge feelings were just on the surface, but I wouldn't let them come out, I was too terrified and too proud. I couldn't even answer when he spoke to me and eventually he left the house, fed up. I was in a terrible state and phoned Babs with an end-of-the-world feeling. Then Steve returned looking like thunder and I knew *he* would need help, so I went for a walk on my own in the park to get things into perspective. I saw how I was really behaving most confusingly for him because big things were happening to me that I couldn't cope with, and he couldn't either. He is not a therapist, just a very good friend, and he goes by his feelings, not by what is therapeutically best for me at any given moment. I went back to talk to him and found him crying.

Soon I was up and bouncing again and getting things together and we left for Spain that very night. It was raining and we sat at the busstop waiting for a 49 to take us to Spain and Steve was excited at our mad relationship and our mad journey and I was happy.

On the boat to Dieppe, we paid for a cabin because I was feeling vulnerable and messed up. Steve slept all night, but I kept waking up with night terrors, feeling Jerry's face in front of mine, and calling out to him: he seemed to represent safety and all that is steady in my world. I was scared of being stuck in Pepe's tiny flat in Spain where you can't really make a noise, terrified of having screams and anger locked inside and not being able to let them out. My body had gone still and dead and my head was whirling. Once more I went on the trip about Jerry being right, I'd done my therapy wrong and now it is too late, I can't bear the thought of starting all over again. I turned the light and the day on, pushed away my fears of the journey ahead, took over once more and we began our surprisingly easy hitch towards the sun.

After we crossed the Spanish border, we set off to walk through the mountains and to try and find somewhere to sleep. We passed a spring tumbling down the cliffside where we drank and washed, and we passed three lots of Guardia Civil who asked us inquisitive questions and pored over our passports and pondered over each item in our suitcase. I laughed the whole time, guessing the boredom of being a policeman, and the novelty of seeing two brown brightly-clad people actually *walking* through their mountains.

There was a smooth river where we waded, with Spaniards

watching us from the bushes and a zillion tiny frogs hopping around us. We walked on then, weary, and got an unexpected lift, ending up in Pamplona in the middle of a bull fiesta. We scampered through the raging crowds to the quiet outskirts, still seeking a corner to curl up, and got a lift instead all through the stormy night, lightning lighting up the sky ahead like a cinemascope screen. After an aching night, we arrived in the tired morning in Zaragoza and were picked up in a cafe by a young drunk Spaniard with a sensitive upper-class face who bought us coffee and told us his troubles for hours on end and who needed to cry. Then finally, a lift to Barcelona, six-hours long with a lecherous driver who made my life a misery while Steve slept peacefully in the back of the cab, and I stored up anger enough to cause trouble for a whole day.

Arriving in Barcelona, I hated the city and the Catalans and their built-over countryside, their dry hills and mad streets. I fumed and needed comfort from my ordeal, but Steve retreated inside and there we were, in a morass once more, and my period starting.

Becky welcomed us at the door of Pepe's flat, she'd flown to Spain. Also there was an acquaintance of Pepe's from ten years back who is murdering her child with her own misery, and outside the window, a beautiful tied-up puppy, yelling night and day with boredom and frustration, living victim of dead owners. In the evening, with my body hurting all over, I tried to get help from Steve, but was on a terrible headtrip, having sold my soul for a mess of potage, my anger for a six-hour lift. I was too split and proud again to breathe deep into my body without the right encouragement. Eventually, I brought you near to me, David, I cried for you so far away and brought you to me because I needed help. I asked you to touch my body and tell me to breathe, and at last the tears came through, I could cry and you gave me a session, and I could sleep that night.

Another bad morning then, but in the afternoon, Pepe found us on the beach and it felt good to see him. I talked over the journey and the bad times and he seemed so glad to have me there, the sky turned brighter.

Well, since then, things have been good, with me and Steve —

not with Becky, though, who is very jealous of our being together.

Somehow we have come through and somehow this strange intricate Reichian way of slow-moving with sudden changes has its effects on me when I least expect them, like weird energy effects in sex that make me faint or cry for my mother or look into Steve's eyes and say, 'maybe I *can* live'. And that seems to be what I am doing, in my own way, accepting the ruination of my childhood, and that I cannot miraculously change back into a sixteen-year-old with a smooth stomach and free-moving limbs, but I can be very much in love indeed and know my fears and my insecurity and suddenly in the middle of sex which is so grown-up, my chest and stomach can break with a crying that is thirty years old, a hot feeling of giving in, so good to give in, and I thought I never could.

With love to you, David,

Jenny.

Dear Jen,

You are strangely vulnerable when away from home — it's a different kind of voice that seems to come out of you. Is it harder to be a frightened girl crossing the road, than a queen of passions? I am interested in what is different about you when you are out of your nest, and therapy of some kind not on tap very easily.

What happens is you seem to get more confused, with more space around you and the tide of other people running slower: big breakthroughs and big clarities are harder to find on trips without acid. Spain is hot and dry and hard to scream in.

What seems to happen then is you need to listen to the confusion, and not rush out of it. Bad times turn into good times if you give them time. In the absence of your therapy group, you cannot draw on other's energy to help yours, and it may be good that Steve cannot help you therapeutically. It may be better that he be a very good friend and a lover, give you space to have your own feelings in, but not be therapist too. Because when you are deprived, you dip into your own resources which you trust so little, you draw on the good things in you, and if I can give you a session when I am in Colorado and you in Spain, then that is a kind of minor miracle that is too easily glossed over. When people are not there you do not think about them, you forget them, their faces dull over: but to draw on my energy, distant, that far, and turn it to your own good, means your still, your dead body is only a small part of the truth about you, your fear to be yourself, and under it your live, your moving body that can sleep and wake up in the morning and love Steve again.

Somehow you come through, and that is also the truth; if you would just accept; if you would lie down in the bad times in the knowledge better times will come out of them if you give up that struggle; if you would just accept the slow moving and the sudden changes.

OK, your mother worked a ruination, she created a monster of need who fought terribly to prove she was alive against a terror of becoming small and engulfed again. I worked to soften and melt down the spectres of your past all the time I was with you. If out of all that, in spite of all doubts, beyond the scars and the fact life will never be perfect, you can come to begin to believe that maybe you can live, maybe it is worth it, maybe you are beautiful sometimes, maybe you can love beyond your hate and your pride, maybe you can draw love to you without having to struggle to keep it, maybe inspite of all insecurity the warm and the good things can still flow into and out of your body, — then these are the quiet gains of a slow therapy, less spectacular than the breakthroughs, but they are what I believe in, and when you say you cried like a thirty-year-old, all my energy swings out to you with support, because for so long you have lived as if only by playing sixteen or retreating to the hot fires of infancy could anyone believe in you, or want to relate to you.

What will happen, one day, if, as you grow, the energy-bank of infancy gets exhausted, will you one day go back to the ruins for the last time? Is your fear that with no mother alive or father alive you will forget, everyone will forget, no one will know, the reality of that childhood that makes you real, that terrible childhood that no-one can grasp, — if you gave it up would you be nothing? Just a woman of thirty-one on holiday with her man in a hot and sometimes boring country. To be grown-up is most frightening of all; it means the child in you dying and you are so loth to say goodbye. The miracle would not be changing back into a sixteen-year-old with a smooth stomach, the miracle would be to be Jenny daring to be thirty-one, and no buts. Accepting when you need to be curled up small, or abandoned, or howling — but ready also when that strange tide turns and brings you back to adult tears or adult joy. To give in to being grown means to feel the life in Steven here and now, and the life in your body here and now. It means to draw things from the present, or the recent past, to know that there is nourishment here as well as in the emotions of infancy.

So have respect for *your* way of being, when you are not working 'therapeutically' and not doing anything great except meandering in Spain, and being sometimes with your man, and sometimes with your self. Trust the small things to work for you, the strange nights of Spain that come to you when you least expect them.

I still don't understand why you seem closer when you are geographically further away. Perhaps there is a rhythm in all this we may understand one day.

Love, David.

Dear David,

Once more the cosmic whirl brought Sitges its first summer rain, and a scattering of letters to my stagnated doorstep. Your letter, David, and Mike's book; and twenty pages of sensitivity from Laszlo, and a flash of lightning from Alex, and a telegram to say 'arriving' from my sister. No time to absorb each drop of energy, please take back your words and send them to me one at a time . . .

The first time I read hungrily, not tasting. Now, alone in the house, with the enormous task before me of relating out of chaos, I can hardly bear to re-read your words. I have been experiencing bewitchment: Pepe is my witch-mother, and Becky as his accomplice; me, the caster-of-spells and also the spellbound. Jerry says you have the uncanny knack of sending exactly the fitting words. I do not want uncanniness or knacks! Anything that 'fits' terrifies me, because then I think someone has made it up. I have made it up? My terror is a daytime sunshine one: am I in fact David sending myself these words? They hit my centre like arrows. David, my book cannot stand, it must be destroyed, because it pretends to form and process, and natural logicality. No year of gentle climax this, but a year of self-doubt and chaos; the Ramblings of a Schizophrenic Girl, no Room to Breathe.

'You are strangely vulnerable when away from home.' Why then, if you wrote that to me, it seems something did come through to you from my felt chaos. So it seems I *can* express myself; horror is not being free to express pain. So clarity did come to you, David, and you fed it back to me? How difficult it is to take responsibility for my own clarity! Ironically, in order to shift the dead weight of my accumulated terror-bound DOR (Wilhelm Reich's Deadly Orgone Radiation), I sought solace in the head-trips of Gestalt Therapy. They loosened me a little; what was alive in Perls seeped through the sickening garbage of his competitors in Gestalt Therapy Now.

Yes, it is harder to cross the road and show my tears to the woman who owns the dog that is chained up night and day crying, than to scream my anger at my safe friends back home. But I did it, this morning, and she responded kindly, and I broke a week-old impasse that had reached that terrible moment before a climax-that-never-comes when I planned to steal the dog away in the night and set it free. The man with the light made my desperate plan pointless; my words and tears to the lady herself this morning restored my self-respect.

Spain is hot and dry and indeed difficult to scream in. So I retreated into Instant Illness, total body pains that laid me out, that took me over on receiving yet another ungrounding-letter from Jerry. I should not be with Steve, he says. I am uncreative and dead, selling myself for the sake of safety, that's what he says.

Oh, I stood up, answered him back magnificently. But his punches threatened my roots, hit at my nerve-cores and my body collapsed. For two days, just pain, all over; relieved, immediately, by a very small session, crying; horrified by a sudden thought that all my guys hate me as soon as I won't sleep with them, want to destroy me; that, without sex, I am nothing.

I had noticed that the couple of times I got into quite deep things out here was when I just went and collapsed on my bed and did it. As soon as I try to drag Steve into helping me, there is a stagnation of energy, nothing good happens. I am sucking on him, dragging; he is resisting me, deadly. Perhaps the time has come to stop this stagnating therapy game. A kind of twitch takes hold of me where, if my energy dies on me, I feel I must have a session. It seems I have a lot of work to do not lying on a bed.

I have been clinging to memory, that they wanted to take away; yelling at Jerry who tells me to give up the past; and I do not erase that clinging or that yelling. But something new is dawning on me today. I fight furiously to hold on to my past so that I will not become schizophrenic, rootless. Is this just another catastrophic expectation, unfounded? I felt a jolt of fear when Pepe told me it was Friday, and I thought it was Thursday. I had lost a day! From the age of ten till I was twenty, I wrote compulsively — happenings, not feelings — covering every day of my tiny diaries. A space unwritten was a day lost; I would even make up something so as not to leave a blank. Yesterday, I was attacked by fear when a string of days stretched out behind me, and I couldn't remember what sessions I'd had, what feelings. Now, it seems, to write my sessions is to cling. How many more things must I let go of in this horrid journey?

I have clung so long to clarity, to seeing the perfectly defined waves of my therapy journey, to delineating the ups and downs, coming to you, thirsty, when I was in confusion. All that had its healing place. But now I feel I am scared of diving into the flood of Life, going with the swell instead of standing back and painting it. At home, the problem does not show up: I am already in a flood and do not have to jump in; but it is not always *my* flood, often other people's and I have welcomed the

chance to swim in it; their deaths are easier to die than mine.
Now, in Spain, the stark colours once more, no watercolours or
gently shaded edges, as I wrote from here so many painful years
ago. And when there is no flood or current, but just still water?
Then the terror is greatest and my death-obsession returns in
full strength. I even plot death, angry at having to wait for it to
come to me when I am not expecting it, I plot sulkily to go out
and meet it.

David, when I had all those mountains to climb, I could be
totally absorbed in the climbing. I find this stage so painful. It is
the quiet gains of a slow therapy that I cannot sit down with. I
wanted eternal life, my Dad made flesh, and a return to lost
youth. I don't yet know what being thirty-one means, David. I
get a whiff of it on the beach with Becky — it lies somewhere
between giving my life up to her because I cannot live; and
sacrificing her in my frantic struggle to make up for lost time.
On trips, and occasionally not on trips, I have felt the centre
road: to stand back and let her take the stage, in full awareness
of myself as a creature from whom life has come. It is terribly
painful, David; my friends in therapy without children cannot
know this split.

Steve and I, who for a while were like some soft four-eyed
eight-limbed creature, have retreated for a while back into our
own separate worlds. I like this; I do not feel threatened.
Another catastrophic expectation bites the dust. We snarl good-
naturedly at one another, amazingly confident through having
lived through our insecurities. A forever kind of connection
that blows with the wind and not away with it.

One thing I do not like in Mike Barnett's book: he writes
almost sarcastically of where he was at. He is speaking
pompously against a human being that was himself. I do not
want to do that: and that is what I start to do when I get
criticized by Jerry and start to criticize myself for where I'm at.
David, never let me put you down or your therapy. I think the
sessions now should be about us, not about me. I want to hear
your side of our story now, sod you being good god for so long!
Where are your angers and despairs and fears provoked by my
rocky ride, by my stormy growing-up, bombarding you with my
hopes and terrors?

I am so loth to say goodbye, David! I feel myself clutching at you at the very thought. How will I maintain a connection with you? Must I forcibly give up something so beautiful and precious? How can I visit you once a fortnight as an adult? Will you lie on the couch next time while I feel out your armchair? I need you, but often I don't need a session with you. No, I don't *need* you, but I want you very much indeed. Must I artificially end our relationship? I am asking myself these questions, I will let them ferment in my mind.

'Send me news of the humdrum' you say. I have still to accept that *I* am something for *you*! I am still partly fixed in wondering, as I did four years ago, 'Will he charge me per line for answering my letters?'

There is a rhythm in all this that we will understand one day.

Dear Jen,

There is a lot to say in reply to your letter. Your absences are hinges when doors open and light gets in. It is good to stand back from the day-in, day-out therapy and allow a kind of confusion to come out which has a lot to teach us behind it.

A neurosis is a life-raft. When I met you, you were clutching at straws, really capable of drowning. Out of the therapy, you constructed some sort of boat that could carry you through the floods. You never drowned. But now you say lying in a boat is stagnation.

A neurosis is, to a child, a life-saver: your energy-pattern saved you from smothering. If you had given it up *then*, if it had been plucked from you then, you might have become a Janice, a mute with dumb eyes. Hysteria saved you from schizophrenia, then. To give it up now is like getting out of a boat after you've grown old enough to be able to swim.

How can you keep the connection, you ask? Let me answer that straight away — from now on, we need talk no more of 'sessions'; let's think in terms of meeting. A 'session' is something taken by a person who feels sick, a crippled child, who spends a lot of time lying on a bed working with something called 'energy' on something called 'memory'. Meetings are between people who can offer each other something worth having, sessions if necessary, but much else beside. 'Sessions' end if the sick child gets healthy; and staying sick is the only way to keep 'sessions'. Meetings go on as long as both people like having them.

Let me talk a little about my angers, fears, despairs, and also joys as I keep you company on this journey. My anger has been rare because I have not felt provoked by you, your course has not involved the need to destroy me. My despair was strongest in the poems – they are what I had to say about it, and they contained also my hope. My fear is that you would break the connection before it had served its vital purpose, that you would abandon the therapy with me and go goose-hunting with some high-energy therapist armed with five hundred gimmicks. My joy was those times you broke out of your trap, and a singing in my arteries when you found yourself real. You know also how I had to learn to contain that excitement and not spill it all over you. Sometimes since Christmas, I have been bored by some of the yellow pages of someone's childhood I know so well coming through the letter box like a kind of duty. Like homework. And I think: it's Jenny, this is part of her therapy, this is one of her 'sessions' she has with her friends, when she lies down to work on her past; but occasionally also a sadness that sometimes I am dead to them, these pages, they belong to a time so long ago I was not around; sometimes when you write from the centre of your circle surrounded by people giving you help and people you give help to, when you write from your centre of high energy and intense moments, and so much activity, you seem further away than when you come to rest in a dead space in a far away country. And when you write to me out of your confusion, I feel almost a relief from your diary-of-sessions, that here is a present-day person speaking to me who I can answer.

The primal assumption is that going back to the pain of the past is the way to let go of neurosis. But healing old wounds may have as much to do with taking in as with pressing out. You can't prise people's fingers off the life-raft – they need to hold it for long enough to know it is there, it is for them, it is something they have a right to. You have a right to your

memory, to your childhood and to your pain. But to cling
always is to hold back from learning to swim. To come to the
point of risking drowning by taking the fingers off is harder the
greater the fear of going under was, as a child. Hysteria is a net
to cling to when there are no other ways of surviving.

The energy assumption is that people with fire in them are
more alive than people with slow-burning systems. You are an
Aries, and you see your struggle as the constant need to fan the
ashes into flame in case the fire should die out. Here is the
death that haunts you: the no-energy death. What you fear, as
you say, is still water, liquidity, the life that lies under the
banked fires. Sometimes therapeutic energy-work can act
without touching the deeper flow.

Often I wish you would 'die': lie down and see what arises
when the fire is not stoked. And sometimes I miss the
experience of sharing that kind of death with you — of proving
to you that it is possible to stop twitching and not be deserted.
A person is more than an energy-system. 'Death' for you would
not be met with a scream, but a whimper: it is the loss of
struggle you are afraid of, the acceptance of ordinariness.
Beyond that you deny yourself the chance to learn that you can
be loved for who you are when you let go of the fire-child and
the hope to recover your lost youth which has found what life
it can only in sessions, and the vibrant words that rip out of
your past. You will never get youth back beyond that, but the
struggle to find it keeps you old-at-heart, it keeps you chained
to your task, the therapy-task.

Therapy can get like acid: acid takes people into an energy-
stream, it proves people are not dead. But the spaces between
are very important. Unlike the typical acid-head, you have the
sense to leave long spaces between acid trips, the spaces are
vital, they stop you blowing your mind. Spaces in therapy are
equally vital, to stand back from it all, and allow time for new
things to start working.

So let your book rest for a while. It records your struggle to
get here, it honours your determination not to drown. Now I
want to meet you beyond that and when your letter writes to
me from a place where you can see the trauma of clinging to

memory, you seem nearer to reach than sometimes when I sit with you in the same room. It could be fun to discover what tides run in you if you get off the therapy-treadmill.

Your letter is not little, and does not speak from the past. It may be confused, but it's far from schizophrenic. It may lack energy but it transmits important reality. The words are less charged with intensity, but there is more humanity in them. You may ramble, but you don't sound so driven. Some of your therapy-writing has a deep blood magic in it, it is born out of the guts of your myth. But it is possessed. I marvel at your intensity, I am moved by your passion, I am bored when therapy becomes a duty, but my love is for Jen who is much fuller than anything she is possessed by. You will never bewitch me, I am not going to bewitch you.

To say goodbye to your old life-style is to make opportunity to say a new kind of hello to people. I think there are plenty of signs it's already happening quite a bit with Steve. If Steve is your therapist, he is blocked from saying hello to you in the here and now, he has to relate to you then. Your yellow pages of therapy often don't say hello. I noticed I was writing to you less. But your confused letter with no home-work in it draws from me a long response. I am excited again to be hearing from you.

'Therapy' is the name of the spell you have to break, to make more life possible. What you and I have built, slowly, through contact, is fuller than 'therapy' and does not need to be broken. If any of your people tell you it's all transference, sick need, and the rest, they are just dead wrong.

How could you listen to Jerry telling you to give up the past? — he speaks from his truth and his distortions. But if in your own time and from a different direction, you start speaking your own truth about clinging to insight, and the fight to stay in the current, that is what matters, and that is what you must listen to. When writing becomes a task or a duty, believe in your body's taste. Lay the sessions down, and the recording of sessions, so you can find who you are without them. Do lost days make a schizophrene? I am looking forward to meeting you in your vulnerability.

Every split is a disused pathway, a neglected route, an unexplored connection. It is not a chasm that can only be jumped over with fire in one's belly. Fire in your guts was needed to melt the ice in your head. But if the fires slow down now, you won't freeze to death; or fall down the chasm of the dream: you will begin walking some of the unexplored pathways — your letter is littered with signposts.

The message boils down to this: I don't have to drop out of your life when you start to grow up. I don't have to die on you when your struggle to recover your Dad in the flesh ends. If the journey changes from being-hurt to being-alive, I can still keep you company on it. Even if it means being beside you as your neurosis dies to remind you there is someone left, called Jen.

One day it will sink into your beautiful sick healthy schizophrenic possessed creative mind that the only way I can stand the pain of your struggle is because it is out-weighed by the excitement of meeting your clear spaces, of being with you when you become real to yourself. To need a womb to grow in if one is cold is a need that can be out-grown; to be enriched by good contact is basic to health.

I was very moved by what you wrote about our therapy: You said you didn't need therapy, you needed David. I am humbled by this: there was nothing I did to win this kind of loyalty. Except be in the room with you. I wanted to see you happy with no strings attached. No strings means: you don't have to act from sickness to keep the connection. You don't have to prove need to satisfy want. You can, when you are ready, give up the doctor, but you can keep the connection built in love and friendship.

Gentle climax? Year of chaos? The year is not run yet, Jen, there is time and room for other tides to start turning. New signposts to follow if you read the signs in your letter.

Write again soon Jenny. At least we seem to talk the same language.

Love, David.

Letter to Jerry, 13th July, 1973

Hello Jerry,

So many changes here, movements day by day, but at this moment I feel dead because everything on the outside is so good and that leaves me to know my frightened energy is mine. After two days of very bad times with Becky, now she is good with Steve and me for a bit, and a five-year-old boy who is being killed is to stay with us for a week; I'll be glad to let him know there *are* people in the world who won't slap him every time he moves and that he doesn't have to eat when he doesn't want to. Also, the puppy outside has stopped crying for a while.

Pepe has goggles and a snorkel and has shown me how to enter the slow-moving world of underwater sea swimming, following the shoals of completely relaxed fish, and breathing slowly, moving silently, entering their world.

My feelings about therapy have been undergoing a slow and big change since my mother's death; this could be an enormous blocking, or it could be a readjustment to reality. I guess I always saw therapy as miraculous, because I experienced so many miracles within it. Somewhere inside me I have always believed that I would wake up one morning and find my stomach smooth and firm again, that I would be a child with no child and would find once more my springtime. I guess I had visions of my energy flowing as freely round my body as the wind through the trees, of juices springing from me as easily as from a newborn baby, of no more nights of terror nor mornings of stiffness or evenings of sadness or afternoons of lethargy. I would be sixteen forever and shine through the misty world like the sun in Spain, spreading love and harmony around me and healing with my touch.

It is a white withheld terror I experience to see Sitges once more and this stone flat, scene of so many silent scenes of despair and deadness. I do not want to remember, do not want to know I am once more here and so little has changed except the love around me which I am so seldom free to absorb, the love of Pepe matured and grown despite the cloud of his tensely-held anger keeping him in chains, the love of Becky, despondent and depressed so often, constantly conscious of her hunger and furious at the inadequacy of her irresponsible parents; of Steve, just starting to struggle with the phantoms of his nights; of Laszlo back home, frowning and caring and working, carrying a load which he is only just beginning to identify, and Babs my only woman, and you too, Little Big Man once, now big little man, a warm change, and good to know you you.

You know, here there is time to listen and absorb your words, and a welcome in me for them, so speak freely. I can't say the Time is Now, but moments of it are, they slip through into the present in spite of the debris of the past.

Love to you, Jenny.

Another letter to Jerry, 19th July, 1973
Dear Jerry,

Through the labyrinths of your everstrange spelling, I see you are turning poet; a very clear dream you had, which makes me feel sad. Well, you should wear that midnight robe with the stars behind and the smiling sun to the fore.

How can I speak to you across the months of loneliness, across our different trails? Well, what I need is continuity, and if you go I will lose that. Who is left? No-one from my pre-therapy past. Steven is present, maybe future. But I need connections with the past. My parents are dead, my sister silent; my stepparents coldly killing, my old friends flown in hostility, the girl I loved married and with a new child. The Americans have moved on, the Englishmen never stayed; one Hungarian to warm my roost and a strange clouded Spaniard to provide me unclear security; David a phantom still on a palm-tree in southern England, forever a warm help, but forever at the other end of a postage stamp. I return to you, communicating some-how through spiderstrong threads so fragile and so tenacious, across webs of hostility and mists of fear. I have so readily owned guilt, never asserted my hurt; easy to be the baddy, so new to be the spurned. A betrayal so big inside me — maybe without Steve even now I would still look past you and not at you. I realized too late I would have to pay a big price for my newly-flowing blood, I struggled on believing in one basic thing:

that we were side by side; I never saw till too late that it was 'every man for himself'. I believed still blindly, desperately, in communists' and christians' 'each for one another'. Wrong, I know now, but a year to recover from the blow, a year's set-back and growth, but this journey has been so painful, some-times I regret birth.

Today Carlos harpooned a squid. It took centuries of sea-memory to die, pulsating in pain. It was not worth being born to suffer such a death.

I tried to cut you out to rid myself of the despair and horror of me building sandcastles in a raging torrent and a boat sails by and you hop on it, leaving me to fight the current.

Your letter pulls me: 'Your place is by my side, when will you come home and admit it?' I can give you much love, but I would fear to risk myself in your stormy seas when I have found some peace and security through all our daily difficulties. I have no hate for you. I have hurt and bruised mistrust in my eyes and anger which flares when you string too many words together and a burning jealousy when I hear you speak of the people who took you from our makeshift cave into their plush drawing-rooms. I am fierce, but I am loyal in my own way and I do not leave people who keep my love warm. And I see that you do not leave either, there is a steadfastness in you, Taurus, which earths my tribal spirit.

In the height of midsummer, I have only autumn feelings; the loss is thick and unresolvable inside me, clouding my days and nights. My parents are dead, and maybe I will dream forever.

My answer to Jerry's answer
Hello Jerry,

I came home from the beach in my usual state of mediocre health, read your letters, noted with disgust the amount of money you'd spent on express postage which is a capitalist con (send me the money next time), and reacted very strongly to your words, giving myself a long session whilst the brush-strokes of Steve continued scratching on the wall regardless, driving me to greater fury. I felt No Better At All after the session, and soon fell desperately ill. Many hours later, I am still getting worse, in pain all over my body. Quite a bullseye to lay me out from such a distance. I creep away on hands and knees to see what is left of me.

What I agree with in your letter is that my feelings have blinded me to 'exploring' you, except at our last couple of meetings. The rest of your letter is bog-paper. I never said you were Past, silly prickly old sod, I said you were an important *present* link with my recent past. And I am not 'tied down' to Steve: I have never been more open to you than now that I am with him. 'Standing alone', Jerry, will you please get this into your thick nut, can be a DEFENCE, and although I go through hell when I am not relating, it is thoroughly unconstructive hell, in which I am stony and blocked and cold. I am not dead and safe in my relationship with Steve — he makes bloody sure of that. You try being dead or safe with Steve in the room and you'll soon find out what I mean and I'll snigger up my sleeve and rub my hands in glee to see you twist and turn. You might as well try being quiet in a room with Joey and Judy on heat. My 'commitment' to Steve as you put it, is a thoroughly organic one, like you become committed to health-foods if you like the effect they have on you. The 'doomed mood' of my letter was because of doom feelings in me about myself and not a feeling of doom about you and me, Jerry.

You talk about 'need' pushing me into relationships as if 'need' were a dirty word. Well, it's not, unless it's covered over and unrecognized, as mine was. Now my need is on the surface all the time, and causing me all hell, and I don't intend to deny it by walking off alone into the sunset when it's nice here by the fire.

And I don't need you, prick-face, to lecture me about standing alone. I'd like to scream in your feather-bedded, silver-spooned Jewish face for the utter cheek of *you* saying that to *me*. When will you grant me my *totally different past*, my pocket-moneyless, homeless, pioneering, non-arse-licking past? It is a *step forward* for me to be flabby and floppy and openly dependent. Right on, I'm still a baby, it's taken me enough time to uncover my defences against knowing that.

You *are* Now, because you are brave and funny and good at sorting out messes and very young and open at times. When you start to squint like a professor and get a twitch in your right lecturing hand, you are Past for me.

You got the Zen parable completely wrong, and your anarchic spelling and inability to keep the intellectual bit together make you thoroughly human and lovable. I won't let go of the good things in you. And I certainly won't let go of Steve without a fight, he's the most precious thing that's happened to me and I'd be an idiot to throw him away. What exactly is this mythical 'me' you think I'm giving up to pay for love?

To me it feels like every time I take a new step towards openness and happiness, you swoop down and pounce and scream in my face and try to frighten and unground me in what I'm doing. I am not a confident person, Jerry. I cannot stand alone. I need my perceptions confirmed, my beliefs tested out; I need the warm aura of my friends to help me along. Our paths are so different, Jerry: you were dependent, on drugs, on magazines, on film-making ego-trips, on my mothering. Your path had to lead via the painful spikes of independence. My history has been exactly the reverse. I allowed myself no softness, no flinching, no slacking, no comforts. I drove myself mercilessly at school, at work, in politics. I had nothing to give up except my stiff-upper-lip, my pride and arrogance. In the absence of any real self, I had an iron mask. Now the mask is rusty, I am left feeling like a badly sewn-up patchwork quilt. You can undo me with a few words. Hence my terrible body-pains at the moment.

In spite of which, Jerry, believe it or not, I am very fond of you and still hope we may salvage some of the fun I'd hoped for with you and my amazing friend. Let all three of us discover one another and ourselves without image or prejudice. Love is now, here for the taking. We all have warm skin and good energy and lively eyes and wild hair and creative minds. Come!

○　　○　　○

Trip, 4th August, 1973

Peter came in right at the beginning with some Tarot cards. I'd
never thrown the Tarot before. Instead of asking them a
question, I made a wish: I asked to become unrecognizable to
myself and others, to go back to a time before my parents
distorted me, to lose all ego and to become as one with nature
without struggle. I spent a long time on the Tarot reading, every
detail making amazing sense to me. Although it was a non-body
thing, I did not criticize it but could see layers upon layers of
meaning in it, I felt it as breathtakingly symmetrical and based
on some ancient understanding of the journey of human life
that has long ago been lost.

After this, I needed space to breathe and shiver, so I asked
Pete to go and spent some time alone. My body had flopped
though, through concentrating on my head, so I needed help.
I got Becky in; she and Babs' two kids spent some time with
me. My teeth were chattering wildly and I offered ten thousand
pounds to any of the children who could cure me of my
juddering jaw. Rachel suggested I stop breathing and kept
putting her hand over my mouth; Paul tried warming my back
by rubbing it; Becky tried putting peaches in my mouth. Then
they tried making faces to frighten me. Nothing worked, but
we had a marvellous time. The kids really loved me saying,
'Don't let any of the grown-ups in'. 'But you're a grown-up', said
Rachel. 'Not today she's not', said Becky. All the children really
helped me. I lay for some time with Paul cuddled up to me and
thought to myself: *this* is what really matters, this is what's
important. These children are in my world and my time should
go to them and to nothing Outside. I felt with a shudder how
awful it would have been if I'd had another baby, like I so often
want, when I don't even have enough to give to the children
who are here already. I felt disgusted by the whole therapy
world and the position I'd had in it for so long and wanted to
withdraw completely into obscurity. Becky threw the Tarot
that day too. She got the same answer as me: The Hermit. Then
Steve threw it, and he got the same answer too.

Becky came and lay with me then and talked to me for a long
while. She seemed very grown-up to me, a girl approaching

puberty. She told me of her worries about growing up, how to live, how to get money. It took me a while to let it sink into me that she really experienced this as a problem. It was a jolt for me, to have to realize my blindness: that these material things which warrant no more than a shoulder-shrug from me are really important to her. Then she told me how she wants her Dad and me all living together in one house and how it made her sad we had never had a house of our own and that 'nothing is ever *certain*'. I began to get caught up in my guilt about all this, I could feel my mind rushing off into working out how I could 'make it all better' for her, make her dreams come true. But I put the brakes on, forcing myself to see, this is how it is, this is how I am, I cannot metamorphose into a perfect mother, all I can do is know myself. I have suffered long enough from having a 'perfect' mother myself. Then Becky told me about her Dad, 'He's not really a father,' she said, 'I've given him up. When he's talking to his friends, he's like glass, I have to shout to make him notice me. He doesn't want me, he's always playing tricks on me, trying to find ways of getting away from me.' I felt upset again, thinking how she could easily say the same things about me. I saw her as alone, a separate young human being with a life story all her own and quite a heavy burden to carry.

Later I went into the room where the 'grown-ups' were, but I couldn't sit there, I was too tense and paranoid. I thought they were seeing me as someone completely lost and blocked and out-of-touch and were just being kind about it. I felt I was saying ridiculous, out-of-touch things. It was quite late at night now. I asked Steve to come in and help me because I felt lost. We decided to go out for a walk.

My period started today. I didn't want to use a tampax ever again; I felt rebellion, a revulsion against putting them in me. I wore a long dress and just let my period flow. Steve was supportive and kept making jokes about telling people I'd cut my feet if anyone stared. I was sucking my thumb and felt weak; I didn't like walking past the crowds. I didn't have my body or my legs and walked relying on Steve. I kept feeling he was ashamed of me, but he said he was quite proud. It took so

long to get down to the big dark beaches, and even there there
were so many people hovering around. I noticed how clumsy I
was as I crossed the rocks: I'd lost touch with the earth and was
so fearful of unseen dangers ahead that I wasn't looking at the
real dangers just under my nose. When I jumped down from
some rocks into the sand, I liked the jolt that went all through
my body. I wanted to do it again. I walked through the water
and felt how cotton-woolly my sensations were compared to
how sharply I can feel sometimes. The waves were frightening
me. I was jumpy and knew I needed somewhere where it was
safe to scream without anyone rushing up to 'help'. We kept
walking, nowhere was safe, there were always people around.
Finally I stopped, facing the sea. It was no good going any
further; I had work to do.

I stood there, looking out to sea, nothing in front of me but
a pitch-black sky with stars and a black sea with its suddenly-
appearing white waves that would rush up and break near me,
terrifying me. I knew what I had to do. I stood at the edge of
the sea in my long dress, letting my blood and my piss go into
the sea, join up with it. I let the sea and sky and ground swirl
around me, gave myself over to them, opened myself to my
fear. The energy of the sky and sea and earth was coming
straight at me, pointing at me, converging on me. I started to
collapse inside, to melt. I screamed again and again, fear
breaking warm in me as the waves pounced and broke near me.
I was frightened of my own screams, frightened too of
frightening Steve. But I could feel my ice breaking, could feel
myself coming back to life. The sea was my mother, coming at
me, coming to get me, shocking me, making me go stiff and
dead with held fear. I had found a new therapy room, a way to
open when all my doors were closed.

People came near, curious. We moved on to another beach.
I shouldn't have moved. I needed to let the fear of these people
also climax in me. I found a new place and faced the water
again, staying there for ages. I said to my mother, the sea, 'I'm
so frightened, so frightened of you, please don't, please don't
come.' I was crying and it felt good to melt. I started crying
more desperately, this time for my sister, she was my last hope,

she was the only person there with me in those times when my
mother came at me and frightened the life out of me; she was
the only person who could really know. I cried more and more
frantically for her to come and save me, but suddenly knew, it
was no use, she couldn't help me, I was alone in my fear, she
couldn't feel it for me; we'd both been alone in that bedroom as
kids when Mum came up. I had to face Mum alone, no-one else
could be with me any more. I opened my legs, sitting there in
the sea, opened my body and let the sea come at me. I let
myself join up with it to heal me of my fear. I did as much as
I could that night, which wasn't much, but I'd found a way, my
way, which isn't in the books, but it brought me back after
being away a long time.

I sat with the sea for ages. Looking out to sea, I talked one
by one to the people closest to me. I talked to Becky and cried,
'I cannot give you back what you didn't have, I can't do it, I
can't'. I saw how I keep tying myself up with guilt, trying
desperately to make up for my cruelty and emptiness when she
was a baby, how in a way I am trying to treat her as a baby,
protect her from bad, wipe out pain; and now what I see is that
she is nearly eleven, with her own sadnesses and tragedies to
face, and all I can do is be honest with her and be her friend,
and see her as a whole, responsible person. I have to give up her
babyhood as lost, give up my own as lost, and live with her
now. I must listen to her instead of trying to cuddle her feelings
away; that's not what she wants.

I saw Babs and Peter and cried, seeing how my mother stops
me from being with my best friends. I told her to get out of me
and imagined the sea healing me, cleansing me of my evil spirits.
Then I started getting quite cold. I made humming sounds and
looked at the town lights and the stars up above and had a rest
from traumas. Steve got bored and said he was going off into
the streets, he wanted to smoke. I was shocked and panicked.
For a moment I felt the bottom had fallen out of my world: I'd
felt protected by him sitting behind me, and now I felt I'd
really been alone. His face suddenly looked ugly and distorted;
I saw his big body as deformed. But then, just as suddenly, I
realized I *could* manage alone and said, 'You'd better go then.'

But his tension was broken and now he didn't want to. So both thoroughly wet and covered in sand, we started for home. I knew that when I'd gotten dry and warm at home, I would come back and do it all again, alone.

At home, I sat under the warm shower with my dress on, the warm water tumbling all over me till I had thawed out. I spent some time selecting long loose clothes I would feel right in. I looked at myself in the mirror. I looked thirty, weather-beaten, grown-up, and definitely not glamorous. Wrapping my Indian bedspread around me, I went out, barefoot. I was scared as I went down the stone stairs, knowing I was going on a mission and that it was a long one, and that there was no alternative. It was about one o'clock. Guys were hanging around. They looked at me, some called out; some followed me. My hair was wet from the shower, I must have looked strange. People stared and some made remarks. This was a thorny path for me: I had to steer my way between letting them get right on top of me, and putting on a brazen, don't-care strength. When some crippled, bent character seemed to be following me for too long, I suddenly burst into quick running and got to the sands. I thought aggressively to myself, 'These fat pigs are going to get some exercise if they want to catch me.' I remembered with disgust my past when I would think I had to care and cater to all the lonely freaks. Now their clutching just made me angry.

I retraced my footsteps, all the journey I'd been with Steve there to look after me. I was extra careful on the rocks, feeling how easy it would be not to notice danger, I was so busy fleeing from potential pursuers. At one point, I started to climb down in a difficult place, then stopped, went back and found a better route. That gave me confidence: once upon a time, pride would not have allowed me to go back, I would have forced myself onward into danger.

I found a place to sit and look at the sea. Soon, guys started calling out. I moved on, angrily, and sat down again. They came right up to me, asking if I was English. I said firmly, bristling with hostility: 'I DON'T WANT TO TALK.' They kept on, and I repeated it several times, then got up and moved angrily away, backwards a few paces. They just stood there and I knew I was not going to let them block my journey. I chose flight once more, dashing past them suddenly at full speed. I ran for a long while, across the sands, then up to the road and the lights, just in case. I walked quickly along the road and sat on a wall high above the beach, thinking, 'I too can sometimes be ON TOP, looking down from a safe position, surveying the situation, and watching for danger. I don't always have to sit in the shadows waiting for it to get me.' Then it was time to move, and I went back down to the dark beach, my heart beating wildly and very aroused. I thought: 'Enough of running, now I am going to have to FIGHT for the space I need to live and breathe.' I chose a place on the beach by the water's edge. There were guys creeping around behind me. I stayed. I was stiff and hurting with tension and fear, but I held my ground.

I lay down to breathe, resisting as much as possible the temptation to look around me and check up. I could feel people near, threatening. The sky was cloudy now, not perfectly dark like earlier, and it was no longer so easy to let the sea threaten me as I felt in such danger from the human world. It was all I could do to stay there and breathe a little into my swollen stomach. I took some clothes off and moved down to sit nearer the water, and stayed there for a long time.

When I decided to walk home, my stomach was still stiff and swollen from unresolved tension. I was doing a lot of thinking. I thought about David and knew I had to give him up; I had leaned on him so long and now I had to stand alone, face the world alone, grow up. I could no longer be his beautiful and absent daughter. I could not go running and crying to him when people upset me with their letters or reactions to me. I had to relate directly to the people around me and not use him as my ultimate support to fall back on when all else failed. I had to risk all else failing, or remain a child forever. To be thirty, I have to say goodbye to David. And NO MORE LETTERS. I would have to live without the support of his beautiful letters, without displaying my life to him.

I spoke to David in my mind, flooding with tears, saying, 'You have helped me so much, you have been with me so long, it is going to be painful to give you up.' But I knew I couldn't get any further on my journey unless I did. My crying came, and came for Jerry too, for how good we'd been together, a really strong pair, finding each other at just the right time, and having so much influence on one another and on those around us. I saw Jerry now as dedicated to himself as I am to myself, and felt, 'our story is not finished, you are someone maybe I don't have to say goodbye to.'

I crossed the rocks, crying to myself. Just then, a man moved right up to me. He was in uniform and flashed a torch right in my face. I asked him in Spanish who he was and he said, 'Police'. I quelled the bubble of paranoia that started to rise inside me, and said calmly, 'I am not in need of help.' He said, 'But you are crying, what's the matter?' I said, 'Something personal. I don't need your help.' He said, 'Well, tell me what it is then.' I said, 'NO, I DON'T NEED YOUR HELP.' Then he gave up, reluctantly, shrugged his shoulders and turned slowly away saying, 'Oh, well, if, as you say, you don't need any help. . .'

○   ○   ○

Letter from David, August 13th, 1973
Dear Jen,

You are very brave. I did not see you were ready yet to find your feet so fully.

I know you are not 'cured'. But you can stand in the sea without drowning. You don't have to damage yourself and I don't have to tell you any more who you are.

How did you fix it that, just now, Lorton can be your home instead of London? I think you need fields, and stones, and lots of sky, instead of tarmac with the grass crushed and a therapy room with no windows.

I am coming down to London on September 8th. Please don't bring any money.

There is nothing more I can give you except my love that you can live without now.

I want to hold you before you go.

David

Letter to David, same day

Yesterday was very hot, the sea calm as a lake.

I never swim very far from shore. I have never learnt to swim 'properly'. But I can move through water calmly when there are no waves to confuse me.

I started off on a long swim. I'd already gone further than ever that day, across the harbour and back. Now I took off along the cliffs, along the coastline where no-one can see because there are no beaches, just sheer cliffs. I thought of trying to make it to a tiny little bay I know, reachable otherwise only along the train tracks.

Going was easy. Smooth water, fresh energy. I tried out different strokes that I daren't use when people are watching. Some Spaniards whistled at me from a dinghy. I ignored them, no time now to express my indignation, stuck here in the water.

I saw our bay in the distance, crawling with ant-size people. I did not dare to land. I fantasied I would hit underwater rocks and my stomach would be ripped open from underneath. I know I can open my eyes under the clear water to check, but I know also of a strange fear that comes over me when I am under water, and this was no place to panic.

I had to decide: land and rest, or go straight back. I turned round. I noticed how on a calm, safe day, fears from the sea inside can bring death. I understood the mariners' tales, the disappearances in the midst of calm, the tables laid and cigarettes still smoking, and not a soul on board. In order to make sure I *could* land on the beautiful rocks along the coast if I needed to rest, I swum nearer the cliffs. No waves to buffet me, no clouded sea to confuse me. But now, instead of the yellow seabed beneath me, dark massed shapes. I was looking down, and fear was creeping up. I imagined my mother looming down there, smiling slyly, beckoning, saying, 'Oh, so you've come at last. You're alone now, aren't you? I knew you'd come in the end. It's time to join me.' I could feel her pull. A fear so insidious, it would be sweeter to give in and slip down to her, and die. Is it so easy to die?

I looked up quickly. This is no time for a session.

It was a long, long way back to the beach. I could feel the

fear sapping my energy and strength. My body could make it, a little weary and faint maybe, but fear was draining my power. I knew I mustn't look down; those dark shapes would turn immediately into the face of my mother and swallow me up. I felt how fear stunts my life. The caverns and cliffs were beautiful, harmless, yet I was giving them the power to destroy me.

A strange, axe-shaped rock loomed out of the water, standing all alone. I had passed it on my journey there; now I had to look away quickly, take control of myself and my feelings. I looked at the bubbles directly in front of me. I concentrated on my movements. I tried out different strokes again, noting calmly how my strength had dimmed.

Quite suddenly, the danger was passed. Now it was just a question of getting home. It was a long way, but I have the body for it.

I lay, later, a little dizzy, on the beach beside Steve who was sleeping peacefully.

○   ○   ○

I had one more session with David, and then went home with him, for the first time, to his family, and his village near the sea. We spent a lazy autumn day on the beach, a shingly beach, wide and magnificent, with an iron sea that made the Mediterranean look like your local swimming pool. The day after my visit, I left London for good and went to live with Steve, Babs, Peter and our four kids in the Lake District. David sent me one last poem:

Wave

The ocean was resting from rage
and held you lazily.
The killer rocks smiled five fathoms up.
Chin cupped in a hollow wave you swam
dark head in the blue of a slow swell:

the horizon let you go.
Hands on the brown sand told me
the sea gave up its young.
Your jaw juddered, but not with cold,
a small wave broke,
the wind had forgotten to cry,
light moved on a face of water.
It was a slow day
I caught the breath of your long goodbye.

David.

○   ○   ○